Princes and Peoples:
France and the British Isles,
1620–1714

Princes and Peoples: France and the British Isles, 1620–1714

An anthology of primary sources

edited by
Margaret Lucille Kekewich

at The Open University

Manchester University Press
– Manchester and New York –
in association with The Open University
distributed exclusively in the USA and Canada by St. Martin's Press

Published by Manchester University Press
Oxford Road, Manchester M13 9NR, UK
and Room 400, 175 Fifth Avenue,
New York, NY 10010, USA

Distributed exclusively in the USA and Canada
by St. Martin's Press, Inc.,
175 Fifth Avenue, New York, NY 10010, USA

British Library Cataloguing-in-Publication Data
A catalogue record for this book is available from the British Library

Library of Congress Cataloging-in-Publication Data
Princes and peoples : France and British Isles. 1620–1714 : an
   anthology of primary sources / edited by Margaret Lucille Kekewich.
      p.   cm.
   "This book forms part of an Open University course A220."
   ISBN 0–7190–4572–X. — ISBN 0–7190–4573–8 (pbk)
   1. Great Britain—Civilization—17th century—Sources.   2. Great
Britain—Civilization—18th century—Sources. 3. France–
–Civilization—17th century—Sources.   4. France—Civilization—18th
century—Sources.   I. Kekewich, Margaret Lucille. 1939–
DA370.P75   1994
941.06—dc20   94–5406

ISBN 0 7190 4572–X *hardback*
ISBN 0 7190 4573–8 *paperback*

This book forms part of the Open University course A220 *Princes and Peoples: France and the British Isles, 1620–1714*
For information about this course, please write to: Central Enquiry Service, The Open University, PO Box 200, Walton Hall, Milton Keynes MK7 6YZ, UK.

Photoset in Linotron Sabon
by Northern Phototypesetting Co. Ltd, Bolton

Printed in Great Britain
by Redwood Books, Trowbridge, Wiltshire

CONTENTS

Contents

Contents

Contents

Contents

LIST OF ILLUSTRATIONS

ACKNOWLEDGEMENTS

The editor and publishers wish to thank the following for permission to use extracts:

The Marquess of Bath, Longleat House, for material from the Portland Papers Volume II, f.262, updated in *Calendar of the Manuscripts of the Marquess of Bath*, II, Historic Manuscripts Commission, 1907, pp.170–1; A & C Black (Publishers) Ltd. for material from H. C. Barnard, *Madame de Maintenon and Saint-Cyr*, 1934, republished 1971, pp.231–2; Bodleian Library for 'Visitation articles of the Diocese of Hereford', B 7 9 Linc.(21), pp.1–3; Blackwell Publishers for material from Thomas Hobbes, *Leviathan or the Matter, Form and Power of a Commonwealth Ecclesiastical and Civil*, ed. Michael Oakshott, 1946, pp.113–5, 144–5; David Campbell Publishers Ltd. for material from R. Baxter, *The Autobiography of Richard Baxter: being the Reliquae Baxterianae abridged* ed. J. H. Lloyd Thomas, Everyman's Library, 1931, pp.77–9; Cambridge University Press for material from John Locke, *Two Treatises of Government: A Critical Edition*, ed. Peter Laslett, 1967, pp.398–401; N. Williams, *The 18th Century Constitution*, 1960, pp.364–6; J. P. Kenyon, ed., *The Stuart Constitution 1603–88: Documents and Commentary*, 2nd edn., 1986, pp.54–6, 98–9, 149–51, 324–5, 328, 331–2; Essex Record Office for material from J. A. Sharpe, ed., *William Holcroft His Booke*, 1986, pp.32–3, 54, 56; Libraire Arthème Fayard for material from R. Mandrou, ed., *Relation Des Journes de la Fronde*, 1978, pp.102–3. Copyright © 1978 Libraire Artheme Fayard; Macmillan Ltd. for material from R. Bonney, *Society and Government in France under Richelieu and Mazarin*, 1988, pp.97, 164, 203–4, 207–8; and Roger Mettam, *Government and Society in Louis XIV's France*, 1977, pp.18–24, 29–30, 90–1, 255–9; Methuen & Co. for material from E. Curtis and R. B. McDowell, eds., *Historical Documents 1172–1922*, 1943, pp.152–8; J. S. Morrill for material from *The Revolt of the Provinces: Conservatives and Radicals in the English Civil War, 1630–1650*, Historical Problems and Documents, No.26, 1976, Allen & Unwin, pp.145–6, 199–200; Open University Press for 'The Putney Debates, 1647', A203 Supplementary Material, Cassette Notes 5, 1981, pp.19–24; Oxfordshire Archives for 'Instructions for levying the poor rate in the parish of St Martins, Oxford, 1620', Ms d.d. Par Oxford St Martins c.29 item a.; Penguin Books Ltd. for material from Blaise Pascal, *Provincial Letters*, trans. A. J.

Acknowledgements

Krailsheimer, Penguin Classics, 1967, pp.132–4. Copyright © 1967 A. J. Krailsheimer; Phillimore & Co. Ltd. for material from E. R. C. Brinkworth, *Shakespeare and the Bawdy Court of Stratford*, 1972, pp.148–51; Princeton University Press for material from W. F. Church, trans. *Richelieu and Reason of State*, 1972, pp.213, 215, 246. Copyright © 1972 by Princeton University Press; Scottish Academic Press for material from G. Donaldson, ed., *Scottish Historical Documents*, 1970, pp.94–201, Nat. MSS Scot.iii, no.xcviii; The University of Massachusetts Press for material from Barbara Rosen, *Witchcraft in England, 1558–1618*, 1991, pp.57–8; Copyright © 1991 by The University of Massachusetts Press; Walpole Society for material from Abraham van der Doort, *Catalogue of the Collections of Charles I*, ed. O. Miller, 1960, Vol.37, pp.76–7; Wiltshire County Record Office for material from Paul Slack, ed., *Poverty in Early Stuart Salisbury*, Wiltshire Record Office, 31, 1975, pp.52–64, G23/1/228; and with Lord Radnor for 'Regulations for the Hungerford Almshouses at Corsham, Wiltshire, 1668', Wiltshire Record Office, WRO 490/11.

Every effort has been made to trace all the copyright holders but if any have been inadvertently overlooked the publishers will be pleased to make the necessary arrangement at the first opportunity.

SCOTLAND

Forth

Edinburgh

Clyde ● Glasgow

Carrickfergus

ULSTER

CONNAUGHT

Galway ●

Shannon *Liffey*

LEINSTER ● Dublin

MUNSTER

Cork ●

ENGLAND

York ●

Chester ●

WALES

Severn

Norwich ●

Cardiff ●

Bristol ●

London ●

Thames

0	50	100	150 kms
0		50	100 miles

NORMANDY

Rouen

Paris

ILE-DE-
FRANCE

Seine

BRITTANY

ANJOU

Loire

Dijon

BURGUNDY

Nantes

Tours

POITOU

La Rochelle

Lyon

Grenoble

Rhône

DAUPHINÉ

Bordeaux

GUYENNE

Garonne

GASCONY

Toulouse

LANGUEDOC

Avignon

PROVENCE

Marseille

Rhine

| 0 | 50 | 100 | 150 kms |
| 0 | | 50 | 100 miles |

- - - - - 1620 French frontier

- - - 1715 French frontier

xiv

GENERAL INTRODUCTION

Seventeenth-century Europe occupies an unenviable position in the minds of many people as uncertainties surround the question of its place in history. The religious reformations of the previous century, accompanied by the artistic and educational changes of the Renaissance, give that period a particularly glamorous character. The Enlightenment and economic expansion of the eighteenth century, followed by the French Revolution, is often hailed as the period when 'Modern Europe' emerged. There is much good sense to be found in these propositions, yet neither century can be satisfactorily defined without a knowledge of the intellectual, political, social and economic developments of the intervening period: they brought to fruition much which was only potential in 1600 and initiated ideas and practices which were later to be refined and extended.

France and the British Isles provide excellent evidence of the processes of consolidation and change which were taking place throughout seventeenth-century Europe. They also serve a comparative study well, as the similarities and differences which can be identified in both states illuminate the reasons for the way in which many of their national attitudes and institutions developed. English historians in the nineteenth and early twentieth centuries, many of whom subscribed to Whig/Liberal ideology, tended to trace the irresistible advance of democracy through the victories of parliament and the rule of law in the 1640s and in 1688:

> this revolution [1688], of all revolutions the least violent, has been of all revolutions the most beneficent. It finally decided the great question whether the popular element . . . found in the English polity, should be destroyed by the monarchical element, or should be suffered to develope itself freely, and to become dominant.
>
> (Macaulay, 1858, p.668)

Verdicts on the rule of Louis XIV were equally assured:

1

> All power came from the king, and it was a fixed determination of Louis
> XIV that this fact should be recognised by all the officials of the State . . .
> the nobility were excluded [from office] with jealous care . . .
>
> (Grant, 1908, pp.2–3)

After the Second World War a generation of historians, many of them
Marxist, were prepared to question these long-held assumptions.
Christopher Hill (1980), for example, found it much more interesting to
attempt to recover the political aspirations of the artisans and yeomen who
were the rank and file of the New Model Army, than continually to agonize
about the motivation of Charles I, Strafford and Laud. Rather later, John
Morrill (1976) and his followers, who have produced between them a growing number of local studies, added yet another dimension to the causation
and course of the civil wars. The final decades of the century present
difficulties to any commentators with firm political convictions, since they
have to pick their way through the labyrinthine complexities of the factional
politics of the reigns of the later Stuarts. Those on the left would, however,
question Macaulay's delight at the 'Glorious Revolution', observing grimly
that it simply confirmed the control that the ruling classes exercised over all
means of production and communication.

In France historians of the *Annales* school have, to some extent, influenced
the work of English historians like Hill and Brian Manning (1976), by
concentrating on the details of the structure of society, how it was administered and the economy. Writers such as Roland Mousnier (1976) and
Emmanuel Le Roy Ladurie (1974) have looked for their evidence beyond the
centre of government and have found that studies of communities and
provincial hierarchies yield a far more complex picture of the workings of the
state than had previously been imagined.

A major preoccupation for contemporary writers is the phenomenon of
'absolutism'. How should it be defined? Was the concept understood at the
time? When did it become the means by which France was governed? Did it
ever really penetrate the British Isles and if not, why not? Even the most
sceptical of historians, such as Roger Mettam (1988), find it difficult to deny
that, once he became an adult, Louis XIV did wield a formidable amount of
authority. His writ did not always run amongst rebellious, heretical
Camisards and, from time to time, he had to compromise with recalcitrant
provinces over the taxes they were to pay but, in other respects, his will seems
to have been irresistible. Kevin Sharpe (1989) suggests that Charles I enjoyed
something like absolute power, during the eleven years of rule without
parliament, and that he used it well. The 'revisionists', those who tend to see
the triumph of parliamentary rule as neither inevitable nor inherently
desirable, writers such as Robert Beddard (1991), can find positive things to
say about James II and subject the exact share of power enjoyed by the Stuarts
and their parliaments, both before and after 1688, to close scrutiny.

The documents in this collection throw light on the issues raised above and provide a wealth of evidence about many aspects of life in the French and British states. Yet the objection might well be raised that such a book as this one can only have a limited usefulness for two reasons. The first relates to the nature of the selection of documents, which is entirely under the control of a group of historians who are probably far from neutral in their opinions about the interpretation of the seventeenth century. The second should query the extent to which the documents can be relied upon and address the difficulty that a particular piece of evidence may only tell a partial story.

The intention in compiling this book is that it will only contain primary sources, that is accounts which were written at or fairly close to the time when the events to which they relate happened. The time-scale will necessarily vary; the National Convenant, for example, dates from 1638, the year in which it was drafted, whereas the Earl of Clarendon's *History of the Great Rebellion* was mostly composed several decades after the end of the civil wars. In both cases the essential attribute of the documents is that they are primary sources and thus worthy of attention. Another question to ask relates to the nature of the source. The Covenant, a political and religious document to which a large number of people subscribed in a short period with a particular set of objectives in mind, will certainly differ from the *History* of one distinguished but disgraced statesman, looking back with the benefit of hindsight. If these kinds of factors are borne in mind, the assessment of the quality of evidence becomes a practical proposition. The status of the person or people who produced the document is a matter of concern: how much or little did they really know about the subject? Sometimes a humble record, such as a laundry list, or a routine one like a gaol delivery, can tell the historian more than a flattering account of a great lord's household or a florid but inaccurate parliamentary speech. If it is at all possible, documents of different kinds which relate to the same historical circumstances should be examined before any conclusions are drawn.

There is also the challenge of 'cracking the code' in documents: what did they mean to contemporaries? Jokes, references to popular songs and recent events, slang, cant, words that have changed their meaning and many other features can obscure the significance of some sources. In this collection footnotes may help, but there are bound to be some hidden meanings that we have missed. This reiterates the question of the usefulness of a selection of documents, namely the nature of the choices. A book like this is not intended to be read in isolation from other primary and secondary works on the subject. These documents represent a reasonable selection and provide a supplement to fill the gaps which, inevitably, do exist in the coverage of such a large subject. Most of the documents are extracts, often quite short, and this means that sometimes important aspects of an issue have been omitted. Similarly if a document has been translated into English this is stated, and allowance must be made for the possibility of slight changes in the meaning.

The limited potential of one anthology of documents, however carefully selected, to provide evidence to answer some of the great questions of the period also applies to the comparative nature of this collection. The juxtaposition of an account of a French popular revolt being suppressed with great ferocity, and a gentlemanly English court case in which the royal right to taxation triumphed, does not necessarily prove that the French regime was more despotic than the English. Again, the acceptance or rejection of arguments about such matters should be determined by reviewing a number of different sources, some primary and some secondary; the latter will themselves invariably have been based on large quantities of original material as well as on the work of earlier historians.

No attempt has been made to achieve an exact balance between the types of French and British documents in the selection. Apart from the obvious problem that there were sometimes no closely equivalent institutions or events to cite (e.g. the French academies or English justices of the peace), each state produced records which were unique to a particular person or occasion. Conversely some well-known sources have not been used because they did not suit the purposes of this collection: sadly, writers such as Samuel Pepys and Madame de Sévigné have been omitted. In compensation, it is hoped that the more obscure documents, some printed and/or translated here for the first time since they were originally produced, will promote an understanding of how two great states developed and related to one another during the seventeenth century.

This anthology has been planned as a source book for students taking the Open University undergraduate course entitled *Princes and Peoples: France and the British Isles, 1620–1714*. The course includes a variety of materials: television programmes, audio- and video-cassettes, an illustration book and two history set books. The selection of documents has also been assembled with the interests and needs of the general reader and other students in mind but, since it is linked to a particular course, it should be helpful to outline its main features and to relate them to some of the documents printed here.

The course, which is at the second level, concentrates on the changes which took place in the politics, religion, economies and societies of France and the British Isles. In the exercise of comparison we hope to illuminate, by discussing both similarities and differences, the reasons why both countries experienced major upheavals in the seventeenth century, and why those upheavals had very different outcomes. A major subject of the course is the development of the state, the institutions within it and the ways in which state power was extended or curbed.

The first part of the course concentrates upon what the societies and institutions of France and the British Isles were like in 1620. It is concerned with the breakdown of relations between rulers and ruled in the 1640s and 1650s and with the restoration of stability in the 1660s. It begins with an introduction to comparative studies and to the French and British states: their institutions, the extent of their competence and their impact upon the population. In this context documents are cited which attest to the efforts of subjects to resist royal taxation and the means by which the poor were provided for at local level. This is followed by a comparative study of the courts of Charles I and Louis XIII, which is used to test the thesis of David Starkey (1987, pp.1–24) that during the first part of the seventeenth century the court remained an important focus of political power and a means by which monarchs extended their authority. Letters, a catalogue and a treatise on *The Art to Please in Court*, are some of the evidence which are assembled to assess the theory. The civil wars which followed on from the heyday of the two courts are then discussed, especially how much they had in common and how much they differed. Some documents illuminate the way in which the protagonists sided with the monarchs or their enemies: such are the National Covenant of the Scots and the apology for the *Ormée* revolt in Bordeaux. Anne Laurence marks a pause in the unfolding of events by giving some consideration to the reasons historians have suggested for the instability in the states during the middle part of the century. Was this part of a general crisis in which Europe's structures showed the strain of social, political, economic and religious changes? Or were short-term and local factors such as the personality of Charles I and the disaffection of merchants in Bordeaux responsible? Some of the answers to these problems may be sought in the way in which the states returned to stability in the 1650s and 1660s. Arthur Marwick studies the effects of the wars on the societies and their politics. Evidence, such as the brutal repression of a rebellion in northern France and the compromise with his subjects over the amount of power he would enjoy proclaimed in Charles II's Declaration of Breda (1660), demonstrates how continuity and change were both inherent in the accomplishment of political equilibrium.

The second part of the course is concerned with longer-term developments in education, religion, local administration, the regulation of the community and the family in the seventeenth century. It commences with a review of the opportunities which existed for the acquisition of a formal education in France and the British Isles and of the associated question of the incidence of literacy. The development of political propaganda through a spate of pamphleteering linked to the upheavals of the mid-century, and the issue of censorship are addressed through examples such as the polemics of John Lilburne the Leveller and the later writings of the Huguenot exile, Pierre Bayle. The importance of religion in understanding the motivation of many of those who were engaged in controversy and conflict is discussed with illustrations drawn from the different confessional groupings, and the issues they reflected, that existed throughout the century. A variety of religious experience is presented, from the Puritan Richard Baxter's account of his ministry to Pascal's ridicule of the way in which the Jesuits encouraged popular credulity about the powers of the Virgin Mary as an intercessor. Bill

Sheils goes on to survey the extent to which units of local government reflected central policy and how far they showed autonomous or oppositional features. In particular, evidence is considered which either confirms or challenges theories that France was moving towards an increasingly absolutist and Britain towards a more limited form of monarchy. Some examples of how the states exerted control at a local level are presented; they particularly relate to the relief of poverty and the control of witchcraft. Chilling evidence of the processes of accusation, condemnation and execution shows that the persecution of witches was not so predominantly a Protestant practice as has sometimes been claimed. This part of the course progressively narrows the focus down to the smallest units of society: it concludes with a discussion by Rosemary O'Day of the family and why it was so important an institution for contemporary politicians, clerics and philosophers. Sir Robert Filmer's *In Praise of the Virtuous Wife* gives a traditionalist's view of some of the issues involved.

The third part of the course is concerned with the development of Louis XIV's absolutist monarchy, the establishment of a constitutional monarchy in England and the suppression of overt discontent in Scotland and Ireland. The manifestations of political opposition amongst the nobility and gentry are exemplified in documents such as the Duke of Monmouth's proclamation in 1685 when he laid claim to the title of 'king'. His was by no means a primarily dynastic rebellion; few of the commoners who followed him would have supported an illegitimate son of Charles II had his successor, James II, not been a Catholic. Evidence such as the Article of Impeachment of Dr Sacheverell in 1710, undertaken by some extremely heavy-handed Whig ministers, shows that confrontations over religion did not go away after 1688. Popular protest occasioned by grievances such as food shortages and high taxation were endemic in France, even under Louis XIV: several documents show his anxiety to keep a firm control over potential trouble spots by browbeating, via his minister Colbert, hapless governors, *intendants* and minor officials. Bill Purdue concentrates on the reigns of the later Stuarts and the regime of the adult Louis XIV to assess the degree to which the former ushered in a limited form of monarchical government whilst the latter confirmed the earlier tendency under Louis XIII and Richelieu to absolutism. The Revocation of the Edict of Nantes in 1685 was certainly one of the most authoritarian acts of any potentate during the period. The Bill of Rights, of four years later, was partly an expression of English fears that their state would go the same way under an over-powerful monarch and of a determination to stop that from happening. The emergence of political ideas used to be regarded as a kind of intellectual process that developed apart from the practicalities of daily life. Recent writers have been inclined to associate them much more closely with the aspirations and conflicts which were observed by the political theorists. The particular combination of reverence and moral censure that bishop Bossuet offered to Louis XIV would have been unthinkable under a different regime. It seems unlikely that John Locke's *Two Treatises of Government* would have been written in the same way had the circumstances in England in the 1670s and 1680s been otherwise. Antony Lentin considers one sphere, that of the Arts, in which France was supremely successful: her literature, music, architecture and couture were emulated by the rest of Europe, even by Protestant countries. The admiration of Christopher Wren for the work at the Louvre transcended religious and political prejudice, although contemporaries such as Addison and Wycherley mocked the excesses of French influence. Clive Emsley shows that France also led Europe in her development of military expertise. Extracts from the works of Vauban, her greatest engineer, demonstrate the links between strategy and building policy. James II is to be given some credit for his plans for the navy and his experience as a soldier, but his successor, William of Orange, was a much more seasoned and formidable general. The campaigns of Marlborough demonstrated that Britain, albeit aided by many foreign troops, could surpass the French. The deadly capacity of warfare to kill and maim, however, meant that both sides avoided battles, except when conditions were very favourable, and most hostilities were conducted by siege warfare. The course ends with a summary of how the states developed in their political and socio-economic functions over the period. Some conclusions are also drawn about the extent to which there really was a contrast between the so-called absolutism of the French state and the so-called limited monarchy in Britain.

Each of the three parts of this anthology has a brief introduction, and each document is preceded with details of its immediate provenance and a headnote which gives more background information. Some documents are presented in modern English, either in a translation made specially for this book or, if it is an English text, taken from a modern printed edition. The rest retain the original language but, except in the case of words for which no modern equivalent exists, the spelling has been modernized. A few numbered footnotes have been added to explain obscurities in the text, editorial additions are enclosed in square brackets and deletions within the text are indicated by three ellipses, but no such indication is given at the beginning or end of extracts.

Margaret Lucille Kekewich edited this anthology as a member of the course team of *Princes and Peoples*, and the rest of the team chose many of the documents especially those which related to the units they wrote. This involved abridging them and writing headnotes and footnotes. Members of the team were: Henry Cowper, Ian Donnachie, Clive Emsley, Anne Laurence, Antony Lentin, Arthur Marwick, Rosemary O'Day, Bill Purdue, Bill Sheils and Kevin Wilson. Angela Scholar made a number of the translations from French and advised authors on others. We are also very grateful to the course editor, Anne Howells, to the course managers Pat Caldwell and Lydia Chant, and also to Kate Richenburg, and Lyn Camborne-Paynter, Janet Fennell, Nicki Merridan, Sarah Mowatt, Cheryl O'Toole, Angela Redgewell,

Rochelle Scholar and Sophie White. Colin Jones is the external assessor of the course and the authors of its two set books are Robin Briggs and Barry Coward.

References

Beddard, R.A. (ed.) (1991), *The Revolutions of 1688: the Andrew Browning lectures, 1988*, Clarendon Press, Oxford.

Grant, A.J. (1908), 'The Government of Louis XIV', in A.W. Ward, G.W. Prothero and S. Leathes (eds), *The Cambridge Modern History*, vol.V, Cambridge University Press, Cambridge.

Hill, C. (1980), *The Century of Revolution, 1603–1714*, Nelson, Surrey.

Le Roy Ladurie, E. (1974), *The Peasants of Languedoc*, translated with an introduction by J. Day, University of Illinois Press, Urbana.

Macaulay, T.B. (1858), *The History of England*, vol.2, Longman, London.

Manning, B. (1976), *The English People and the English Revolution*, Heinemann, London.

Mettam, R. (1988), *Power and Faction in Louis XIV's France*, Basil Blackwell, Oxford.

Morrill, J.S. (1976), *The Revolt of the Provinces: Conservatives and Radicals in the English Civil War, 1630–50*, Historical Problems and Documents, no.26, Allen and Unwin, London.

Mousnier, R. (1979), *The Institutions of France under Absolute Monarchy, 1598–1789*, University of Chicago Press, Chicago.

Sharpe, K. (1987), 'The image of virtue: the court of Charles I, 1625–42', in D. Starkey.

Starkey, D. (ed.) (1987), *The English Court: from the Wars of the Roses to the Civil War*, Longman, London.

PART I

Traditional society and the civil wars, 1620–1660

Introduction

The first part of this collection is concerned to establish the political, ideological and economic bases of society in France and the British Isles during the early and middle decades of the seventeenth century. Both states were still adjusting to the great upheaval which had been caused in Europe by the Protestant and Catholic reformations. Initially these had started within the late medieval Catholic Church as attempts to discourage practices which were seen as corrupt or superstitious and to improve the educational standards and commitment of the clergy. The emergence of Protestant churches, which were distinct and independent from the Catholic Church, by the middle of the sixteenth century, was only possible because some secular rulers were prepared to support them. The authority of such rulers was increased, yet princes who remained Catholic also tended to become more powerful as the papacy was desperate to retain their loyalty and made concessions which enhanced the integrity of their states.

The reformations also, paradoxically, led many members of the middle and lower ranks of society to question the right of their political and ecclesiastical masters to impose their authority upon them. Commercial expansion, industrial enterprise and the opportunities offered by newly discovered and exploited lands gave ever-increasing numbers of men, and a few women, greater levels of prosperity and economic independence. This led many to aspire to enjoy some measure of influence over the political decisions which affected their lives, as well as to have the freedom to choose their own religion. Many of the documents in this part of the book reflect the anxiety of the monarchs and their ministers to preserve (or even to extend) their power and the established state religion, and the determination of many of their subjects to challenge their right to do so.

The volatile condition of politics and religion combined, in the early years of the seventeenth century, with instability within the monarchies themselves to threaten the well-being of the states. The Stuart line of Scotland replaced the long-lived Elizabeth I of England, Ireland and Wales in 1603, bringing with them a rather more optimistic view of the plenitude of royal power than had been held by their predecessor. The Bourbon dynasty suffered a terrible setback in 1610 when the assassination of Henri IV put his young son on the throne and made his unreliable widow regent for too many years. One means by which contemporaries defined the strength of a state at this time was through the uniformity of religious observance accepted by its citizens.

The extract from David Calderwood's *The Pastor and the Prelate* (I.1) exemplifies several characteristics of the British opposition to royal religious policy. Contemporary Huguenot leaders were less concerned to vindicate their religious beliefs than to safeguard them, by protecting the areas of France where they were tolerated under the terms of the Edict of Nantes (1598). Louis XIII in the 1620s was not prepared to allow 'a state within a state' to exist and with the efficient support of his minister, Cardinal Richelieu, successfully dismantled the Huguenot strongholds. They continued to enjoy religious toleration until the adult rule of Louis XIV.

The growth of the power of states is often equated with the extension of government to influence and control new areas of national life. In the first part of the seventeenth century this was perceived by the kings' subjects to be happening with regard to taxation. This led them to mount challenges: in France they often took the form of riots, abuse of tax collectors and even revolts; in England the limits of the royal power to levy taxes were normally questioned through the law courts or parliament. Historians used to see the Stuarts' and Bourbons' anxiety to extract extra monies from their people as a manifestation of their absolutist policies. In recent decades many detailed studies, the work of Lublinskaya (1968) on France, for example, have emphasized the harsh economic realities, such as inflation and the cost of waging war, which forced the kings to look for increased revenues. The accounts of Bate's case in 1606 (I.2) and the sedition in Agen in 1635 (I.3) record reactions to means of raising royal income which were considered to exceed the legitimate exercise of the prerogative.

Various forms of direct and indirect taxation existed in both states, the main difference was that in England direct taxes fell most heavily on the upper classes; in France many of the wealthiest regarded their exemption from direct taxation (mainly the *taille*) as part of their privileged status. Indirect taxation also differed in its forms between France and the British Isles. In the former, goods which were transported within the country could be liable to a whole series of internal customs dues. Both states had means of financing local needs such as the maintenance of highways and the support of the very poor. In France seigneurs, officials and the Catholic Church all had a part to play. In England the parish was the unit which defined local financial responsibilities, although its officers were under the supervision of the justice of the peace, usually a member of the gentry and often the squire. The largest sums of money that parishes had to raise were for the relief of the poor and this unattractive task fell to the churchwardens as the extract from the parish of St Martin, Oxford (I.4) makes clear. In Scotland many of the responsibilities held by JPs in England were exercised by kirk sessions.

The most interesting question to ask about the way in which France and the British Isles were governed in the seventeenth century is whether they promoted or impeded the advance of the absolutist policies, which the Bourbons and Stuarts are accused by some historians of wishing to promote. Did royal victories against indignant taxpayers in the English courts ultimately make Charles I more powerful? Did the fall of the great Huguenot stronghold of La Rochelle enhance the long-term authority of Louis XIII? One answer to these conundrums could be that royal successes did strengthen monarchs when the policies concerned were pleasing to a majority of the influential people in the country. So Charles I only won Pyrrhic victories in the courts because most of the property owners identified with his opponents. Louis XIII, on the other hand, delighted his predominantly Catholic subjects by ending the political independence of the Huguenots. As Gerald Aylmer has observed, what made for the effective implementation of absolutist policies was

> ... the relative ability of the central government to harness national resources in a successful partnership with the dominant groups or classes.
>
> (Aylmer, 1990, p.102)

The way in which the royal courts enhanced the image of the monarchs and their families was an essential factor in determining the prestige that they would enjoy in the eyes of their subjects and also with foreign powers. Contemporaries were well aware of this; the letters of James Howell (I.5) make clear both his regret that the king did not grace the sad palace and the new parliament building at Edinburgh with his presence, and his deference towards Thomas Wentworth (Earl of Strafford) who kept great state as Lord Deputy of Ireland in Dublin. Not all observers of the Bourbons and Stuarts were so respectful, and John Chamberlain's lively account of the reception in London of Henrietta Maria after her marriage by proxy in 1625 to Charles I (I.6) combines the hearty support of a loyal subject with a realistic approach to the financial advantages of the transaction.

The pressures put upon successful ministers and courtiers to sustain their positions against the hostility of rivals are graphically described by Wentworth in his letter of 1637 to his friend archbishop Laud (I.7). It also provides evidence about some of the financial pitfalls which high office could entail: if you lived in a becoming style you would probably bankrupt yourself. If you took measures to finance the expenses of office you would be accused of corruption by your enemies.

An important part of the image of kingship, that those who aspired to wield absolute power had to convey, was to own an impressive selection of palaces, castles and hunting lodges built and furnished, if possible, in accordance with the most modern taste. The monarchs inherited a goodly number of residences together with quantities of worm-eaten furniture and old-fashioned pictures. The French kings were more fortunate than their British counterparts as they possessed, in the Louvre, a palace which had been built during the previous century in the grand, classical style of the Italian Renaissance. The Banqueting House of Inigo Jones in Charles I's palace at Whitehall, decorated by Rubens, exemplified the same style and, arguably, the same pretensions to absolute power. It should have been the first part of a great new palace which was planned but never built. Charles did, however, indulge his considerable love and knowledge of art in acquiring a collection of pictures, many painted in the high Renaissance style which had become fashionable during the previous hundred years. An extract from the catalogue of his collection (I.8), compiled in 1639, just before the outbreak of the civil war led to its gradual dispersal, demonstrates his discrimination as a connoisseur of art. Yet this was not the kind of pursuit which was likely to enhance his popularity with the majority of his subjects.

An important aspect of the court was the impact it made on popular opinion: the choice of companions made by the kings was crucial. One of the origins of the political problems encountered by Charles I in the 1620s was that the Duke of Buckingham was perceived as a rapacious, lowly born upstart. Louis XIII made a wise decision in making cardinal Richelieu his first minister: it was hard to object to an aristocrat who was also a great prelate. Writers did their best to promote the kind of conduct which would improve the repute of the courts and, with it, of their monarchs. Nicolas Faret's *The Honest Man or the Art to Please in Court* (I.9), as its title implies, attempted to achieve the seemingly impossible task of persuading courtiers that they could be successful and, at the same time, observe decent standards of moral behaviour.

The career of the Duke of Épernon was more typical of how ambitious men actually rose to fame and fortune through royal favour. The two extracts from his biography (I.10), written by an admiring secretary, show how, even late in life, such a career could go into serious decline. He demonstrated his power in Guyenne by living in great state; when Louis XIII visited him he may have found him to be too grand for a mere subject. Many complex factors brought about Épernon's eventual fall; one which worked against him was his bad relationship with some of the leading citizens of Bordeaux. Provincial governors under the centralizing regime of the Bourbons had a fine balancing act to perform: they had to keep order but they must not become too powerful in their own right.

In some ways the French kings and their ministers encountered greater difficulties in dealing with lesser provincial bodies than with the great nobles, such as those who were governors. Marillac's letter to Richelieu of 1630 (I.11) records a fairly common phenomenon in the dealings of central government with local interests. The Estates of Burgundy were trying to retain their traditional rights of assembly against a royal attempt to devolve their tax-voting function on to a court of venal officials. The fact that the

Estates survived, after placating the king by voting him a huge sum of money, indicates the limitation placed in practice on the exercise of absolute royal power. Robin Briggs has written of France:

> However much the kings believed in their ultimate sovereignty, they all recognized that they could only infringe the innumerable particular rights of their subjects when the supreme needs of the state required it.
>
> (Briggs, 1987, p.208)

In delineating the limits of absolutism Briggs offers an insight, which applies just as well to the British Isles as to France, into the origins of the civil wars which afflicted both states in the mid-seventeenth century. In the former case, a number of factors had combined by 1642 to undermine the authority of Charles I: even when he scored a technical victory, as in the case against John Hampden in 1637 (I.12), who was arraigned for his failure to pay ship money. More seriously, in 1638, the Scots drew up the National Covenant (I.13) in direct defiance of the king's religious initiatives. Royal policy in Ireland suffered an equally disastrous reverse: the conflicting demands of Catholics and Protestants in 1644 (I.14) bear out the view of historians such as Conrad Russell (1990) that the Stuarts' rule of multiple kingdoms was a major cause of instability in the state.

By 1648 the French monarchy, during the minority of Louis XIV, was also experiencing organized defiance from large sections of the population. The Frondes lacked the religious dimension which was a characteristic of the British civil wars but in other respects the insurgents had much in common: dislike of arbitrary taxation, hatred of royal ministers and an anxiety to retain old customs and rights which seemed to be endangered by the centralizing policies of the royal government (I.15, 16). The possibility that some of the leaders were influenced by the example of the successful British revolution is raised by Morosini's letter (I.17).

A consideration of the nature of the mid-century uprisings in France and the British Isles leads to the question of why they occurred. The explanation of what happened in England favoured by historians in the post-war years, including Marxists such as Christopher Hill, concentrated on the emergence of new classes, eager to share power with the monarchy and landowners. The extract from the Putney Debates, especially the contribution from trooper Sexby (I.18), lends credence to the idea that political activism had extended at least as far down as the artisans by the middle of the century. A more recent tendency to look at what happened in the British Isles in terms of the networks of relationships within parliaments, or local communities, or the tensions which arose between the three kingdoms, has been termed 'revisionism' as it shuns 'the big explanation' of the Marxists.

Since the outcome of the Frondes was not, perhaps, as spectacular, or their impact as climactic as the British civil wars, debate over their causes has never raged so fiercely. Much of what happened looked like the assertion of personal, privileged interests by members of the royal family, the nobility, the *parlements* and their supporters. The ardent royalist Bossuet's verdict in 1685 (I.19) neatly avoided these unpleasant facts, and he hailed the Frondes as 'the labour pains of France about to give birth to the miraculous reign of Louis XIV'. Clarendon, writing (in exile and disgrace) about the causes of the 'Great Rebellion' (I.20), apportioned some blame to the personality of Charles I as well as to the inflammatory impact of Puritan preachers upon the people.

The way in which stability was restored in both states after the upheavals of the mid-century is interesting for what it tells us about the nature of seventeenth-century societies and governments. Contemporary leaders of opinion are unencumbered by the deference for their superiors, reverence for tradition or deeply held religious convictions which dictated the behaviour and attitudes of men and women in earlier centuries. The inability of Cromwell and his associates to find a means of authorizing their rule in the eyes of the people, after the abolition of the monarchy, led to constant shifts in the devices by which they governed. After the death of the only man who could control the Army, the Restoration of the Stuarts and legitimacy was only a matter of time. The problem facing the government in France was similar but not identical: technically Louis XIV had never ceased to rule during the Frondes. When they ended and Mazarin recovered his grip on affairs there had to be a laborious process by which the Bourbon dynasty regained its prestige and power.

Baron de Lanta's efforts on behalf of the Estates of Languedoc in 1656 (I.21) record a case where the reassertion of central control was in danger of going too far. The royal government did a deal with the nobles and bourgeoisie whose interests were threatened: its power was acknowledged but only on condition that it recognized the limitations imposed by law and custom. The documents which deal with the revolt in the Boulonnais in 1662 (I.22) show the terrible repercussions on subjects who were unable to reach a compromise with their king. Nobles and common people had united in this uprising, always a dangerous situation for the government, but the Boulonnais was much nearer to the capital than Languedoc and proved easier to control.

The next three documents show how Cromwell and parliament in the 1650s wrestled with the problem of the four nations within the British Isles. The Ordinance for the Union of Scotland and England (I.23) followed the defeat of the Scots; they were to be united with England on very unfavourable terms. The Humble Petition and Advice (I.24) confronted the problem, mentioned above, of how the government was to be authorized. The solution that parliament came up with was to treat Cromwell in almost every respect like a traditional monarch and hope that he would stabilize the volatile political situation: his death, of course, had the reverse effect. Thomas Burton's diary (I.25) records the grievances of the longer established Protestant settlers in Ireland who feared that their interests would be swamped by those of the new settlers from the Army.

The last two documents in this part show two young kings flexing their muscles. The message from Louis XIV to his chancellor in 1661 (I.26), after the death of Mazarin, announced that he would in future personally direct the government. The conditions under which Charles II was to regain control of the British Isles dictated the adoption of a conciliatory tone in the 1660 Declaration of Breda (I.27), but it soon became evident to his subjects just how duplicitous their king could be. This duplicity was necessary to the continued survival of the Stuarts. The ruling classes would be quite prepared to turn against the restored monarchy if it exceeded what they perceived to be the traditional limits to its power.

References

Aylmer, G. (1990), 'The peculiarities of the English state', *Journal of Historical Sociology*, 3.

Briggs, R. (1987), *Early Modern France, 1560–1715*, Oxford University Press, Oxford.

Lublinskaya, A.D. (1968), *French Absolutism: The Crucial Phase, 1620–29*, Cambridge University Press, Cambridge.

Russell, C. (1990), *The Causes of the English Civil War*, Clarendon Press, Oxford.

1
David Calderwood: *The Pastor and the Prelate* (1628)

Source: David Reid (ed.), *The Party Coloured Mind: Prose Relating to the Conflict of Church and State in Seventeenth Century Scotland*, Scottish Academic Press, Edinburgh, 1982, p.4.

David Calderwood (1575–1650), a Scottish divine and indefatigable student of the relations of civil and spiritual authority, was deeply opposed to the introduction of bishops into the Church of Scotland. He was banished from Scotland in 1617 for opposing the king's right to direct the policy of the kirk through the bishops. He remained in exile in Holland until 1625 when he returned to Scotland. He was one of those who drew up the *Directory for Public Worship* and he wrote a monumental history of the kirk of Scotland.

For as Scotland, albeit far from Jerusalem, was one of the first nations that the light of the gospel shined on when it appeared to the Gentiles and one of the last that kept the light when the shadows of the hills of Rome began to darken the earth, so when the sun came about again at the Reformation, if this blessed light shined first upon others, all that had eyes to see both at home and abroad, have seen and said, that it shined fairest upon us, divine providence delighting to supply the defect of nature with abundance of grace and to make this backside [i.e. the back of] of the earth, lying behind the visible sun, by the clear and comforting beams of the sun of righteousness, to be the sunny side of the Christian world.

2
The judgement of Bate's Case (1606)

Source: J.P. Kenyon (ed.), *The Stuart Constitution 1603–1688: Documents and Commentary*, 2nd edn, Cambridge University Press, Cambridge, 1986, pp.51–6.

In 1606 John Bate, a merchant, refused to pay the import duty levied by the crown on currants and was prosecuted in the court of exchequer. The judge, Chief Baron Fleming, found in favour of the crown.

[Chief Baron Fleming]

To the king is committed the government of the realm and his people;

. . . The matter in question is material matter of state, and ought to be ruled by the rules of policy; and if it be so, the king hath done well to execute his extraordinary power. All customs, be they old or new, are no other but the effects and issues of trade and commerce with foreign nations; but all commerce and affairs with foreigners, all wars and peace, all acceptance and admitting for current, foreign coin, all parties and treaties whatsoever, are made by the absolute power of the king; and he who hath power of causes hath power also of effects. No exportation or importation can be but at the king's ports, they are the gates of the king, and he hath absolute power by them to include or exclude whom he shall please; and ports to merchants are their harbours and repose, and for their better security he is compelled to provide bulwarks and fortresses, and to maintain for the collection of his customs and duties collectors and customers; and for that charge it is reason that he should have this benefit. He is also to defend the merchants from pirates at sea in their passage. Also by the power of the King they are to be relieved if they are oppressed by foreign princes . . .

It is said that an imposition may not be upon a subject without parliament. That the king may impose upon a subject I omit; for it is not here the question if the king may impose upon the subject or his goods, but the impost here is not upon a subject, but here it is upon Bate, as upon a merchant who imports goods within this land charged before by the king; and at the time the impost was imposed upon them they were the goods of the Venetians and not the goods of a subject, nor within the land, but only upon those which shall after be imported; and so all the arguments which were made for the subject fail. And where it is said that he is a merchant, and that he ought to have the sea open and free for him, and that trades of merchants and merchandise are necessary to export the surplus of our commodities and then to import other necessities, and so is favourably to be respected; as to that, it is well known that the end of every private merchant is not the common good but his particular profit, which is only the means which induceth him to trade and traffic. And the impost to him is nothing, for he rateth his merchandise according to that . . .

And whereas it is said that if the king may impose, he may impose any quantity what he pleases, true it is that this is to be referred to the wisdom of the king, who guideth all under God by his wisdom, and this is not to be disputed by a subject; and many things are left to his wisdom for the ordering of his power, rather than his power shall be restrained. The king may pardon any felon; but it may be objected that if he pardon one felon he may pardon all, to the damage of the commonwealth, and yet none will doubt but that is left in his wisdom . . . And the wisdom and providence of the king is not to be disputed by the subject; for by intendment they cannot be severed from his person, and to argue *a posse ad actum* to restrain the king and his power because that by his power he may do ill is no argument for a subject. To prove the power of the king by precedents of antiquity in a case of this nature may easily be done, and if it were lawful in ancient times it is lawful now, for the authority of the king is not diminished and the Crown hath the same attributes that then it had . . .

[After reviewing the precedents he concluded:]

. . . All these statutes prove expressly, that the king had power to increase the impost, and that upon commodities of the land, and that he continually used this power notwithstanding all acts of parliament against it . . . Wherefore I think, that the king ought to have judgment.

3

Sedition at Agen (1635)

Source: R. Bonney, *Society and Government in France under Richelieu and Mazarin*, Macmillan, Basingstoke and London, 1988, pp.203–4. Translation from French.

The town council of Agen reported on the riot which broke out in Agen on 17 June 1635 at the rumour of a new imposition of the *gabelle*, the tax on salt. Such riots were common in many parts of France in the 1630s and were as often against rumours of taxation as against actual levies. It was rare for riots to be as violent as this one. (The mob claimed twenty-four victims.)

collectors of salt taxes

On Sunday 17th of the month at 9 o'clock in the morning the riot and popular sedition on the rumour of the *gabelle* began . . . Plenty of people assembled and began to troop together, shouting that 'we must kill the *gabeleurs*' and 'long live the King without the *gabelle*' . . .

This riot and popular sedition was so great and arose so suddenly among the plebs and common people of Agen that when the sieur Meja met the sieur d'Espalais, a town councillor and captain of St. Caprazy at the St. Gilles road, he ordered him to go to his quarter and prevent the evil plans of this mob. The said sieur d'Espalais placed himself in front of his house in a state to rally the good inhabitants among his neighbours to resist the mob on the road, but was killed and butchered on the spot and his house sacked, pillaged and put on fire; his eldest son killed, together with the La Tour sieur de Sauvebère, a councillor of the *Cour des Aides*[1] who had taken refuge there; he was killed and butchered, as well as a man named Guérineau, a student, who was thrown from the window and burnt alive. The adjoining house of the sieur de Barbier, a councillor in the *Cours des Aides*, was also pillaged and burnt. The

19

sieurs de Maures, the father a town councillor, the son an *élu*,[2] were murdered, killed and butchered in the convent of the Carmelites where they had taken refuge. The house of the sieur Codoing, an *élu*, was pillaged and he was killed, butchered and dragged to the river. Thomas, the jailkeeper was killed and butchered in front of the jail. Messieurs president Dubernet and other Messieurs of the chamber,[3] of the Catholic or Protestant faith, went with Monsieur Delpech, the *lieutenant criminel* and the sieurs Meja, Grousses and Cancer, town councillors, to protect the town hall with certain town councillors and bourgeois of the rue de Garonne, and established barricades and fortified the doors of the town hall. At this moment, certain gentlemen, seigneurs and litigants at the chamber offered themselves to assist us and serve the King and the town by defeating the incendiaries and seditious persons . . .

The town hall was menaced with arson. We got out the cannon and other pieces and falconets [light cannons], established barricades at the four corners and approaches to the town hall, installed a good guard throughout, even at the five gates and at the St. Caprazy church. The people barricaded themselves throughout the streets and alleys.

Behind the barricades, the mob discussed who they intended to kill if the rumoured *gabelle* was not abolished. They demanded a decree of amnesty for their murders and incendiarism and forced Messieurs of the Chamber to draw up this declaration and have it printed. If they had not agreed, everything would have been put to fire and blood. As long as the *gabelle* was abolished they said that they would return to obedience. The decree was announced by trumpet call throughout the town . . .

[1] A court with powers to oversee the tax system.
[2] A venal official responsible for levying taxation.
[3] Of the edict (*chambre de l'édit*). This was one of several special tribunals set up under the terms of the edict of Nantes to hear cases involving Protestants.

4

Instructions for levying the poor rate in the parish of St Martin, Oxford (1620)

Source: Oxfordshire Archives, St Martin's Parish, Oxford C29(a) 121.

At the quarter sessions local justices of the peace gave instructions to the churchwardens and overseers of the poor for each parish to levy the poor rate from all householders.

Civitas Oxon [the city of Oxford]

To the churchwardens of the parish of St Martin and to Thomas Crompton and Thomas Cooper overseers for the poor within the same parish for this year 1620 appointed.

These are in his Majesty's name to charge and command the one and every of you presently to demand of all and every the persons of your parish, being assessed and rated to contribute towards the relief of the poor of your said parish all and every the several sums of money severally and respectively assessed and rated upon them together with the arrearages [arrears] for and towards the necessary relief of the poor of your said parish according to the form of the statute in that behalf lately provided. And if they or any of them shall refuse to pay the said several sums so rated upon them, that then presently you levy the same by distress and sale of the offender's goods, rendering to the party the surplus that shall remain upon the sale of their said goods. And this shall be your sufficient warrant therein. Dated the first day of June anno Domini 1620.

Jo. Prideaux, vicecan[1]

Oliver Smith, mayor

[1] The vice-chancellor of the University of Oxford and the mayor of the city were *ex officio* justices of the peace and members of the quarter sessions for the city.

5

Howell's *Familiar Letters* from Edinburgh and from Dublin (1639)

Source: J. Howell, *Familiar Letters or Epistolae Ho-Elianae*, Dent, London, 1903, vol.2, pp.60, 63–5.

James Howell (*c*.1594–1666), the son of an impecunious Welsh curate, was a writer who made a precarious living on the fringes of the court. He was variously a businessman, a tutor and, for eight years, a resident as a debtor in the Fleet, where he paid his way by his prolific writings. After the Restoration, Charles II awarded him a salary as 'historiographer royal of England'. His career demonstrates how able people, without inherited wealth or titles, could advance by gaining favour at court.

A.   *To my Lord Clifford, from Edinburgh*

MY LORD,

I have seen now all the King of Great Britain's dominions; and he is a good traveller that hath seen all his dominions. I was born in Wales. I have been in

21

Figure 1 Title page of James Howell's, *Epistolae Ho-Elianae*, 1650 (second edition).

all the four corners of England, I have traversed the diameter of France[1] more than once, and now I am come through Ireland into this Kingdom of Scotland. This town of Edinburgh is one of the fairest streets that ever I saw (excepting that of Palermo in Sicily); it is about a mile long, coming sloping down from the Castle . . . to the Holyrood House, now the Royal Palace; and these two begin and terminate the town. I am come hither in a very convenient time, for here is a National Assembly and a Parliament, my Lord Traquair being His Majesty's Commissioner. The bishops are all gone to wreck, and they have had but a sorry funeral, the very name is grown so contemptible, that a black dog if he have any white marks about him is called Bishop. Our Lord of Canterbury is grown here so odious that they call him commonly in the pulpit the Priest of Baal and the Son of Belial . . .

There is a fair Parliament House built here lately, and it was hoped His Majesty would have taken the maidenhead of it, and come hither to sit in person; and they did ill who advised him otherwise.

I am to go hence shortly back to Dublin, and so to London, where I hope to find your lordship, that, according to my accustomed boldness, I may attend you. In the interim I rest your Lordship's most humble servitor.

J.H.

Edinburgh 1639.

[1] English kings still styled themselves 'king of France'. This was based on a dynastic claim to the throne which originated in the fourteenth century.

B. *From Dublin to Sir Edward Savage, Knight, at Tower Hill*

I am come safely to Dublin over an angry boisterous sea. Whether 'twas my voyage on salt-water, or change of air, being now under another clime, which was the cause of it, I know not, but I am suddenly freed of the pain in my arm, when neither bath, nor plaisters [ointments or medicated bandages], and other remedies could do me good.

I delivered your letter to Mr James Dillon, but nothing can be done in that business till your brother Pain comes to town. I meet here with divers of my northern friends whom I knew at York. Here is a most splendid court kept at the castle, and except that of the viceroy of Naples I have not seen the like in Christendom, and in one point of grandeur the Lord Deputy [Sir Thomas Wentworth] here goes beyond him, for he can confer honours and dub knights, which that viceroy cannot, or any other I know of. Traffic increaseth here wonderfully, with all kind of bravery and buildings.

I made a humble motion to my lord that in regard businesses of all sorts did multiply here daily, and that there was but one clerk of the council (Sir Paul Davis) who was able to despatch business (Sir William Usher, his colleague, being very aged and bedrid), his lordship would please to think of me. My lord gave me an answer full of good respects to succeed Sir William after his death.

No more now, but with my most affectionate respects unto you I rest, your faithful servitor,

J.H.

Dublin, *3 May 1639.*

6

John Chamberlain to Sir Dudley Carleton, London (1625)

Source: J. Chamberlain, *The Court and Times of Charles I*, pub. Henry Colburn, London, 1848, vol.1, pp.34–5.

John Chamberlain (1553–1627) was the younger son of an alderman of London. He was left sufficient money to live a life of leisure and maintained a wide circle of correspondents. One of these was Sir Dudley Carleton (1573–1632), a diplomat who was favoured by Buckingham and in 1625, after many years as ambassador at the Hague, was made vice-chamberlain of the royal household and privy councillor.

John Chamberlain Esq. to Sir Dudley Carleton, London, June 25, 1625
Though the sickness increase shrewdly upon us, so that in this week died in all 640; of the plague 239; and though this term [the legal term of Trinity] be abridged to the three first days, and the three last, yet we cannot find in our hearts to leave this town, as long as such doings, by reason of the Queen's arrival, and the sitting of the parliament.

The feast that should have been on Sunday, by reason of the Queen's indisposition, or that all was not ready, was deferred until Tuesday, when the publication and confirmation of the *articles* [articles of the marriage treaty] was solemnized in the Great Room at Whitehall, where also the ambassador and all the French were feasted, but neither the King nor Queen present, nor likewise the next night at York House, whither they were all invited by the duke of Buckingham, and entertained with such magnificence and prodigal plenty, both for curious cheer and banquet, that the like hath not been seen in these parts. One rare dish came by chance; a sturgeon, full six feet long, that afternoon leaping into a sculler's boat, not far from the place, was served in a supper. In all these shows and feastings, there hath been such excessive bravery [ostentatious display] on all sides, as bred rather a surfeit than any delight in them that saw it. And it was more fit, and it should have become us to compare and dispute with such pompous kind of people in iron and steel, than in gold and jewels, wherein we came not near them.

The Queen hath brought, they say, such a poor, pitiful sort of women, that there is not one worth the looking after, saving herself and the duchesse of Chevreuse, who though she be fair, yet paints foully.[1] Among the priests, you would little look for Monsieur Lancy, that went ambassador to Constantinople, when we were at Venice, and is become a 'padre del oratorio' [oratory priest]. I doubted poverty or desperation had driven him to it, but they say he is rich and hath good means.

Six score thousand pounds of her dowry is come along with the Queen, which will work no great effect, if it be true that fifty thousand pounds of it be allotted to the earls of Carlisle and Holland for their services, and that she require thirty thousand to distribute among her servants. We were in hopes that the best part of them would have been packing away the next week, but she hath persuaded and prevailed with the duke and his lady that she shall lie in here,[2] which cannot be but to our great charge and incommodity.

[1] The duchess amazed Londoners by swimming across the Thames one warm evening as well as by painting her face.

[2] The duchess of Chevreuse should be delivered of the child she was expecting.

7

A letter from the Earl of Strafford to Archbishop Laud (1637)

Source: W. Knowler (ed.), *The Earl of Strafford's Letters and Dispatches*, printed for the editor by William Bowyer, London, 1739, vol.2, pp.105–7.

Thomas Wentworth, Earl of Strafford (1593–1641), was appointed Lord Deputy of Ireland by Charles I in 1632, and was made an earl in 1640. Soon afterwards he was promoted to the rank of Lord Lieutenant. He was installed in Dublin in July 1633. He derived comfort during his years in Ireland from his correspondence with his friend and kindred political spirit, William Laud (1573–1645), Archbishop of Canterbury. Wentworth showed some signs of paranoia in these letters, constantly imagining attacks from unspecified enemies and seeking reassurance from Laud.

The *Lord Deputy to the Archbishop of Canterbury, A.D. 1637.*
May it please your Grace,
No sooner am I got home, but the gout hath laid fast hold on me, yet gives me leave to think the more, as it renders me able to do the less; and in taking the view of my buildings, as I came along, they put me in mind of some things,

which have run in my thoughts ever since, so as I shall crave your leave to count them over with your Grace. And as I shall deal most ingeniously with you as my ghostly father, so do I beseech and promise unto myself your advice and counsel.

I have good advertisement that some, who sure find that I serve the Crown too entirely for their purpose, do yet endeavour to persuade his Majesty, that I serve myself too well in this place, so to bring me into suspicion with my master, and through that open a way to my prejudice. To evince this belief from his Majesty they fetch their calumnies from every side.

Their first charge is, that I have two or three and twenty thousand pounds a year coming in. And should it be forty, were I to be condemned for that, more than themselves, that comparatively have forty times as much as other men, that for any thing I know, may deserve as much better than they, as they themselves deserve better than I? It is very true that I have under the blessing of Almighty God and the protection of his Majesty six thousand pounds a year good land, which I brought with me into his service; I have a share for a short time in these customs, which whilst his Majesty's revenue is there increased more than twenty thousand pounds by year, proves nevertheless a greater profit to me than I ever dreamt of. Besides I have nothing but those gracious entertainments, which others before had, and those which succeed me must have, saving only that my troop consists of a hundred horse, where theirs were but forty. Yet let them take this truth along, my hundred hath stood me in gathering, furnishing, and maintaining, some thousands more, than ever I must see again forth of his Majesty's pay: where other former Deputies have known how out of the pay of their forty to clear into their own purse about five hundred pounds yearly; nor is this a riddle, lest it be I will expound it: they kept in their stable half a dozen hackneys; I a hundred horse, in every respect able and fitted for his Majesty's service.

Next they say I build up to the sky. I acknowledge that were myself only considered in what I build, it were not only to excess, but even to folly, having already houses moderate for my condition in Yorkshire: but his Majesty will justify me, that at my last being in England, I acquainted him with a purpose I had to build him a house at the Naas [Jigginstown], it being uncomely that his Majesty should not have one here of his own, capable to lodge him with moderate conveniency (which in truth as yet he hath not) in case he might be pleased sometimes hereafter to look upon this kingdom; and that it was necessary in a manner for the dignity of this place, and the health of his Deputy and family that there should be one removing house of fresh air, for want whereof I assure your Lordship, I have felt no small inconvenience, since my coming hither; that when it was built, if it liked his Majesty it should be his, paying me as it cost; if disliked *a suo damno* ['at his loss'], I was content to keep it and smart for my folly. His Majesty seemed to be pleased with all, whereupon I proceeded and have in a manner finished it, and so contrived for the rooms of State and other accommodations which I have observed in his

Majesty's houses, as I have been indeed stark mad, ever to have cast it so for a private family . . . If I be made so happy as to see his Majesty on this side, he will give me thanks . . . and then I am at the height of my ambition, and these my well-wishers fairly hounded on the very place to accuse me.

Dublin, this 27th of   Your Grace's
September, 1637   most humbly to be commanded.
                  Wentworth

8
An extract from Abraham van der Doort's catalogue of the collection of Charles I (*c*.1639)

Source: Abraham van der Doort, *Catalogue of the Collections of Charles I*, edited by O. Miller, Walpole Society, Glasgow, 1960, vol.37, pp.76–7.

Abraham van der Doort (?1575–1640) was a Dutch craftsman and printer who probably came to England in 1609 and entered the service of Prince Henry. From 1625 he was a Groom of the Chamber to Charles I, earning 5/6d a day, and subsequently received three salaries of £40 a year for the care of the king's collections, for making patterns for coins for the Royal Mint and as Surveyor of the King's Pictures. He was very conscientious, and anxiety about the trust reposed in him may have led to his suicide in June 1640. He had compiled an inventory which was probably completed in 1639 and which survives in four contemporary manuscripts. The edition draws on all four of them: Bodleian Library MSS Ashmole 1514, 1513; British Library MS Additional 10112; and a Windsor MS in the Royal Collection.

Windsor MS Version

By your Majesty's especial command your pictures and rarities which you had kept at St. James's in the Cabinet Room, were transported and brought to Whitehall into the Privy Gallery in your Majesty's new erected Cabinet room, whereof the particulars as well of the said rarities from St. James's as also other pictures, medals, agates or the like since by your Majesty augmented, as by the number and bigness particularly specified doth appear as followeth:

Placed around about in the aforesaid your Majesty's Cabinet room 81, whereof 7 are not painted pictures.

1

Done by Giorgone.[1] Bought by your Majesty Matte of Geldrope when you were prince.

Imprimis. A dark painted man's head in a black cap and a cloak without hands or ruff done by Giorgone said to be his picture being painted upon a new board set in a black frame painted upon the right light.

2

Done by Lucas van Leyden and given to your Majesty by the States [Assembly of the United Provinces]

Item, under the said piece leaning upon his right hand holding a dead skull in the other hand – whereby standing a lighted candle, and also hanging at the wall a red cardinal's hat being painted upon a board, being one of the 5 pieces which the States Ambassador gave to your Majesty at St. James in 1635, in a black ebony frame, painted upon the right light.

3

Bought by your Majesty done at Prague by Paul van Vianen

Item, under the piece aforesaid a piece done by Paul van Vianen who was the Emperor Rudolph's man. In chased work hangs a silver plate in a black frame being Our Lady and Christ and some saint with a pair of pincers where she holdeth a tooth with [St Apollonia].

4

Mantua piece done by Titian

Item, a standing Lucretia [Royal Collection] holding with her left hand a veil over her face, and a dagger in her hand to stab herself, an entire figure half so big as in the life. In a black ebony frame, painted upon the right light.

5

Given to your Majesty by Sir Arthur Hopton

Item, a little piece wherein a witch riding upon a black ram goat in the air with a distaff in her hand. 4 little cupids in several actions, said to be done by Elsheimer [not by Elsheimer, Royal Collection] before he went to Italy by a print of Albert Durer, painted upon the right light.

6

Given to your Majesty by Sir Arthur Hopton, your Majesty's Ambassador in Spain, by the young Brueghel

Item, before the chimney under the said Lucretia there hangeth at this time the little landscape picture, containing some 25 country people, being at their harvesting, being in a black ebony frame, painted upon the right light.

¹ Now thought not to be by Giorgione, Royal Collection.

9

Nicholas Faret, *The Honest Man or the Art to Please in Court* (1630)

Source: Nicholas Faret, *The Honest Man or the Art to Please in Court*, translated into English by Edward Grimstone and published in London, 1632, pp.3–8. Dedicated to Richard Hubert Esq., Groom Porter to His Majesty.

Nicholas Faret's treatise is in the tradition of the sixteenth-century work *The Courtier*, by Baldassare Castiglione. Faret wished to instil decent standards of conduct in courtiers by cultivation of the polite arts. The translation for an English courtier, only two years after it was published in France, bears testimony to the close cultural relations which existed at the time between the English and French Courts.

Princes and great men are about a king like goodly stars, which receive all their light from him, but it is all confounded in this great light. And although their brightness doth not appear but when they are remote from him, yet it is never glorious, nor full of lustre, but when as this first fountain of glory pours itself upon them and distributes unto them certain beams of his magnificence.

The greatest part of the meaner sort consume themselves near this fire, before they can be warm, and fortune, who takes delight to display upon this theatre, the most remarkable tricks of her malice and lightness, makes a sport at the ruin of a thousand ambitious men, to raise one to the top of the precipice, which she prepares in a manner for all those which suffer themselves to be blinded with her favours. 'Envy', 'Avarice' and 'Ambition', which always attend her, reign particularly with her about kings, whither they draw an infinite number of mercenary spirits, whom the disorder of insatiable covetousness, will not suffer to contain themselves in a life full of sweetness and tranquillity, to cast themselves into the tumults which great courts (like unto great seas), are continually tossed.

They inspire so many ruinous designs which arm men one against another, and make most flourishing monarchies desolate, and in the end trouble the whole frame of human society, and violate the most sacred laws which are observed in the world. Amidst these most pernicious dangers which they procure, in my opinion, such as follow them, cannot be too well advised, to preserve himself from the misfortunes which do accompany them: and there is not any man settled in so firm a station, whom the authority of those that are more powerful, or the envy of his equals, or the malice of those which are under him, may not pull down from the top of his greatest prosperities.

10
The History of the Life of the Duke of Épernon (c.1640)

Source: Guillaume Girard, *The History of the Life of the Duke of Épernon, the Great Favourite of France*, English edn by Charles Cotton, Esq., London, 1670, pp.378, 419–20. Translation from French.

This biography was written by one of Épernon's secretaries, Guillaume Girard, soon after the duke's death in 1642. Épernon's son, Bernard de la Valette, had spent some time in exile in England, before the deaths of Richelieu and Louis XIII enabled him to return to France and to all his father's titles, possessions and honours. This may explain the English interest in Épernon's career which led to this translation. The two extracts refer to incidents which occurred relatively early in the adult reign of Louis: his visit to Cadillac in 1620, a gesture of forgiveness soon after Épernon had supported Marie de Medici in her second war against the king, and the duke's first confrontation with the *parlement* of Bordeaux in 1623 over his entry as the new governor.

The History of the Life of the duke of Épernon, the Great Favourite of France

His Majesty continuing his way through Guyenne, took occasion to call at Blaye, from whence he removed Lussan, viscount de Aubeterre, to recompense him with the staff of a Marshal of France, placing Brantes in his stead. Whilst these things were in doing, the duke of Épernon (who attended his Majesty on this voyage) took the opportunity to prepare his house for his reception; wherein he ordered all things so admirably well, and with such magnificence, that his Majesty could hardly have been better entertained in any part of the kingdom. The noble furniture, wherewith this house did abound, was now all brought out: the king's apartment all hung round with hangings embossed all over with gold, as also ten chambers more were furnished with the same, to which the beds of cloth of gold and embroidery were richly suited; neither was delicacy, rarity, or plenty of provisions inferior to this outward pomp. All the favourites, ministers and others of the greatest quality at court were commodiously lodged in this stately house, and the provisionary officers there found what was not elsewhere to be seen in the kingdom; which was a vast series of offices underground, so large, and so well fitted with lights, that they were astonished at so prodigious an extent of accommodations; which are indeed, if not the chiefest ornament, at least the greatest convenience of a building.

After his Majesty had stayed two days at Cadillac, where his whole court had been magnificently treated, he parted thence to continue his journey towards Bearne . . .

[The president of the parlement of Bordeaux wrote to Épernon:] 'That a difficulty having been started in the parlement about the manner of his reception, they had determined to moderate the excessive honours [that] had formerly been paid to Sons of France,[1] or the first Princes of the Blood,[2] who had been governors of the province, in going to receive them in their scarlet robes; a punctilio that though it was true, it had been waived in deference to the duke of Mayenne, it had nevertheless been done merely out of respect to the high favour wherein he was, when advanced to the government of Guyenne: but at this time they were resolved to be more reserved.' I never in my life saw the duke more surprised, than at this news, who jealous of his honour and dignity to the highest degree, would rather never have entered Bordeaux, than suffer the least diminution of what had been granted to the duke of Mayenne. He therefore returned an answer . . . wherein he insisted with great vehemency upon . . . those honours . . . paid to his predecessor . . .

The duke, not yet satisfied with delivering his sense of this affair in writing, would moreover dispatch away Constantin, the Comptroller of his House, to Bordeaux to communicate his resolution to several members of that *parlement*, who were his particular friends; wherein he succeeded according to his own desire, and his reception was concluded in the same form his predecessors had been received, some of the company totally disowning all the first president had writ concerning this business: by which the duke having

31

just reason to think him the author of this scruple . . . he from thenceforward entertained very sinister impressions of his friendship: neither was it long before he made him sensible of it.

¹ Legitimate sons of the kings of France.
² Members of the house of Bourbon, such as the prince de Conti.

11
Marillac to Richelieu (1630)

Source: R. Bonney, *Society and Government in France under Richelieu and Mazarin*, Macmillan, London, 1988, p.97.

Michel de Marillac had worked for Sully during the reign of Henri IV. In 1630 he held the important office of Keeper of the Seal and used it to pursue the policy of reducing the power of provincial estates by asserting royal control over the levying of taxes. Later in the year he was to be disgraced for his part in the 'Day of the Dupes' when, in alliance with Marie de Medici, the Queen Mother, he tried unsuccessfully to destroy the power of Cardinal Richelieu.

27 January 1630

The deputies of Burgundy have been heard by the King, with Monsieur de Bellegarde present, concerning the revocation of the *élections*[1] for which they offer 1.8 million *livres*; but the uniformity which the King wishes to establish in his kingdom has led him to refuse these offers and to persevere in the establishment of *élections*. There is one great advantage of them: no taxes can be levied in this province except by letters patent of the King, and the Estates will not be able to burden the people.

I have written to you concerning the *droit annuel*[2] in my previous letters. Yesterday, the King, considering the need to assist your army,[3] resolved to accord it to the financial office-holders and not to the judicial office-holders, whose offices will be abolished on their death. This shows that the failure to renew the *droit annuel* results from the wish to assist the people and for the good of justice. Financial office-holders are a charge on the King because of their great salaries, but judicial office-holders are a charge on the people because of their great number, and draw from the people in fees what they do not receive in salaries. I consider that, if this is carried out carefully, there will soon be a great diminution in the number of these offices and a great help to the people, besides which it will considerably reduce the price of offices, which may not be significant at the beginning but subsequently becomes the main wealth of the most notable families. This would also gain support for this measure and remove the opinion that it is just an expedient to gain vacant offices which can then be granted out by the crown.

¹ These were lesser finance courts concerned with the levy of direct taxation. They existed throughout much of France (the so-called *pays d'élections*), but were not in the provinces with provincial estates (the so-called *pays d'états*).
² The so-called annual right (sometimes called the *paulette*) was an annual payment by an office-holder for the privilege of resigning his office to his heir.
³ Richelieu was lieutenant-general in the army of Italy at this moment.

12
The speech of Oliver St John in the ship money case (1637–8)

Source: J.P. Kenyon (ed.), *The Stuart Constitution 1603–1688: Documents and Commentary*, 2nd edn, Cambridge University Press, Cambridge, 1986, pp. 98–9.

Oliver St John (*c*.1598–1673) made his reputation as a lawyer and politician by his eloquent defence of Lord Saye and John Hampden in this ship money case. He continued supporting parliament, and later Cromwell, actively until the Restoration. He was Chief Justice, Common Pleas from 1648 to 1660.

Rex v Hampden, 1637–8 (ship money)
[Oliver St John, November 1637]

My Lords, . . . it must needs be granted that in this business of defence the *suprema potestas* [supreme power] is inherent in his Majesty, as part of his crown and kingly dignity.

So that as the care and provision of the law of England extends in the first place to foreign defence, and secondly lays the burden upon all, and for ought I have to say against it, it maketh the quantity of each man's estate the rule whereby this burden is to be equally apportioned upon each person; so likewise hath it in the third place made his Majesty the sole judge of dangers from foreigners, and when and how the same are to be prevented, and to come nearer, hath given him power by writ under the Great Seal of England, to command the inhabitants of each county to provide shipping for the defence of the kingdom, and may by law compel the doing thereof.

So that, my Lords, as I still conceive [it] the question will not be *de persona*, in whom the *suprema potestas* of giving the authorities or powers to the sheriff, which are mentioned in this writ, doth lie, for that is in the king; but the question is only *de modo*, by what medium or method this supreme power, which is in his Majesty, doth infuse and let out itself into this particular . . .

His Majesty is the fountain of justice; and though all justice which is done within the realm flows from this fountain, yet it must run in certain and known channels: an assize in the King's Bench, or an appeal of death in the Common Pleas, are *coram non judice* though the writ be his Majesty's command; and so of the several jurisdictions of each Court . . . If the process be legal, and in a right court, yet I conceive that his Majesty alone, without assistance of the judges of the court, cannot give judgment. I know that King John, H.3 and other kings have sat on the King's Bench, and in the Exchequer; but for ought appears they were assisted by their judges . . .

And as without the assistance of his judges, who are his settled counsel at law, his Majesty applies not the law and justice in many cases unto his subjects; so likewise in other cases neither is this sufficient to do it without the assistance of his great Council in parliament. If an erroneous judgment was given before the Statute of 27 Eliz. in the King's Bench, the king could not relieve his grieved subjects any way but by Writ of Error in parliament; neither can he out of parliament alter the old laws, nor make new, or make any naturalisations or legitimations, nor do some other things; and yet is the parliament his Majesty's court too, as well as other his Courts of Justice. It is his Majesty that gives life and being to that, for he only summons, continues and dissolves it, and by his *le volt* [it is agreed] enlivens all the actions of it; and after the dissolution of it, by supporting his Courts of Justice, he keeps them still alive, by putting them in execution. And although in the Writ of Waste, and some other writs, it is called *commune concilium regni* [common council of the realm], in respect that the whole kingdom is representatively there, and secondly, that the whole kingdom have access thither in all things that concern them, other courts affording relief but in special causes, and thirdly, in respect that the whole kingdom is interested in, and receive benefit by the laws and things there passed; yet it is *concilium regni* no otherwise than the Common Law is *lex terrae* [law of the land] . . .

My Lords, the parliament, as it is best qualified and fitted to make this supply for some of each rank, and that through all the parts of the kingdom being there met, his Majesty having declared the danger, they best knowing the estates of all men within the realm, are fittest, by comparing the danger and men's estates together, to proportion the aid accordingly.

And secondly, as they are fittest for the preservation of that fundamental propriety which the subject hath in his lands and goods, because each subject's vote is included in whatever is there done . . .

My Lords, it appears not by anything in the writ, that any war at all was proclaimed against any state, or that if any his Majesty's subjects had taken away the goods of any prince's subjects in Christendom, but that the party might have recovered them before your Lordships in any his Majesty's courts; so that the case in the first place is, whether in times of peace his Majesty may, without consent in parliament, alter the property of the subject's goods for the defence of the realm.

Secondly, the time that will serve the turn for the bringing in of supplies and means of the defence, appears to your Lordships judicially by the writ, that is seven months within four days, for the writ went out 4 August, and commands the ship to be at Portsmouth, the place of rendezvous, the first of March following; and thereby it appears that the necessity in respect of the time was not such, but that a parliamentary consent might in that time have been endeavoured for the effecting of the supply . . .

13
The National Covenant (1638)

Source: Nat. MSS Scot. iii, no.xcviii, in G. Donaldson (ed.), *Scottish Historical Documents*, Scottish Academic Press, Edinburgh, 1970, pp.194–201. (Adapted for clarity.)

This document represents the culmination of the hostility felt by the Scottish subjects of Charles I to many of his policies. The strongest grievance which they harboured against him was that he systematically attempted to impose the Anglican canons, liturgy and Prayer Book on the Church (Kirk) of Scotland. The members of that church were Presbyterians, most of whom found the doctrines and practices of the Laudian Church of England (Anglican Church) unacceptable. The Covenant was drafted by Alexander Henderson and Archibald Johnston of Wariston, two leading critics of royal policies in Scotland. It was given its final format and signed by a group of Scots nobles, in Greyfriars Church, Edinburgh, on 28 February and 1 March 1638, and distributed throughout the country for signature. The Scots pledged themselves, in the Covenant, to resist the religious changes introduced by the king and defend their Presbyterian Church.

The Confession of Faith of the Kirk of Scotland, subscribed at first by the King's Majesty and his household in the year of God 1580; thereafter by persons of all ranks in the year 1581, by ordinance of the lords of the secret council and acts of the general assembly; . . . now subscribed in the year 1638 by us noblemen, barons, gentlemen, burgesses, ministers and commons under subscribing; together with our resolution and promises for the causes after specified, to maintain the said true religion, and the King's Majesty, according to the confession aforesaid and acts of parliament: the tenor whereof here followeth: . . .

Figure 2 The Arch-Prelate of St Andrews comes under attack whilst reading from the Revised Prayer Book for Scotland in St Giles Cathedral in Edinburgh in 1637, contemporary woodcut.

That all Kings and Princes at their Coronation and reception of their Princely Authority, shall make their faithful promise by their solemn oath in the presence of the Eternal God, that, enduring the whole time of their lives, they shall serve the same Eternal God to the uttermost of their power, according as he hath required in his most Holy Word, contained in the old and new Testament. And according to the same Word shall maintain the true Religion of Christ Jesus, the preaching of his Holy Word, the due and right ministration of the Sacraments now received and preached within this Realm (according to the Confession of Faith immediately preceding) and shall abolish and gainstand all false Religion contrary to the same, and shall rule the people committed to their charge, according to the will and command of God, revealed in his foresaid Word, and according to the laudable Laws and Constitutions received in this Realm, no ways repugnant to the said will of the Eternal God; and shall procure, to the uttermost of their power, to the Kirk of God, and whole Christian people, true and perfect peace in all time coming: and that they shall be careful to root out of their Empire all Heretics, and enemies to the true worship of God, who shall be convicted by the true Kirk of God, of the foresaid crimes, which was also observed by his Majesty, at his Coronation in Edinburgh 1633, as may be seen in the order of the Coronation.

In obedience to the Commandment of God, conform to the practice of the godly in former times, and according to the laudable example of our Worthy and Religious Progenitors, and of many yet living amongst us, which was warranted also by act of Council, commanding a general band to be made and subscribed by his Majesty's subjects, of all ranks, for two causes: One was,

For defending the true Religion, as it was then reformed, and is expressed in the Confession of Faith above written, and a former large Confession established by sundry acts of lawful general assemblies, and of Parliament, unto which it hath relation, set down in public Catechisms, and which had been for many years with a blessing from Heaven preached, and professed in this Kirk and Kingdom, as Gods undoubted truth, grounded only upon his written Word. The other cause was, for maintaining the Kings Majesty, His Person, and Estate: the true worship of God and the Kings authority, being so straitly joined, as that they had the same Friends, and common enemies, and did stand and fall together. And finally, being convinced in our minds, and confessing with our mouths, that the present and succeeding generations in this Land, are bound to keep the foresaid national Oath and Subscription inviolable, We Noblemen, Barons, Gentlemen, Burgesses, Ministers and Commons under subscribing, considering divers times before and especially at this time, the danger of the true reformed Religion, of the Kings honour, and of the public peace of the Kingdom: By the manifold innovations and evils generally contained, and particularly mentioned in our late supplications, complaints, and protestations, Do hereby profess, and before God, his Angels, and the World solemnly declare, That, with our whole hearts we agree and resolve, all the days of our life, constantly to adhere unto, and to defend the foresaid true Religion, and (forbearing the practice of all novations, already introduced in the matters of the worship of God, or approbation of the corruptions of the public Government of the Kirk, or civil places and power of Kirk-men, till they be tried and allowed in free assemblies, and in Parliaments) to labour by all means lawful to recover the purity and liberty of the Gospel, as it was stablished and professed before the foresaid Novations: and because, after due examination, we plainly perceive, and undoubtedly believe, that the Innovations and evils contained in our Supplications, Complaints, and Protestations have no warrant of the Word of God, are contrary to the Articles of the Foresaid Confessions, to the intention and meaning of the blessed reformers of Religion in this Land, to the above written Acts of Parliament, and do sensibly tend to the re-establishing of the Popish Religion and Tyranny, and to the subversion and ruin of the true Reformed Religion, and of our Liberties, Laws and Estates, We also declare, that the Foresaid Confessions are to be interpreted, and ought to be understood of the Foresaid novations and evils, no less than if every one of them had been expressed in the Foresaid confessions, and that we are obliged to detest and abhorr them amongst other particular heads of Papistry abjured therein. And therefore from the knowledge and consciences of our duty to God, to our King and Country, without any worldly respect or inducement, so far as human infirmity will suffer, wishing a further measure of the grace of God for this effect, We promise, and swear by the Great Name of the Lord our God, to continue in the Profession and Obedience of the Foresaid Religion: That we shall defend the same, and resist all these contrary errors and corruptions, according to our vocation, and to the uttermost of that power that God hath put in our hands, all the days of our life: and in like manner with the same heart, we declare before God and Men, That we have no intention nor desire to attempt any thing that may turn to the dishonour of God, or to the diminution of the Kings greatness and authority: But on the contrary, we promise and swear, that we shall, to the uttermost of our power, with our means and lives, stand to the defence of our dread Sovereign, the Kings Majesty, his Person, and Authority, in the defence and preservation of the foresaid true Religion, Liberties and Laws of the Kingdom: As also . . . whatsoever shall be done to the least of us for that cause, shall be taken as done to us all in general, and to every one of us in particular . . . And because we cannot look for a blessing from God upon our proceedings, except with our Profession and Subscription we join such a life and conversation, as beseemeth Christians, who have renewed their Covenant with God; We, therefore, faithfully promise, for our selves, our followers, and all other under us, both in public, in our particular families, and personal carriage, to endeavour to keep our selves within the bounds of Christian liberty, and to be good examples to others of all Godliness, Soberness, and Righteousness, and of every duty we owe to God and Man, And that this our Union and Conjunction may be observed without violation, we call the living God, the Searcher of our Hearts to witness . . . that Religion and Righteousness may flourish in the Land, to the glory of God, the honour of our King, and peace and comfort of us all.

14
Irish Catholic and Protestant demands in petitions to Charles I (1644)

Source: E. Curtis and R.B. McDowell (eds), *Irish Historical Documents 1172–1922*, Methuen, London, 1943, pp.152–8.

A. *Catholic petition to Charles I, presented at Oxford*

In 1640 the strong hand of the Lord Lieutenant, the Earl of Strafford, was removed from Ireland and the following year the Catholics rose in rebellion. They continued to profess their loyalty to Charles I, but this was really dependent on the redress of their grievances. The great majority of the native Irish were Catholic and many had lost their land under English rule. The 'Old English', who had been settled in Ireland for a long time, had mostly been able to keep their land but, because of their Catholic faith, still felt themselves to be second-class citizens. These two groups combined in the Confederation of Kilkenny where a government was set up under the direction of Catholic bishops. It was responsible for the petition to Charles I from which extracts are printed below.

That all acts made against the professors of the Roman Catholic faith, whereby any restraint, penalty, mulet [mule bit, i.e. bridle], or incapacity may be laid upon any Roman Catholic within the kingdom of Ireland may be repealed, and the said Catholics to be allowed the freedom of the Roman Catholic religion . . .

That the offices and places of command, honour, profit and trust within that kingdom be conferred upon Roman Catholic natives of that kingdom, in equality and indifference with your majesty's other subjects.

That the insupportable oppression of your majesty's subjects for reasons of the Court of Wards, and respite of homage be taken away and a certain revenue in lieu thereof settled upon your majesty without diminution of your majesty's profit . . .

That an act of oblivion be passed in the next free parliament, to extend to all your majesty's said Catholic subjects of that kingdom, for all manner of offences, capital, criminal and personal, with a saving and reservation to both houses within six months next after the passing of the said act, to question any person or persons of any side for any notorious murders, cruelties, rapines and robberies against public faith, and such persons as have privately or publicly in their councils or actions joined against your majesty with the rebels at Westminster, and the same to hear and determine according to law, honour, and justice, and the said act to extend to all goods and chattels, customs mesne [land in feudal tenure], profits and prizes, arrears of rents, received or incurred since these troubles. Forasmuch, dread sovereign, as the ways of our address unto your majesty for apt remedies unto our grievances was hitherto debarred us, but now at length through your benign grace and favour laid open, we therefore in pursuance of our remonstrance formerly presented, do humbly offer these, which granted, your said subjects will readily contribute the ten thousand men, as in the said remonstrance is specified, towards the suppressing the unnatural rebellion now in this kingdom, and will further expose their lives and fortunes to serve your majesty as occasion shall require.

B.   *Protestant petition to Charles I, presented at Oxford*

Many of the Protestant settlers in Ireland originated in Scotland and had brought with them an uncompromising hatred of Catholicism. They tended to sympathize with the English parliament which, by 1644, was winning the civil war against Charles I. These extracts from their petition to the king particularly address the need to enforce the laws against the Catholics. Charles, in return for financial support, had made concessions to them known as 'the Graces'. The Irish Protestants wished to reverse that policy and to suppress the rebellion with armed force.

We most humbly desire the establishment of the true Protestant religion in Ireland, according to the laws and statutes in the said kingdom now in force. That the popish titular archbishops, bishops, jesuits, friars and priests, and all others of the Roman clergy be banished out of Ireland, because they have even been stirrers up of all rebellion, and while they continue there, there can be no hope of safety for your majesty's Protestant subjects: and that all the laws and statutes established in that kingdom against popery and popish recusants may continue in force, and be put in due execution . . .

That the establishment and maintenance of a complete Protestant army, and sufficient Protestant soldiers and forces, for the time to come, be speedily taken into your majesty's prudent, just and gracious consideration, and such course laid down and continued therein, according to the rules of good government, that your majesty's right and laws, and the Protestant religion and peace of that kingdom be no more endangered by the like rebellion in time to come . . .

That some fit course may be considered of to prevent the filling or over-laying of the commons house of parliament in Ireland, with popish recusants, being ill affected members, and that provision may be duly made that none shall vote or sit therein, but such that shall take the oaths of allegiance and supremacy [i.e. oath of obedience to Charles I and recognition of royal supremacy over the church].

15
Abraham de Wicquefort describing the Fronde (1648)

Source: R. Mandrou (ed.), '*Chronique*' *Discontinué de la Fronde (1648–1652)*, Abraham de Wicquefort, Paris, Fayard, 1978, pp. 102–3. Translated from the French by Arthur Marwick.

Abraham de Wicquefort (1606–82) was born in Amsterdam. He spent much of his life in France; at the time of writing the history of the Frondes, he was representing Augustus, Duke of Wolfenbuttel, a German prince, at the French court. He was expelled a few years later, possibly for writing too freely about the love affair between Louis XIV and the niece of Cardinal Mazarin. He spent his last years in obscurity, recording his experiences of life as a diplomat. The incidents described in the extracts printed below took place in Paris, on 28 August 1648, during the Fronde of the *parlements*. These assemblies of lawyers enjoyed considerable popular support as they were opposing the right of the royal government to impose new taxes. 'Fronde' is the French word for 'sling'; the rebels saw themselves as weak but virtuous, defying the royal government, just as young David had slain the giant Goliath with his sling.

And indeed it seemed that, with the arrival of night, peace and calm had returned, when, yesterday morning, the chancellor was attacked on his way to the *parlement* by the people, who killed the officer accompanying him and pursued him right into the Duc de Luine's [Duc de Luynes] mansion, which, when they could not find the Chancellor, even though he was hiding there, they sacked. Four companies of guards and the king and queen's light cavalrymen, commanded by the Maréchal de la Meisleraye, went in and brought him out more dead than alive, and themselves came under several volleys of hostile fire as they made their retreat, which they were forced to do as though from an enemy. A company of Swiss guards, which had been positioned at the end of the Pont Neuf, facing the *faubourg*, were forced to take the same course of action, having lost their lieutenant and twelve or fifteen soldiers. After this the approaches to the main streets were blocked by barricades which were pushed to within 200 yards of the Palais Royal. At mid-day the *parlement* went to the Queen and asked her to return their colleagues, which she was at first unwilling to do, but tried to obtain from them the promise that the *parlement* would discontinue its assemblies: but this they refused to do; they then proceeded to the Croix-du-Trahoir fountain, where the people, discovering that the prisoners were not with them, seized the first and second presidents, forced them into a tavern, threatened them with a pistol to their throats, and sent them back to the Palais Royal, insisting that they must not return without Messieurs du Blancmesnil and de Broussel. On their arrival there this second time, they turned their attention to the Queen's demands, and decided to defer their assembly until the feast of Saint Martin, except for the question of the Tariff, the *rentes*[1] due to the Hôtel de Ville, and the implementation of the resolutions reached on the Chambre Saint Louis' proposals, which is all the *parlement* will be able to do before the recess, which begins on the seventh day of the coming month. Two of the King and Queen's carriages were immediately despatched to bring the two prisoners, of whom one was in the Bois de Vincennes and the other on his way to the Havre de Grâce. Meanwhile, in an attempt to get the people to disarm, M. de Broussel's nephew led the *parlement* out to assure them that his uncle had been freed: but in spite of this they would not relinquish their arms, but set up units of guards every 100 yards and continued to fire all night as though conducting a siege . . . I hope that when the Councillors arrive the people will lay down their arms. They were still armed when they saw M. de Broussel return today about mid-day. I have not been able to ascertain what the Parliament decided this morning. That will be for my next bulletin.

Paris, 28 August 1648

---

[1] A system of concealed borrowing at interest under which fixed annual or quarterly payments were sold for cash. The crown's credit was often so bad that some *rentes* were nominally assigned to the municipality of Paris and other third parties.

16
The Apology for the *Ormée* (1651)

Source: S.A. Westrich, *The Ormée of Bordeaux: A Revolution during the Fronde*, Johns Hopkins University Studies in historical and political science, 89th series, 2, Johns Hopkins University Press, Baltimore, 1972, pp.21–2. Translated from French.

Between 1648 and 1650, Bordeaux, led by its *parlement*, had participated in the first Fronde to protest against the level of royal taxation. The leaders of the protest had been unable to make much headway against the governor, Bernard de la Valette, Duke of Épernon. Cardinal Mazarin, however, wished to restore peace and offered the Bordelais an amnesty and withdrew a tax on wine: they accepted his olive branch with alacrity. Yet a few months later, during the Fronde of the nobles, some aristocratic refugees were admitted to Bordeaux by popular demand, despite the fact that the *parlement*, on this occasion, was unwilling to defy the royal government. Louis XIV came to the city at the head of his army and another peaceful compromise was concluded. This was the background to the growing discontent of the ordinary people and their alienation from the *parlement*, which is described in an extract from a pamphlet, 'The Apology for the *Ormée*', probably written in 1651. The *Ormée* took its name from the platform planted with elm trees (*ormeaux*) on which the meetings took place.

It was customary for the more prosperous bourgeois – those not having to remain in their shops – to gather on an elevated platform in a corner of the city. Their discussions turned to the troubled times: the exactions, the forced contributions, the misappropriations, the fact that one who collected revenues had purchased a piece of land worth 6000 *livres* per annum, that another had used the money to pay back a debt of 40,000 *livres* . . . The public's curiosity having been aroused, the assemblies became longer and more frequent, with the result that the *parlement*, whose ire had been provoked, ordered that they be outlawed.

17
The Venetian Ambassador on the Origins of the *Ormée* (1652)

Source: A.B. Hinde (ed.), *Calendar of State Papers and Manuscripts, Venice 1647–52*, vol.28, HMSO, London, 1927, pp.238–9. Translated from Italian.

Michiel Morosini was a member of one of the great patrician families of Venice. His state had pioneered the notion that permanent representatives might be kept at foreign courts to safeguard the interests of their country and relay information which might be useful. Since this letter was sent from the royal court of St Germain, on the outskirts of Paris, we may deduce that Morosini had received this news from Bordeaux: Venetian commercial interests were widespread and merchants were likely to be eager to render service to their state by gathering information.

The opportunity enjoyed by the English of going yearly to Bordeaux in order to ship wines had given them ample means not only of establishing many connections there but, under existing circumstances, of impressing their own opinions on the inhabitants of the city. The people there used to assemble daily at a certain spot, more to hear the news than from any idea of insurrection or of anything else. But meeting there in great numbers, they began to discuss the badness of the times, contrasting it with the peculiar prosperity of England. This seems to have led to speeches in favour of liberty, advocating the expulsion of the *parlement* and the forming of a more popular one and, in short, governing themselves.

18
The Putney Debates (1647)

Source: A203 Supplementary Material, Cassette Notes 5, The Open University, 1981, pp.19–24. Based on the transcription by S. Aylmer, *The Levellers in the English Revolution*, Thames & Hudson, London, 1975, pp.106–16.

These debates within the Parliamentary Army took place in Putney church, during late October and early November 1647. Charles I was in their hands and they wished to agree upon the terms they would offer him.

The Levellers and their supporters in some of the regiments were afraid that the senior officers (grandees), led by Oliver Cromwell and his son-in-law Henry Ireton, would make a settlement which would exclude all but the small minority of substantial property owners from political power. They hoped to prevent this from happening by reforming the House of Commons: equalizing the size of constituencies and widening the franchise to include many or most adult males. It is not clear just how far down the social scale most Levellers wished to go; they certainly did not agree amongst themselves on this matter. See *The Agreement of the People* (III.21), which best records Leveller thinking at this time. Members of the General Council of the Army participated in the debates; some were officers and soldiers from the ranks (called 'agents') who had been elected as representatives by their regiments. Others, like Cromwell and Ireton, were officers of the general staff; some civilian Levellers such as Maximilian Petty had also been invited. These extracts come from the debate on the second day, October 29. They include a brief interjection by a conciliatory army officer, Colonel Nathaniel Rich, and speeches by two radical Levellers, Colonel Thomas Rainsborough and Trooper Edward Sexby.

Cromwell Mr Petty

Petty I desire to add one word, concerning the word property. It is for something that anarchy is so much talked of. For my own part I cannot believe in the least, that it can be clearly derived from that paper. 'Tis true, that somewhat may be derived in the paper against the King, the power of the King, and somewhat against the power of the Lords; and the truth is when I shall see God going about to throw down King and Lords and property,[1] then I shall be contented; but I hope that they may live to see the power of the King and the Lords thrown down, that yet may live to see property preserved. And for this of changing the representative of the nation, of changing those that choose the representative, making of them more full, taking more into the number than formerly, I had verily thought we had all agreed in it: that more should have chosen, all that had desired a more equal representation than now we have. For now those only choose who have forty shillings freehold. A man may have a lease for one hundred pounds a year, a man may have a lease for three lives; but for this, that it destroys all right that every Englishman that is an inhabitant of England should choose and have a voice in the representatives, I suppose it is the only means to preserve all property. For I judge every man is naturally free; and I judge the reason why the men when they are in so great numbers that every man could not give his voice, was that they who were chosen might preserve property; and therefore men agreed to come into some form of government that they might preserve property, and I would fain know, if we were to begin a government: you have not forty shillings a year, therefore you shall

Figure 3 Pikemen marching to battle to the rhythm of fife and drum, woodcut detail from the ballad *The Protestant Triumph: or the signal victory of K. William over the French and Irish*, 1690.

not have a voice. Whereas before there was a government every man had such a choice, and afterwards, and for this very cause, they did choose representatives, and put themselves into forms of government that they may preserve property, and therefore it is not to destroy it.

Cromwell Commissary-General Ireton

Ireton If you admit any man that hath a breath and being, I did show you how this will destroy property. It may come to destroy property thus: you may have such men chosen, or at least the major part of them, why those men may not vote against all property? You may admit strangers by this rule, if you admit them once to inhabit, and those that have interest in the land may be voted out of their land; it may destroy property that way: for that by which you infer this to be the right of the people, of every inhabitant, and that because this man hath such a right in nature, though it be not of necessity for the preserving of his being; therefore you are to overthrow the most fundamental constitution for this. By the same rule, show me why you will not, by the same right of nature, make use of anything that any man hath. Show me what you will stop at, wherein you will fence any man in a property by this rule.

Thomas Rainsborough I desire to know how this comes to be a property in some men, and not in others . . .

45

Cromwell   Commissary-General

Ireton   Let the question be so: Whether a man can be bound to any law that he doth not consent to? And I shall tell you, that he may and ought to be, and I will make it clear. If a foreigner come within this kingdom, if that stranger will have liberty who hath no local interest here, he is a man, it is true, hath air, that by nature we must not expel our coasts, give him no being amongst us, nor kill him because he comes upon our land, comes up our stream, arrives at our shore. It is a piece of hospitality, of humanity, to receive that man amongst us. But if that man be received to a being amongst us, I think that man may very well be content to submit himself to the law of the land; that is, the law that is made by those people that have a property, a fixed property in the land, though he nor his ancestors, not any betwixt him and Adam, did ever give concurrence to this constitution; that is my opinion. A man ought to be subject to a law, that did not give his consent, but with this reservation, that if this man do think himself unsatisfied to be subject to this law, he may go into another kingdom; and so the same reason doth extend in my understanding, that a man that hath no permanent interest in the kingdom, if he hath money, his money is as good in another place as here; he hath nothing that doth locally fix him to this kingdom.

Cromwell   Colonel Rainsborough

Thomas Rainsborough   I do very well remember that the gentleman in the window [said] that, if it were so, there were no propriety to be had, because five parts of the poor people are now excluded and would then come in. So I say, if otherwise, then rich men shall be chosen; then, I say, the one part shall make hewers of wood and drawers of water of the other five, and so the greatest part of the nation be enslaved. And truly I think we are where we were still; and I do not hear any argument given but only that it is the present law of the kingdom. I say what shall become still of those many that have laid out themselves for the parliament of England in this present war, that have ruined themselves by fighting, by hazarding all they had. They are Englishmen. They have now nothing to say for themselves.

Cromwell   Colonel Rich

Rich   I should be very sorry to speak anything here that should give offence, or that may occasion personal reflection. But all that I urged was this: that I think it worthy consideration, whether they should have an equality in their interest, but however, I think we have been a great while upon this point, and if we be as long upon all the rest it were well if there were no greater difference than this.

Cromwell   Trooper Sexby

Sexby   I see that though liberty were our end there has been a degeneration from it.

We have engaged in this kingdom and ventured our lives, and it was all for this: to recover our birthrights and privileges as Englishmen; and by the arguments urged there is none. There are many thousands of us soldiers that have ventured our lives; we have had little propriety in the kingdom as to our estates, yet we have had a birthright; but it seems now, except a man hath a fixed estate in this kingdom, he hath no right in this kingdom. I wonder we were so much deceived. If we had not a right to the kingdom, we were mere mercenary soldiers. There are many in my condition, that have as good a condition; it may be little estate they have at present, and yet they have as much a right as those too who are their lawgivers, as any in this place. I shall tell you in a word my resolution.

I am resolved to give my birthright to none, whatsoever may come in the way; and be thought that I will give it to none. I do think the poor and meaner of this kingdom, I speak as in that relation in which we are, have been the means of the preservation of this kingdom, I say, in their stations and I really think that to their utmost possibility; and their lives have not been dear for purchasing the good of the kingdom. Those that act to this end are as free from anarchy or confusion as those that oppose it, and they have the law of God and the law of their conscience. We must be plain. When men come to understand these things, they will not loose that which they have contended for. That which I shall beseech you is to come to a determination of this question.

Thomas Rainsborough I see that it is impossible to have liberty but all property must be taken away. But I would fain know what the soldiers have fought for all this while; he hath fought to enslave himself, to give power to men of riches, men of estates, to make him a perpetual slave.

Cromwell I confess I was most dissatisfied with that I heard Mr Sexby speak of any man here, because it did savour so much of will.

Thomas Rainsborough I wonder how that should be thought wilfulness in one man that is reason in another; for I confess I have not heard anything that doth satisfy me.

Cromwell Trooper Sexby

Sexby I am sorry that my zeal to what I apprehend is good should be so ill resented. I am not sorry to see that which I apprehend is truth, but I am sorry the Lord hath darkened some so much as not to see it, and that is in short. Do you think it were a sad and miserable condition, that we have fought all this time for nothing? All here, both great and small, do think that we fought for something. I confess, many of us fought for those ends which we since saw was not that which caused us to go through difficulties and straits to venture all in the ship with you; it had been good in you to have advertised us of it, and I believe you would have fewer under your command to have commanded. But if this be the business, that an estate doth make men capable, it is no matter which way they get it, they are capable to choose those that shall represent them; but I think there are many that have not estates that in honesty have as much right in the freedom of their choice as free as any that have great estates.

---

[1] A reference to an earlier statement by Ireton.

19

Bossuet's reflections on the Frondes (1685)

Source: L'Abbé J. Lebarq (ed.), *Oeuvres Oratoires de Bossuet*, Hachette, Paris, 1923, vol.6, p.297. Translated by A. Lawrence.

Jacques Bénigne Bossuet's (1627–1704) reflections on the Frondes, from a sermon preached at the funeral of Anne de Gonzaga de Cleves, Princess Palatine, at the church of the Grands Carmelites in Paris, 9 August 1685. He had recently become Bishop of Meaux. The Princess Palatine was active in the Frondes, both for and against Mazarin.

What trouble! What a frightful spectacle confronts me! The monarchy shaken to its foundations, civil war, foreign war, conflagration within and abroad; the cures on all sides worse than the ills; the princes arrested with great danger and then released with as much danger; the prince [Condé] whom we regarded as one of the great heroes of the century rendered useless to the country whose support he had been, and then, I don't know how, against his true interests, taking up arms against it; a minister [Mazarin] persecuted and made indispensable, not only by the importance of his services, but by the misfortunes which implicated the monarch's authority. What shall I say? Was it here that one of the tempests by which the heavens sometimes discharge themselves raged and did the peace of today have to be preceded by such storms? Or, better, was this the last efforts of a restless freedom making way for legitimate authority? Or, better still, the labour pains of France about to give birth to the miraculous reign of Louis?

20

Extracts from *Clarendon's History of the Rebellion*

Source: W.D. Macray (ed.), *Edward, Earl of Clarendon, The History of the Rebellion and Civil Wars in England*, Clarendon Press, Oxford, 1888, vol.II, pp.319–22.

Edward Hyde, Earl of Clarendon (1609–74) was a major figure in English politics from the 1630s. He had promoted the early reforms of the Long Parliament, but had supported the king from 1641. Though a moderate constitutionalist he played an important part in the king's counsels during the civil war. At the Restoration he was chief minister to

Charles II but was disgraced in 1667, spending the rest of his life in exile,
where he wrote his *History of the Rebellion*, first published in 1702–4.

I must not forget, though it cannot be remembered without much horror, that
this strange wild-fire among the people was not so much and so furiously
kindled by the breath of the Parliament as of the clergy, who both administered fuel and blowed the coals in the Houses too. These men having creeped
into, and at last driven all learned and orthodox men from, the pulpits, had,
(as is before remembered,) from the beginning of this Parliament, under the
notion of reformation and extirpating of Popery, infused seditious
inclinations into the hearts of men against the present government of the
Church, with many libellous invectives against the State too. But since the
raising an army and rejecting the King's last overture of a treaty, they
contained themselves within no bounds, and as freely and without control
inveighed against the person of the King as they had before against the worst
malignant; profanely and blasphemously applying whatsoever had been
spoken and declared by God Himself or the prophets against the most wicked
and impious kings, to incense and stir up the people against their most
gracious sovereign.

There are monuments enough in the seditious sermons at that time printed,
and in the memories of men of others not printed, of such wresting and
perverting of Scripture to the odious purposes of the preacher, that pious men
will not look over without trembling . . . It would fill a volume to insert all the
impious madness of this kind, so that the complaint of the prophet Ezechiel
might most truly and seasonably have been applied, *There is a conspiracy of
her prophets in the middest thereof, like a roaring lion ravening the prey; they
have devoured souls; they have taken the treasure and precious things; they
have made her many widows in the midst thereof* [Ezek. 22:25] . . .

And indeed no good Christian can without horror think of those ministers
of the church, who, by their function being messengers of peace, are the only
trumpets of war and incendiaries towards rebellion . . .

If the person and the place can improve and aggravate the offence, (as
without doubt it doth, both before God and man,) methinks the preaching
treason and rebellion out of the pulpit should be worse than the advancing it
in the market, as much as poisoning a man at the Communion would be
worse than murdering him at a tavern. And it may be, in that catalogue of sins
which the zeal of some men [hath] thought to be the sin against the Holy
Ghost, there may not be any one more reasonably thought to be such than a
minister of Christ's turning rebel against his prince, (which is a most notorious apostasy against his order,) and his preaching rebellion to the people as
the doctrine of Christ; which, adding blasphemy and pertinacy to his
apostasy, hath all the marks by which good men are taught to avoid that sin
against the Holy Ghost.

21
The Report of the Baron de Lanta on his visit to the Court (1657)

Source: C. Devic and J. Vaissete, *Histoire Générale de Languedoc*, Recueil des Inscriptions de la Province, edited by E. Roschach, vol.14, Pièces justificatives, Toulouse, Édouard Privat, 1876, no.CCLXV, cols 640–53. Translated by Arthur Marwick.

During the Frondes the Estates and the *parlement* in the Languedoc had formed a successful Union against the crown. In 1656 this Union was revived in protest against the quartering there of the army engaging against the Spanish in Catalonia. In Paris Lanta firmly advocated the rights of the Languedoc before Mazarin. Three days later Mazarin summoned Lanta back to hear his counter-attack. These extracts from Lanta's own report to the Estates contain the important debate which followed. Lanta refers to some of the grievances of ordinary people, but it is clear that basically all he is fighting for is a formal recognition of traditional privileges ('liberties').

His Excellency [Cardinal Mazarin] said he could not conceal the extreme anger with which the King had learned of the deputation which the Assembly of the Estates had sent to the *parlement*; that the times of Unions were over; that it had been said in the Estates that they must equip and prepare themselves in every possible way that could bring ruin to the troops, so that they would never be sent again in the future; that the decrees that the Estates had requested of the *parlement*, prohibiting the Communities from borrowing money, were proof of the matter; that the King was now almost twenty, and that with one breath he would destroy and cast down all these enterprises . . .

To which he [Baron de Lanta] replied that there had never been any talk in the Estates of preparation, nor of seeking means for weakening the troops, but that it was true that, seeing them march into the province, they had sent a deputation to the *parlement* to thank it for certain favourable decrees which it had issued preventing the cutting down of trees in that province and the draining of the salt marsh of Peccais, and had instructed the deputation to request a decree prohibiting the Communities from borrowing money; that the Estates had done this, remembering that after the war of Privas, the debts of the Communities of the province . . . had amounted to nineteen million livres; that the experience of the past and the misery in which those living in the districts of Foix and Bigorre had found themselves, because of the freedom they had had to borrow sums so large that they owed more than they could afford, had forced them [the Estates] to take these steps and that in doing so they had merely followed the will of the Council which had issued several decrees at different times prohibiting the Communities from borrowing; that with regard to the Union being complained of, the Estates had never had any intention of forming one, the very word being obnoxious to them, the truth of which they had clearly demonstrated many times in the recent past; but that there are some Unions which come about naturally, and it was difficult to attack, at the same time and in the same province, what was held most precious and most dear in two Bodies, without forcing them to unite; and that, if liberty prevented this being declared openly, there was no way of stopping common interests resulting in a Union of hearts; that as soon as the people no longer feared the loss of their privileges, and the *parlement* the creation of a new one at Nîmes, with which it was threatened, the province would be calm and peaceful.

22
The Revolt in the Boulonnais (1661–2)

Source: Roger Mettam, *Government and Society in Louis XIV's France*, Macmillan, London, 1977, pp.255–9. Translated from French.

The revolt of the Boulonnais, 1662, was one of several the royal government had to face in the 1660s. Here we have the formal record of the royal decision in the previous year which touched off the revolt. Though Louis presents the levy of 30,000 livres as a concession, in fact (as we learn from the next document) he had no right to make such a levy in time of peace.

A.   *Extract from the Register of the Council of State, Fontainebleau, 19 May 1661*

As the King has been informed that the Boulonnais has suffered heavy damage because of the continual passage of troops, both cavalry and infantry, during the recent wars, and as moreover in those years a number of levies were imposed on that same province for the purpose of provisioning, financing winter quarters, making payments to enemies and other such expenses, and as His Majesty wishes that his subjects living in that province should enjoy the fruits of the peace which he has just procured for the whole of Europe, and to this end will reduce all taxation to very modest sums which are easily raised, His Majesty in council has ordered and orders that through Monsieur d'Ormesson, *maître des requêtes* at the court and *intendant* in the generality of Picardy, he will impose a levy of 30,000 *livres* annually on all his

51

taxable subjects in the province of the Boulonnais, beginning in this present year.

B.–F.   *Letters from Machault, special royal commissioner in the Boulonnais, to Colbert*

Revolt has broken out, and Machault, a special royal commissioner, has been sent to investigate and take appropriate action. These five letters provide a direct account of the origins of the revolt, of the participants in it, of the special tensions in Boulogne, and of the suppression of the revolt and the punishments which followed.

B.

Montreuil, 15 July 1662

The Boulonnais was formerly a county belonging to the family of La Tour du Bouillon. In 1551 . . . its peoples ceded it to King Francis I . . . on the condition that the privileges which they had enjoyed, while under the tutelage of the counts of Boulogne, be preserved . . .

Since 1551 the kings have, from time to time, issued new letters of confirmation of these privileges, in order that they might be thus fully enjoyed, until 1658 when vital needs of state obliged His Majesty to seek some assistance from all his peoples, and he imposed a levy of 81,700 *livres* on the province for the maintenance of his troops . . .

The decree ordering the tax was carried out. The people paid it, and the nobles were exempted on their noble property, the tax-farmers on the profits of their farms, so that all this levy fell on the ordinary people.

As the tax could rightfully last only as long as there was a war, the King immediately after peace was signed reduced it to 30,000 *livres*. And it is currently this tax, which the people believe to have been nullified by the declaration of peace, which has provoked this revolt. The people have risen up; the flame has spread from village to village; numerous vagabonds and layabouts have joined with them; their ranks have swelled; the nobles, who feared that they would not long maintain their exemption and especially so in peacetime when their services were no longer necessary, have not shown anger at this insurrection, preferring that the rebels might succeed and therefore deliver them from the cause of their fear. Thus, Monsieur, has this evil grown . . .

I forgot to tell you that this province does pay an *aides* tax [an indirect tax, mainly on drink].

C.

Montreuil, 10 July 1662

In the meantime, Monsieur, I have spent today gathering information and evidence from the large number of witnesses of the revolt who are here.

They include officials, gentlemen and others, some of whom can give eyewitness reports. There are also many men of noble birth, who have come here because they share our aims, for they have been pillaged and maltreated by the peasantry for refusing to support them.

D.

In Camp at Hucqueliers, 11 July 1662

The plan of which I have already told you, for subjugating the rebels of this province, has had the utmost success. From the moment that all the troops assembled within sight of their positions and made ready to attack them, at this village in which they had barricaded themselves, they took refuge in the castle and then, after some exchanges of musket-shots, surrendered unconditionally and laid down their arms.

Nearly five hundred of them thus fell into my hands, and I have put them under guard prior to taking them to Montreuil tomorrow. You can see from this great number that the King's plans for restoring his galley fleet will be assured of success.

We have taken the rebel leader, a man named Clivet, and one or two of his company, I can think of no torture too severe for such exploits. Meanwhile, Monsieur, the whole province will almost certainly remain completely calm. I am making every effort to press ahead with criminal proceedings so that order may be restored and the law be effectively enforced from the first possible moment.

Monsieur le duc d'Elbeuf under the articles of war has ordered the immediate hanging of three of them. This kind of sentence is customary on such occasions. When I shall have concluded the cases against these rebels and have had them punished, there will be nothing left to do in the King's interest than to ensure that the allocations by Monsieur de Saint-Pouanges[1] of the tax of 30,000 *livres* for 1661 are observed and honoured. I even believe it will be possible to make them pay a further tax for this year as well.

[1] Saint Pouanges was *intendant* at Amiens, and was the second cousin of Colbert.

E.

Montreuil, 27 July 1662

I am sending you a copy of the judgment which I delivered this morning. You will doubtless find it appropriate enough for frightening the whole province, and the examples which have been made will serve to restore everything to the state in which it should be.

I have designated for its execution those places where the revolt was most openly professed . . .

Judgment

. . . We order that the house in which Clivet is living shall be demolished from top to bottom and razed to the foundations, and in its place a pyramid shall be built, and a similar one in both Samer and Marquise, to which shall be affixed a copper frame, holding a summary of this judgment and of the events which gave rise to it.

And moreover that the bells of the said Samer and Marquise, because they served as a means of sounding the alarm, calling together rebels and making them charge the King's troops, shall be taken down for one year . . .

We have forbidden and forbid, also for one year, all fairs and markets in these said towns, and prohibit all subjects of the King from selling, buying, taking, bringing away, or trading in any merchandise and other produce there during that said time, unless they are necessary for the subsistence and life of the people . . .

We expressly prohibit and forbid all inhabitants of the province of the Boulonnais, of no matter what rank and condition, to take up arms, and to assemble or gather together for any kind of pretext, and to utter the word 'Carry' and others tending to provoke sedition, on pain of death.

F.

Boulogne, 19 August 1662

Monsieur, I am sending you a copy of the judgment I delivered this morning against Clivet . . .

Judgment

. . . We have declared and do declare the said Bernard Postel, lord of Clivet, duly guilty in fact and in law of the crimes of sedition, rebellion, disobedience of the King's orders, of armed riot and unlawful assembly, and moreover of having been the leader and commander of the said seditious and rebels, of having pillaged, burned down and raided many houses in the said province of the Boulonnais and further of the assassination committed by him of Monsieur Belleville, in reparation for which we have declared and do declare that all his heirs have forfeited their position and are deprived of the title and quality of a noble, and at the same time we have condemned and do condemn him to make honourable amends, wearing a shirt, with his head and feet naked, a noose around his neck, and with placards in front of and behind him bearing the words 'Chief of the rebels', accompanied by the executioner of the high court, in front of the cathedrals of Our Lady of Boulogne, and there on his knees, holding in his hand a burning torch weighing two pounds, to ask pardon from God, from the King and from the law for his said crimes, which being done he shall be conducted to the main square of the old town of Boulogne where the executioner shall cut off his arms, legs and thighs while he is alive on a scaffold which shall be erected for this purpose, and he shall then be laid and exhibited on a wheel, his face turned heavenward, to live for as long as God shall please.

G.   *Extract from the French Gazette, July 1662*

This is a formal record of a decree of the Council confirming the punitive actions of commissioner Machault in the Boulonnais.

July 1662

Monsieur de Machault has been sent a decree of the council, announcing that proceedings will be instituted against 1200 of the most culpable; that those who are aged twenty and under, or seventy and over, together with the crippled and the sick, shall be set at liberty, and that from the rest, 400 of the fittest shall be selected to serve for ever in the galleys.

23
The Ordinance for the Union of the Peoples of Scotland and England into one Commonwealth (1654)

Source: Acts of the Parliament of Scotland, vi, pt. ii, in W.C. Dickinson, G. Donaldson and I. Milne, *Source Book of Scottish History*, 2nd edn, Nelson, London, 1958–61, pp.816–17.

The Union was a result of Oliver Cromwell's conquest of Scotland. This Ordinance, embodying the Union, was based on the Instrument of Government and passed by Cromwell and his Council (note the significance at this stage of the 'Council' as against 'Parliament') in April 1654.

His Highness the Lord Protector of the Commonwealth of England, Scotland and Ireland, &c., taking into consideration how much it might conduce to the glory of God and the peace and welfare of the people in this whole island, that after all those late unhappy wars and differences, the people of Scotland should be united with the people of England into one Commonwealth and under one Government, and finding that in December, 1651, the Parliament then sitting did send Commissioners into Scotland to invite the people of that nation unto such a happy Union, who proceeded so far therein that the shires and boroughs of Scotland, by their Deputies convened at Dalkeith, and again at Edinburgh, did accept of the said Union, and assent thereunto; for the completing and perfecting of which Union, be it ordained, and it is ordained by his Highness the Lord Protector of the Commonwealth of England, Scotland and Ireland, and the dominions thereto belonging, by and with the advice and consent of his Council, that all the people of Scotland, and of the Isles of Orkney and Shetland, and of all the dominions and territories belonging unto Scotland, are and shall be, and are hereby incorporated into, constituted, established, declared and confirmed one Commonwealth with England; and in every Parliament to be held successively for the said Commonwealth, thirty persons shall be called from and serve for Scotland. . . .

And be it further ordained by the authority aforesaid, that all customs, excise and other imposts for goods transported from England to Scotland, and from Scotland to England, by sea or land, are and shall be so far taken off and discharged, as that all goods for the future shall pass as free, and with like privileges and with the like charges and burdens from England to Scotland, and from Scotland to England, as goods passing from port to port, or place to place in England; and that all goods shall and may pass between Scotland and any other part of this Commonwealth or the dominions thereof, with the like privileges, freedom, charges and burdens as such goods do or shall pass between England and the said parts and dominions, any law, statute, usage or custom to the contrary thereof in any wise notwithstanding, and that all goods prohibited by any law now in force in England to be transported out of England to any foreign parts, or imported, shall be and hereby are prohibited to be transported or imported by the same law, and upon the same penalties, out of Scotland to any foreign parts aforesaid, or from any foreign parts into Scotland.

And be it further ordained by the authority aforesaid, that all cesses, public impositions and taxations whatsoever, be imposed, taxed and levied from henceforth proportionably from the whole people of this Commonwealth so united.

. . .

Passed 12th April, 1654. Confirmed Anno 1656

24

The Humble Petition and Advice (1657)

Source: J.P. Kenyon (ed.), *The Stuart Constitution 1603–1688: Documents and Commentary*, 2nd edn, Cambridge University Press, Cambridge, 1986, pp. 324–5, 328.

The Instrument of Government was the Constitution of the Cromwellian Army. In accepting the humble Petition and Advice in its place, Oliver Cromwell (1599–1658) was moving back in the direction of parliamentary government. It is a recognition that previous constitutional experiments had failed. The Protector already exercised many of the powers previously held by the monarch and this was further to increase them.

25 May 1657

To his Highness the Lord Protector of the Commonwealth of England, Scotland and Ireland, and the dominions thereto belonging, The Humble Petition and Advice of the knights, citizens and burgesses now assembled in the Parliament of this Commonwealth . . .

1. That your Highness will be pleased, by and under the name and style of Lord Protector of the Commonwealth of England, Scotland and Ireland, and the dominions and territories thereunto belonging, to hold and exercise the office of chief magistrate of these nations, and to govern according to this Petition and Advice in all things therein contained, and in all other things according to the laws of these nations, and not otherwise. That your Highness will be pleased during your lifetime to appoint and declare the person who shall immediately after your death succeed you in the government of these nations.

2. That your Highness will for the future be pleased to call parliaments consisting of two Houses (in such manner as shall be more particularly afterwards agreed and declared in this Petition and Advice) once in three years at furthest, or oftener, as the affairs of the nations shall require . . .

3. That . . . those persons who are legally chosen by a free election of the people to serve in parliament may not be excluded from sitting in parliament to do their duties, but by judgment and consent of that House whereof they are members. . . .

8. That none may be admitted to the Privy Council of your Highness or successors, but such as are of known piety and undoubted affection to the rights of these nations, and a just Christian liberty in matters of religion, nor without consent of the Council to be afterwards approved by both Houses of Parliament, and shall not afterwards be removed but by consent of parliament, but may in the intervals of parliament be suspended from the exercise of his place by your Highness, by your successors and the Council, for just

57

cause; and that the number of the Council shall not be above twenty-one, whereof the quorum be seven, and not under; as also that after your Highness's death [the appointment of] the commander-in-chief under your successors of such army or armies as shall be necessary to be kept in England, Scotland or Ireland, as also all such field-officers at land, or generals at sea, which after that time shall be newly made and constituted by your successors be by consent of the Council and not otherwise. And that the standing forces of this Commonwealth shall be disposed of by the chief magistrate by the consent of both Houses of Parliament, the parliament sitting, and in the intervals of parliament by the chief magistrate by the advice of the Council; and also that your Highness and successors will be pleased to exercise your government over these nations by the advice of your Council.

9. And that the chancellor, keeper or commissioners of the Great Seal of England, the treasurer, or commissioners of the treasury, the admiral, the chief governor of Ireland, the chancellor, keeper or commissioners of the Great Seal of Ireland, the chief justices of both the Benches, and the chief baron in England and Ireland, the commander-in-chief of the forces in Scotland, and such officers of state there as by act of parliament in Scotland are to be approved by parliament, and the judges in Scotland hereafter to be made, shall be approved by both Houses of Parliament. . . .

25

Parliamentary Diary of Thomas Burton (1659)

Source: Diary of Thomas Burton Esq. Member in the Parliaments of Oliver and Richard Cromwell, from 1656–59; now first published from the original Autograph Manuscript, edited and illustrated with notes historical and biographical, by John Towill Rultt, Henry Colburn, London, 1828, vol.IV, pp.241–2.

There was no Hansard in the seventeenth century. This record of parliamentary proceedings is from the private diary of an MP (Thomas Burton). Annesley is speaking here as member for Dublin, though during the Long Parliament he had sat for Radnor in Wales, and he returned to a Welsh constituency, Carmarthen, in 1660. Annesley is a supporter of the newly formed 'Protestant Ascendancy' in Ireland and in this extract he is speaking against the abolition by Cromwell of the Irish parliament (mentioning in passing that Ireland has no formal Act of Union either).

Wednesday, March 23, 1659

Mr Annesley . . . England is in no danger of thirty members from Ireland; but if thirty from Scotland should join with them, much mischief might ensue. Whatever has been offered as to the right of Scotland is the same for Ireland, except that of the Act of Union, which is not admitted for a law. If you speak as to the conveniency in relation to England, much more is to be said why they who serve for Scotland should sit here. It is one continent, and elections are easier determined; but Ireland differs. It is much fitter for them to have Parliaments of their own. That was the old constitution. It will be difficult to change it, and dangerous for Ireland. They are under an impossibility of redress.

There is no way to punish judges in case of bribery. To come over here to complain he must bring the justice of his cause. No taxes can be abated, impose what you will.

Anciently, on records, we find that the records of Ireland would never be trusted by sea. Shall we now trust the people, and would not trust the parchments? Ireland must have the disadvantage every way.

As you are reducing yourselves to your ancient constitution, why has not Ireland the same? Why not Lords and Commons there? They have owned the single person. They never forfeited their right. Nothing hinders their restitution but the thirty members coming hither.

Their grievances can never be redressed. Elections can never be determined. Though they were but a province, they were their courts of justice, and Parliaments, as free as here.

Nine thousand pounds *per mensem* [by the month] upon them, and but six thousand upon Scotland; very disproportionable. I shall have my share, what interest soever prevail, whether England or Ireland. You go about to make them foreigners. Scotland pays no customs. Ireland pays not only customs, but increase of customs: 2s. a beast in Lord Strafford's time; and now 6s. 8d. is exacted.

I pray that they may have some to hear their grievances in their own nation, seeing they cannot have them heard here.

26
Louis XIV to his Chancellor (1661)

Source: J.B. Wolf, *Louis XIV*, Gollancz, London, 1968, p.133.

The immediate occasion for this letter was the death of Cardinal Mazarin (1601–61) who had acted as chief minister to Louis since 1643. During that period, in close alliance with the Queen Mother, Anne of Austria, he had suffered many difficulties: foreign wars, financial problems and the Frondes. He had also prepared the young king carefully for his role as ruler of the most powerful state in Europe. Now Louis, nearly twenty-three, announces that he is going to run the government himself.

10 March 1661

Monsieur, I have called you, together with my secretaries and ministers of state, to tell you that up to this moment I have been pleased to entrust the government of my affairs to the late Cardinal. It is now time that I govern them myself. You will assist me with your counsels, when I ask for them. Outside of the regular business of justice, which I do not intend to change. Monsieur the Chancellor, I request and order you to seal no orders except by my command, or after having discussed them with me, or at least not unless a secretary brings them to you on my part. And you, Messieurs, my secretaries of state, I order you not to sign anything, not even a passport . . . without my command; to render account to me personally each day and to favour no one . . . And you, Monsieur the Superintendent [of finances] I have explained to you my wishes; I request you to use M. Colbert whom the late Cardinal has recommended to me. As for Lionne, he is assured of my affection. I am satisfied with his services.

27
The Declaration of Breda (1660)

Source: J.P. Kenyon (ed.), *The Stuart Constitution 1603–1688: Documents and Commentary*, 2nd edn, Cambridge University Press, Cambridge, 1986, pp.331–2.

This declaration was issued by Charles II from his court at Breda in the Low Countries *before* the meeting of the Convention Parliament and was read out to it on its first day, 25 April. The collection of promises it contained helped to smooth the way to Charles's restoration.

The Declaration of Breda, 4 April 1660

Charles, by the Grace of God, king of England, Scotland, France and Ireland, Defender of the Faith, &c., to all our loving subjects, of what degree or quality soever, greeting. If the general distraction and confusion which is spread over the whole kingdom doth not awaken all men to a desire and longing that those wounds which have so many years together been kept bleeding may be bound up, all we can say will be to no purpose. However, after this long silence we have thought it our duty to declare how much we desire to contribute thereunto, and that, as we can never give over the hope in good time to obtain the possession of that right which God and Nature hath made our due, so we do make it our daily suit to the Divine Providence that he will, in compassion to us and our subjects, after so long misery and sufferings, remit and put us into a quiet and peaceable possession of that our right, with as little blood and damage to our people as is possible. Nor do we desire more to enjoy what is ours, than that all our subjects may enjoy what by law is theirs, by a full and entire administration of justice throughout the land, and by extending our mercy where it is wanted and deserved.

And to the end that the fear of punishment may not engage any, conscious to themselves of what is passed, to a perseverance in guilt for the future, by opposing the quiet and happiness of their country in the restoration both of king, peers and people to their just, ancient and fundamental rights, we do by these presents declare, that we do grant a free and general pardon, which we are ready upon demand to pass under our Great Seal of England, to all our subjects, of what degree or quality soever, who within forty days after the publishing hereof shall lay hold upon this our grace and favour, and shall by any public act declare their doing so, and that they return to the loyalty and obedience of good subjects (excepting only such persons as shall hereafter be excepted by parliament). Those only excepted, let all our loving subjects, how faulty soever, rely upon the word of a king, solemnly given by this present Declaration, that no crime whatsoever committed against us or our royal father before the publication of this shall ever rise in judgment or be brought in question against any of them, to the least endamagement of them either in their lives, liberties or estates, or (as far forth as lies in our power) so much as to the prejudice of their reputations by any reproach or term of distinction from the rest of our best subjects, we desiring and ordaining that henceforward all notes of discord, separation and difference of parties be utterly abolished among all our subjects, whom we invite and conjure to a perfect union among themselves, under our protection, for the resettlement of our just rights and theirs in a free parliament, by which, upon the word of a king, we will be advised.

And because the passion and uncharitableness of the times have produced several opinions in religion, by which men are engaged in parties and animosities against each other, which, when they shall hereafter unite in a freedom of conversation, will be composed and better understood, we do declare a liberty to tender consciences, and that no man shall be disquieted or called in question for differences of opinion in matter of religion which do not disturb the peace of the kingdom; and that we shall be ready to consent to such an act of parliament as, upon mature deliberation, shall be offered to us, for the full granting that indulgence.

And because, in the continued distractions of so many years and so many and great revolutions, many grants and purchases of estates have been made, to and by many officers, soldiers and others, who are now possessed of the same, and who may be liable to actions at law upon several titles, we are likewise willing that all such differences, and all things relating to such grants, sales and purchases, shall be determined in parliament, which can best provide for the just satisfaction of all men who are concerned.

And we do further declare, that we will be ready to consent to any act or acts of parliament to the purposes aforesaid, and for the full satisfaction of all arrears due to the officers and soldiers of the army under the command of General Monk, and that they shall be received into our service upon as good pay and conditions as they now enjoy.

Given under our Sign Manual and Privy Signet, at our Court at Breda, this 4 day of April, 1660, in the twelfth year of our reign.

PART II

Society and culture, 1620–1714

Introduction

This part is concerned with general social, religious and economic developments over the whole period 1620–1714. The first group of documents addresses issues concerning education and the extent to which the governments intervened to instil obedience to orthodox religious and political values: they also offer some evidence of how attempts were made to subvert those values. These were made by publicists, preachers and activists who wished to reform or replace the established order. By the end of the century sufficient advances had been made in scientific knowledge and in the gradual emergence of 'toleration' as a concept to encourage writers like Pierre Bayle to advocate freedom of expression for its own sake. In this they were initiators of the Enlightenment, preparing the way for the great changes which were to take place in the eighteenth century, when all the traditional assumptions about the nature of religious, intellectual and political authority were challenged.

The low levels of literacy which prevailed, especially in country areas, in both France and the British Isles in the seventeenth century compound the difficulty of providing accurate estimates, since records left about or by the unlettered are necessarily scanty. Some form of elementary education, often provided directly or indirectly by the official church, was available fairly widely for those who could pay for it: the motivation for acquiring it was more likely to be present in the towns, amongst the artisans and those above them. Did the royal governments regard the education of a substantial proportion of the population as a good or bad thing? The rules laid down by Madame de Maintenon, the morganatic wife of Louis XIV, for her school for girls at Saint-Cyr (II.1) show how anxious the French monarchy was to encourage industry, piety and submissiveness amongst young women who were likely to be some of the wives and mothers of the next generation of officials and minor nobles.

Throughout the century the French government had been concerned to promote the education of the upper classes. By this means the nobility and bourgeoisie could be controlled and a good supply of potential office-holders and army commanders maintained. Early in the century the programmes of riding schools for young nobles were gradually broadened to include some academic subjects on their curricula. Cardinal Richelieu had attended Pluvinel's great riding academy and in later years he founded establishments (II.2) which would serve the needs of the regime. The foundation of the Académie Française was a logical extension of this policy, as it brought advanced learning under royal control. The academies were multiplied, especially by Colbert, in the next reign, giving a level of encouragement to scholars and artists which was unknown in Britain. The absence from this collection of comparable British documents is telling; however, Charles II did extend some vaguely benevolent patronage to the Royal Society after its foundation.

The civil wars in France and the British Isles were the occasion for unprecedented pamphlet campaigns which were waged by all the major parties to the conflicts. This raises the literacy question again; how far down the social scale did the readers of this literature extend? There was a trend for more people to acquire literacy in the course of the century: 'progress . . . undoubtedly did occur' (Cressy, 1980, p.186). Economic factors were one source of motivation, but a desire to engage in a well-informed way in the political and religious controversies of the time was likely to have been another.

The 'Mazarinades', pamphlets produced during the Frondes, took their name from their characteristically virulent condemnation of the person and policies of cardinal Mazarin. Some of them, however, were written in support of the cardinal and the regent. 'The contract of Marriage between Parlement and the city of Paris', 1649 (II.3) created the elaborate fiction advertised in the title to call for unity between two of the leading dissident bodies. The 'Just Defence' of the Leveller John Lilburne (II.4) gives a bleakly factual account of his sufferings as a prelude to a call for all Englishmen, women and children to be allowed to enjoy their God-given freedom. The pamphlets of the mid-century were, to some extent, superseded by journals and newspapers in England by the early eighteenth century. This was made possible by reasonably liberal licensing laws: in France, once order had been restored after the Frondes, the only literature that was more than mildly critical of the government was smuggled in from abroad. No equivalent to the early journals, which the engagement of the English upper classes in politics promoted, emerged in France: only reports on topical events, which were strictly controlled by the authorities, were permitted. The extracts from two leaders in *The Examiner* (II.7) by Mrs Manley in 1711 typify the satirical cut and thrust of adversarial party political journalism of the early eighteenth century. She happened to be writing in support of the Tories' peacemaking, but articles by Whig writers had a similar style.

With the extension of literacy, which was accompanied by increasingly vehement condemnations of the attempts of church and state to control what people read, the issue of censorship was added to the political agenda. After suffering from draconian restrictions under the early Stuarts, publicists enjoyed a brief spell of freedom after the breakdown in authority in the early 1640s. John Milton's *Areopagitica* (II.5) was an eloquent plea for the maintenance of that freedom in the face of moves by the victorious parliament to reimpose censorship, although in later years he was to assist Cromwell in imposing an equally repressive policy. Pierre Bayle, a Frenchman who spent much of his later life in exile, wished to express ideas which could not possibly be published freely under Louis XIV. 'Concerning Obscenities', an extract from *The Dictionary* (II.6) was not an overtly political work as it concentrated on the occasions when it could be proper to publish obscene material. Yet at a time when the church and its moral code were deemed to be an integral part of the fabric of the state, such writings were considered as dangerous as invitations to commit regicide.

At the beginning of the seventeenth century the interdependence of Church and state, mentioned at the end of the last paragraph, was taken for granted. Much of this collection is composed of documents which exemplify the success of the French monarchy in maintaining that situation into the next century, and the differences which arose between the Stuarts and their subjects over the nature of the state religion and the extent to which individuals and localities might dissent from it. Evidence is offered in the following extracts about the claims of the states concerning what constituted conformity and also the deviant beliefs and behaviour of those who were not prepared to accept such claims. 'The Canons' of 1640 (II.8) show Charles I and the Convocation of the Anglican Church desperately attempting to define orthodox religious practice and link it to the concept of obedience to the monarchy at a time when royal authority was breaking down. Two years earlier the reaffirmation by the leaders of Scottish society of their Covenant (I.13) had served notice that the royal government could no longer take religious conformity for granted.

At the grass roots, preachers and their flocks were working out in practical terms what the religious ferment might mean for them. Richard Baxter's memorial of his ministry at Kidderminster (II.9) may sound rather too good to be true; yet one must presume that the most devout Puritans, who really did believe in his ideals, would gather round such a man. Popular beliefs and rituals in France such as semi-pagan celebrations of saints' days characterized a society where the ecclesiastical hierarchy could, in practice, exercise only a weak and spasmodic control over deeply held traditions, although the Catholic Church did manage progressively to modify some of these practices during the course of the century. The question that then could be asked is: did this happen because the authority of church and state were increasing or were the people beginning to reject their old customs as superstitious?

Blaise Pascal's *Provincial Letters* (II.10) lampooned another form of superstition: the way in which the Jesuits (the opponents of his Jansenist sympathies) played upon popular credulity about the ability of the Virgin Mary to ensure salvation for even the most lax believers. Bishop Burnet might have found that he had much common ground with Jansenists, and his account of his episcopal responsibilities (II.11) shows his concern to ensure decent standards of education and morality amongst his clergy. His contemporary, the philosopher John Locke, approached religion in a completely different way. His *Letter Concerning Toleration* (II.12), 1685, written when he was safely out of reach of reprisals from James II in Holland, called for a complete separation of religion from the operation of secular government. The former was entirely a matter for the individual to decide, the latter should be concerned with the protection of the citizen from worldly dangers.

Evidence of the kind of control exercised by the Anglican Church is to be found in the records of the ecclesiastical court at Stratford-upon-Avon (II.13). The punishments were not draconian and even the penalty of excommunication could be lifted upon the payment of a small fine. The final document in the group of those devoted to religious beliefs and observance is the questionnaire issued in Hereford to be administered by clergy and church-wardens. It was part of a survey which took place throughout England to enquire into the state of the church (II.14). After the mayhem of the civil wars and Interregnum the government's concern was to ensure that the outward forms of orthodox Anglicanism were decently observed. They at least betokened complacent clergymen and obedient congregations, the best that the regime of the pragmatic Charles II could perhaps hope for.

Regional and local interests and networks have been a major pre-occupation with seventeenth-century historians during recent decades. The experience of William Holcroft in Essex during the Restoration (II.15) gives an illustration of the very wide range of duties undertaken by English justices of the peace. These officials were technically appointed by the crown but ultimately depended for their authority on their standing in their community. This was a form of institutionalized localism which worked strongly against centralizing tendencies within the state. Sir Anthony Weldon's objections (II.16), not to the principle of ship money but to the way in which it was raised by the decision of royal representatives, rather than by basing it on customary levies, is another manifestation of localism. In France the institution of the *paulette* encouraged office-holders and the monarchy to seek to increase the number of posts available for hereditary tenure. Those who held such offices gained exemption from many taxes such as the *taille* (II.17) but, because they were appointed for life, they had no incentive rigorously to uphold the interests of the central government. The exemption and perceived corruption of such officials was a grievance constantly voiced in peasant revolts (II.18), as the rebels felt that they were expected to bear a disproportionately heavy tax burden. The Bourbons depended too heavily on the revenue from the *paulette* to abolish venal offices. The introduction of *intendants* who were appointed by the crown and answerable to it proved in the course of the century an increasingly effective means of asserting state control over the provinces (II.19).

During the troubled times in the middle of the century, local interests in both the French and British states could assert themselves more strongly than was possible when the central government was stronger. In Dorset and Wiltshire the Clubmen (II.20) provided for the security of their community, which they put before loyalty either to the royal or the parliamentary forces in the war. In Bordeaux the *Ormée* promised protection and support to its members: its ability to deliver these benefits was, however, open to question (II.21): before long the monarchy and the propertied classes were to reassert their power over the artisans and *petit bourgeois*. Even during the relative stability of the later years of Charles II the maintenance of order on the periphery was problematical. The establishment in 1681 of the Commission of Highland Justiciary was an attempt to combat the endemic lawlessness of the area (II.22). The recommendations of the commissioners three years later drew the stark conclusion that only coercion, namely a military presence, would improve the situation. The extent to which the central government and the magistracy were colluding by the 1690s to exert moral as well as legal control over the lower classes is illustrated in a charge given by a local JP to the Surrey Quarter Sessions (II.23). This demonstrates the increasing divergence between the manner in which France and England were ruled in their regions as the century drew to a close. In France the introduction of the *intendants* enabled the monarchy to intervene in most areas of local government. In England securing the Protestant succession consolidated a consensus about government priorities and confirmed an alliance with the nobility and gentry who co-operated in ruling the country through parliament and the commissions of the peace. The next document (II.24) records the details given in the specification to a builder for some of the new houses to be built at Richelieu. The cardinal used some of his great wealth to indulge in a little town planning.

Consideration of regional and provincial affairs leads naturally to the social, ideological and economic realities of the life at local level. The degree to which central government and the authority of the established churches were able to penetrate the lives and value systems of the people will explain much about their reactions to the great political and religious issues of the century. It is notoriously difficult to recover evidence about the lives of ordinary people before the onset of mass literacy: they were most likely to be recorded as individuals if they were accused of some misdeed or were so poor that provision had to be made for them. The extract from the Salisbury Register of passports issued to vagrants (II.25), so that they could be returned to their parish of origin, bears testimony to one of the harshest aspects of the Poor Law. The next two documents show English and French methods of dealing with pauperism (II.26, 27); the French may seem to be more impersonal than the bossy maternalism of Lady Hungerford, yet there is a common factor in both documents and it implies something little short of incarceration.

Witchcraft was a preoccupation for many seventeenth-century communities: the more remote and the less educated they were, the more likely were elderly, isolated, eccentric people to be accused of dealings with the Devil. James I and VI had a positive obsession with the subject: the act of 1604 (II.28) demonstrates his desire to import into England something which had been a great preoccupation of his in Scotland. The account for the expenses of burning a witch in Scotland in 1649 (II.29) is a spine-chilling reminder of the realities of the legislation: it also bears out a point made by Anne Laurence, in Unit 9 of the course, that local communities incurred considerable costs in launching prosecutions. Extracts from cases against a Frenchwoman in 1621 and several Englishwomen in 1645, all accused of witchcraft (II.30, 31), show how innuendo and hearsay were acceptable as evidence.

From an investigation of the nature of society at regional and then at local level it is logical to proceed to a consideration of the family. What kinds of families were produced by economic conditions in France and the British Isles and how did the states expect to use them for the confirmation of government authority and the maintenance of orthodox religious values? The autobiography of William Stout (II.32) offers valuable evidence about the tensions and the location of authority within one English household. The extracts from bishop Bossuet's *Catechism* and Beuvelet's *Instruction* (II.33) emphasize the dominance in France of clerical, celibate modes of thinking about the institution of marriage. The result is that they stress the central role of the church in the relationship between husband and wife, no secular advantages being considered. Sir Robert Filmer's *In Praise of the Virtuous Wife* (II.35) contains some surprises: the author who is associated above all other seventeenth-century theorists with the belief in the maintenance of patriarchal authority places unexpected emphasis on the importance of women in the family. A wife's moral conduct and unselfish devotion to the interests of her husband and children seems to have been, for Filmer, the decisive factor in determining the successful operation of the unit which was, after all, the basic component of the state.

In France, as Robin Briggs has suggested, the church felt the need to control family life by subjecting it to a strict moral code:

> The culture and values of a traditional society were embodied in and transmitted through these immensely resilient and flexible agencies, which were therefore increasingly liable to be seen as centres of subversion.

> (Briggs, 1989, p.275)

Benigne Lordelot's *Domestic duties by the father of a family*, 1706 (II.34), although it was written by a layman, advocated many of the rules of conduct which the ecclesiastical hierarchy wished the fallible, carnal laity to accept. Any doubts about the political as well as the religious purpose of the tract are dispelled by the fulsome dedication to Louis XIV, a virtuous patriarch who should serve as a model to the whole world.

References

Briggs, R. (1989), *Communities of Belief: Cultural and Social Tension in Early Modern France*, Clarendon Press, Oxford.

Cressy, D. (1980), *Literacy and the Social Order: Reading and Writing in Tudor and Stuart England*, Cambridge University Press, Cambridge.

1
Madame de Maintenon and Saint-Cyr

Source: H. C. Barnard, *Madame de Maintenon and Saint-Cyr*, A. & C. Black, London, 1934, pp.231–2 (repubd., 1971). Translated from French.

Françoise d'Aubigny, marquise de Maintenon (1635–1719), was already a widow when she was made a governess of the children Louis XIV had by one of his mistresses. The post brought her into regular and close contact with the king who was very fond of his illegitimate children. She gradually replaced her rivals in Louis's affections and, after the death of the queen, was secretly married to him, probably in 1684. She had owed her rapid rise at Court to her position as governess and this fact, together with her own not inconsiderable education and personal piety, may explain her decision, with the king, to found the school at Saint-Cyr. On the death of Louis in 1715, she retired to Saint-Cyr for the rest of her life. The extent of the influence she exercised over the king is a matter of debate. Saint-Simon disliked her and believed that she had a baleful effect on the king's policies: for example, his decision to deprive the Huguenots of their protection under the Edict of Nantes.

A. *Rules for the Classes (1686)*

1. The first class is usually composed of fifty-six young ladies, without counting those with the black ribbon. The second class usually has sixty-two girls. The 'daughters of Mme. de Maintenon'[1] are counted in the class the ribbon of which they wear, and they follow its curriculum, except in so far as they are prevented by their other duties. Each of the lower classes has fifty-six girls.
2. Although the young ladies should always be subordinate to the the mistresses, they are responsible for their particular duties to the senior mistress only.
3. They read no books other than those given to them by the senior mistress. They wear nothing which is not uniform with the other girls' dress, unless they have special permission.
4. They will be careful never to form special friendships and attachments; but they will have great regard and respect for each other, avoiding the use of the pronoun *tu* or behaving in an unseemly way.[2]
5. They will also be careful to avoid grumbling, complaints, scandal, teasing, disputes, talking about their dislikes, their vexations – in short, everything which is specified in the list of what the young ladies are forbidden to do.

71

6. As it is a mark of a good spirit and of their duty to accommodate themselves to the rules of the house to which they belong, they will observe exactly whatever they are commanded to carry out, avoiding carefully whatever might interfere with this – *e.g.*, talking, making a noise in public places, getting out of place in line, missing the ceremonies, etc.

7. They will be particularly careful never to leave the classroom, whether alone or together, without being accompanied by their mistress or some other person to whom they have been entrusted.

8. Every year the young ladies of the two upper classes will make a retreat lasting several days, unless the superior orders otherwise. It is especially at these times that they will think seriously about the condition of life to which God calls them. This choice is so important that it is not sufficient to think about it when they are getting near the time when they should leave the school; they cannot think of it too soon.

9. They will all be careful to preserve a continual remembrance of those whom God has used for the establishment of this house and to pray every day for them – and especially for the king their founder and for Mme. de Maintenon their *institutrice* [instructress].

10. Finally, they will never forget under what conditions and for what purpose they have been received, and how worthy of blame they would be if they neglected to profit by all the assistance which Providence has afforded in order to give them a truly Christian education.

[1] Those of outstanding merit allowed special privileges and having special duties. They wore the black ribbon.

[2] *Tu* (you) is a familiar form of address in French, *vous* is more appropriate unless you know the person well.

B. *Letter to Madame de Fontaines (1691)*

Source: The Correspondence of Madame, Princess Palatine, Marie Adelaide de Savoie and Madame de Maintenon, selected and translated by Katherine Prescott Wormeley, Heinemann, London, 1899, pp.245–6.

September 20, 1691.

The pain I feel about the daughters of Saint-Cyr can only be relieved by time and by a total change in the education we have given them up to this time. It is very just that I should suffer because I have contributed to the harm more than any one; I shall be happy if God does not punish me more severely. My pride has been in everything concerning the establishment; and its depth is so great it carries the day against my own good intentions. God knows that I wanted to establish virtue at Saint-Cyr, but I have built on sand, – not having that which alone can make a firm foundation. I wanted that the girls should have intelligence, that their hearts should be uplifted, their reason formed. I have succeeded in my purpose; they have intelligence, and they use it against us; their hearts are uplifted, and they are prouder and more haughty than is becoming in the greatest princesses – speaking as the world thinks; we have formed their reason, and we have made them disputatious, presumptuous, inquisitive, bold, etc. Thus it is that we succeed when the desire of excelling makes us act. A simple, Christian education would have made good girls, out of whom we could have made good wives and good nuns; we have made *beaux-esprits*, whom we ourselves who made them cannot endure: there is our blame, in which I have a greater share than any one.

C.   *Letter to Madame de Pérou (1701)*

Source: *The Correspondence of Madame, Princess Palatine, Marie Adelaide de Savoie and Madame de Maintenon*, selected and translated by Katherine Prescott Wormeley, Heinemann, London, 1899, pp.257–8.

February 23, 1701.

It has seemed to me as if you desired that I should write to you on all things that might be of consequence to your establishment. I place in that rank the representations of the beautiful tragedies I caused to be written for you,[1] and which may in the future be imitated. My object was to avoid the miserable compositions of nuns, such as I saw at Noisy. I thought it was judicious and necessary to amuse children; I have always seen it done in places where they are collected; but I wished while amusing those of Saint-Cyr to fill their minds with fine things of which they would not be ashamed when they entered the world; I wished to teach them to pronounce properly; to occupy them in a way that would withdraw them from conversations with one another, and especially to amuse the elder ones, who from fifteen to twenty years of age get rather weary of the life at Saint-Cyr. These are my reasons for still continuing the representations, provided your superiors [the Bishop of Chartres and the confessors] do not forbid them. But you must keep them entirely confined to your own house, and never let them be seen by outside persons under any pretext whatever. It is always dangerous to allow men to see well-made girls who add to the charms of their person by acting well what they represent. Therefore do not, I say, permit the presence of any man, whoever he may be, poor, rich, young or old, priest or secular, – I would even say a saint, if there were such on earth. All that can be allowed, if one of the superiors [priests] insists on judging the performance, is to let the youngest children act a play before him – as, in fact, we have already done.

[1] Racine's *Esther* (1689) and *Athalie* (1691), based on biblical subjects.

2
Richelieu on education and the Academies (1630)

Source: Paris Bibliothèque Mazarine, MS 2117, from E. Schalk, *From Valor to Pedigree: Ideas of Nobility in France in the Sixteenth and Seventeenth Centuries,* Princeton University Press, Princeton, 1986, pp.193–4. Translated from French.

Armand-Jean du Plessis, cardinal and duc de Richelieu (1585–1642), the powerful minister of Louis XIII, was very concerned with the education of the nobility. He created scholarships for poor young nobles, explaining elsewhere in the document that there was provision enough for students of humble birth. In this case he was offering support to young men in existing academies, but he also founded a new one in his town of Richelieu. The desire to provide a practical grasp of the military arts with a decent general education, suitable for prospective public servants, was symptomatic of royal policy. The founding of the Académie Française and later, under Colbert, other academies of the arts and sciences, was a means of regulating the intellectual life of France to serve the purposes of the government.

During the two years of their stay, in addition to the usual exercises of the Academy which will be practised in commmon with all the other students, such as riding and performing on horseback, fencing, studying Mathematics and fortifications and others, they will also, at regular hours, be taught the principles of Logic, Physics, Metaphysics, briefly the French language but a full course on Ethics [la Morale]; and at another convenient hour after dinner they will also be briefly acquainted with map-reading, or Geography, and some ideas about History, the establishment, decline and changing of the Empires of the world, the transmigration of Peoples, the formation and collapse of Cities, and the names and deeds of great men; the students will be also given a brief account of the state of the modern Principalities, and more particularly those of Europe whose interests concern us very much since they are our neighbours. Above all and at full length they will learn Roman History and French History.

3
Marriage Contract between the *Parlement* and the City of Paris (1649)

Source: The Marriage Contract between the Parlement and the City of Paris, 8 January 1649, Paris, veuve Guillemot, 1649, from C. Moreau (ed.), *Choix des Mazarinades*, Société de L'Histoire de France, Paris, 1853, 1, pp.39–41, 48–50. Translated by Angela Scholar.

The *Mazarinades* were pamphlets and poems produced by both sides during the Frondes, 1648–53. They received their name from the fact that many of those written by opponents of the royal government were violently opposed to the chief minister, cardinal Mazarin. The extracts below are taken from a particularly radical and lucidly argued example. The government was quick to respond in the *Mazarinade* 'The blindfold taken from Parisian eyes to enable them to understand the present unrest and to choose the side which they, and all good Frenchmen, should support', 19 February, 1649 (reference as above, pp.228–46). This claimed that 'the Majesty of our kings is the image of divinity', and so there was no justification for any faction to take up arms against them. To do so was impious parricide, similar to the 'execrable barbarity, full of horror', recently committed by the English parliament against its king; it would lead to a total subversion of social and political order in the state.

The Seigneur *Parlement* takes the said Lady the City of Paris to be his wife and legitimate spouse, as likewise the said Lady takes the said Seigneur *Parlement* of Paris to be her husband and legitimate spouse, in order that the said Seigneur and Lady *Parlement* and City of Paris be perpetually and indissolubly joined together and united, and that they may love and cherish one another cordially and sincerely: to this end the said Seigneur and Lady here present, being espoused and conjoined, shall be united and of one accord in all their desires, actions, passions and interests generally and of whatever kind, in accordance with the good of the state and the preservation of king and kingdom; in pursuit of which the present marriage and union shall be concluded, and to which shall give their consent all the other *parlements* of France, younger brothers of the *parlement* of Paris, as they are invited and requested to do, and likewise all the other cities of France, younger sisters of the City of Paris, as they also are invited and requested to do, and all shall enter, if they please, into the present alliance for the universal good of the kingdom and to the glory of God.

The said Seigneur and Lady here present, being espoused and conjoined, take each other with all the rights, titles, reasons and actions, duties and obligations which may apply and belong to them, concern and regard them,

75

generally and of whatever kind, and especially as regards the responsibilities and conditions which follow:

That God shall be always served and honoured, feared and loved, as is right and proper;

That atheists and the ungodly, free-thinkers and the sacrilegious shall be exemplarily punished and tirelessly exterminated; . . .

That the good of the state and the preservation of the king and the kingdom shall always be diligently embraced and pursued;

That relief for the poor people shall likewise be procured in so far as this is possible;

That the king given by God to the kingdom of France shall be served and honoured, loved and obeyed by his subjects; and, so that he may one day know how to command them worthily, that the laws of God and those of the kingdom, along with the other branches of knowledge and the other virtues necessary in a prince, shall be taught to him by learned, virtuous and holy persons such as the said Seigneur *Parlement* of Paris shall deem the most fit and shall appoint, and to whom his education and instruction shall be particularly committed and dearly commended;

That given the young age at which his Majesty at present finds himself, which is still too tender for the government of his state, the said Seigneur *Parlement* shall put forward illustrious persons, who possess the competence required for such an important task, and who will be chosen from among the orders of the clergy, the nobility and the magistracy;

That these wise and virtuous personages shall, after the Princes of the Blood, act as natural councillors and as ministers lending necessary support to the Regency;

That all matters of state and government shall be resolved in accordance with the advice of the Princes of the Blood and the councillors and ministers of state and in accordance with a majority vote, as is appropriate during the minority of kings;

That these councillors and ministers, proposed by the said Seigneur *Parlement*, and accepted and established by the king, shall be dismissed or changed according as their behaviour or incompetency shall give rise;

That in the case of the *parlement* formally requesting the dismissal of those who may have given it cause, it shall meet with no resistance, and those who are appointed in their stead shall be accepted without dispute . . .

And because all these good things cannot come about so long as cardinal Mazarin shall command this state with the insolence and the tyranny with which he conducts himself, who, having perverted all the good rules of a legitimate and reasonable government by extreme ignorance and malice, and committed acts of exorbitant theft from the treasuries of the kingdom, has abducted scandalously and perilously the sacred person of the king and of Monsieur his brother, seduced the other Princes of the Blood and impudently and falsely accused members of this august body of the *parlement* of colluding with the enemies of the kingdom; because of which, having been by a solemn decree [issued 8 January 1649] declared a disturber of the public order and an enemy of the king and his state, he will be tirelessly pursued until he is brought into the hands of justice to be publicly and exemplarily executed;

That the pope, the republics of Venice, Genoa and Lucca and other princes of Italy shall be required and requested to seek out and seize within their territory the movables, precious stones and monies which have been sent there by the said Mazarin, so that they may be restored to the crown and the kingdom from which they were stolen;

That an official declaration shall be drawn up to the effect that no foreigner may ever hold either office or benefice in the kingdom, except for commissions of war only, for those who have proved themselves worthy: . . .

That the governments of all places and towns within a radius of ten leagues of the good city of Paris shall be in perpetuity appointed and retained by the said Seigneur *Parlement* so that they may be held in his name for the welfare and service of the said Lady his wife, unless it is preferred to make them demolish and raze all their fortifications; . . .

That the king shall be humbly begged to return to his throne and to the most secure seat of his empire, which is to say Paris, and from there conduct peace or war, bringing the former to his subjects and waging the latter on his enemies, if appropriate;

That by the grace of God the present marriage may never be dissolved and that none of the parties may ever claim or demand or consent to any separation or estrangement for any cause or occasion whatsoever;

For thus the said Seigneur *Parlement* and the said Lady the City of Paris have promised and sworn on the Holy Gospel in front of the church of Notre Dame in the month of January in the year sixteen hundred and forty-nine; and have signed.

4

The *Just Defence* of John Lilburne (1653)

Source: Taken from an original copy in the British Library, *Leveller Tracts*, edited by W. Haller and G. Davies, Univesity of Columbia Press, New York, 1944, pp.450–5, 463–4.

John Lilburne (1614?–57) was an apprentice to a cloth merchant in London in the 1630s where he came into contact with the other Puritan radicals like John Bastwick. In 1638 he was whipped, pilloried and imprisoned for printing and circulating unlicensed pamphlets and for refusing to take the *ex officio* oath in Star Chamber. On his release by the Long Parliament two years later, he strongly supported moves to curb the king's power and fought with distinction as an anti-royalist in the subsequent war. He was deeply involved in the Leveller agitations for an extension of the franchise and was arrested several times. He was invariably freed because of the support given to him by the London crowds and because Cromwell seems to have had a soft spot for him. He was exiled, however, in 1652, after quarrelling with many of his former political allies. He returned without permission the following year and was immediately imprisoned. The *Just Defence* was one of a number of tracts which he published, in an attempt to vindicate his conduct before his trial. He was aquitted, again enjoying vociferous support from the people of London:

> And what shall then honest John Lilburne die
> Three-score thousand will know the reason why.

Cromwell's regime did not release him from custody until 1655.

THE/JUST DEFENCE/OF/JOHN/LILBURNE/Against/Such as charge him with Turbulency/of Spirit./Job.5.15. *But he saveth the poor from the sword, from the mouth and from the hand of the mighty./*
    Although it be a small thing with me now, after many years of sufferings, to be judged of any, or of man's judgement, knowing how apt men are to judge things hastily before the time, before the Lord come, who will bring to light the hidden things of darkness, and will make manifest the counsels of the hearts, yet considering how vehemently at present my life is sought after (as for a long time it hath been) and that those who so earnestly desire my blood, wanting matter in true law to compass it, have by their politic Agents, filled almost every man's mouth with clamours against me, that I have ever been, and continue a man of a turbulent spirit, always opposing, striving, and flying in the faces of all authorities, restless, and never satisfied whoever is uppermost; yea, though those whom I my self have laboured by might and main to advance and bring into power; and that therefore it is very requisite I be taken off, and that otherwise England must never look to rest long in peace; yea, so turbulent, that if there were none in the world but John Lilburne, rather than want one to strive withall, forsooth, John would certainly quarrel with Lilburne. Finding that this, how slight and unjust soever, hath prevailed more than true Christianity would admit, and threatens my life more than any matter that is against me, most men of judgement evidently seeing that nothing is laid to my charge, worthy either of death or bonds; I take my self obliged to vindicate my conversation from all such wicked and causeless aspersions lest by my silence I should seem guilty, and to have nothing to plead in my defence . . .
    For thus dealt the false prophets with the true, and by their craft and policy

led many people to destroy them; and so likewise dealt the Scribes and Pharisees with the Lord Jesus himself, giving out he was a wine-bibber, a friend of Publicans and sinners, that he cast out devils by Beelzebub the prince of devils: and that for no other cause, but that he published doctrines destructive to their interest of glory and domination . . .

nor should my many imprisonments be more a blemish unto me, than unto the Apostle Paul, who thought it no dishonour to remember those that somewhat despised him, that he had been in labours more abundant, in stripes above measure, in prisons more frequent, in deaths oft . . .

There being not one particular I have contended for, or for which I have suffered, but the right, freedom, safety, and well-being of every particular man, woman, and child in England hath been so highly concerned therein, that their freedom or bondage hath depended thereupon, insomuch that had they not been misled in their judgements, and corrupted in their understandings by such as sought their bondage, they would have seen themselves as much bound to have assisted me, as they judge themselves obliged to deliver their neighbour out of the hands of thieves and robbers, it being impossible for any man, woman, or child in England, to be free from the arbitrary and tyrannical wills of men, except those ancient laws and ancient rights of England, for which I have contended even unto blood, be preserved and maintained; the justness and goodness whereof I no sooner understand, and how great a check they were to tyranny and oppression, but my conscience enforced me to stand firm in their defence against all innovation and contrary practices in whomsoever.

For I bless God I have never been partial unto men, neither malicing any, nor having any man's person in admiration, nor bearing with that in one sort on men, which I condemned in others.

As for instance, the first fundamental right I contended for in the late King's and Bishop's times, was for the freedom of men's persons, against arbitrary and illegal imprisonments, it being a thing expressly contrary to the law of the land, which requireth, that no man be attached, imprisoned, &c. (as in Magna Carta, cap.29) but by lawful judgement of a Jury, a law so just and preservative, as without which entirely observed, every man's person is continually liable to be imprisoned at pleasure, and either to be kept there for months or years, or to be starved there, at the wills of those that in any time are in power, as has since been seen and felt abundantly, and had been more, had not some men strove against it; but it being my lot so to be imprisoned in those times, I conceive I did by my duty to manifest the injustice thereof, and claim and cry out for my right, and in so doing was serviceable to the liberties of my country, and no ways deserved to be accounted turbulent in so doing.

Another fundamental right I then contended for, was, that no man's conscience ought to be racked by oaths imposed, to answer to questions concerning himself in matters criminal, or pretended to be so.

The ancient known right and law of England being, that no man be put to his defence at law, upon any man's bare saying, or upon his own oath, but by presentment of lawful men, and by faithful witnesses brought for the same face to face; a law and known right, without which any that are in power may at pleasure rake into the breasts of every man for matter to destroy life, liberty, or estate, when according to true law and due proceedings, there is nought against them; now it being my lot to be drawn out and required to take an oath, and to be required to answer to questions against my self and others whom I honoured, and whom I knew no evil by, though I might know such things by them as the oppressors and persecutors would have punished them for, in that I stood firm to our true English liberty, as resolvedly persisted therein, enduring a most cruel whipping, pillorying, gagging, and barbarous imprisonment, rather than betray the rights and liberties of every man; did I deserve for so doing to be accounted turbulent? certainly none will so judge, but such as are very weak, or very wicked; the first of which are inexcusable at this day, this ancient right having now for many years been known to all men; and the latter ought rather to be punished than be countenanced, being still ready to do the like to me or any man. I then contended also against close imprisonment, as most illegal, being contrary to the known laws of the land; and by which tyrants and oppressors in all ages have broken the spirits of the English, and sometimes broken their very hearts, a cruelty few are sensible of, but such as have been sensible by suffering; but yet it concerns all men to oppose in whomsoever; for what is done to any one, may be done to every one: besides, being all members of one body, that is, of the English Commonwealth, one man should not suffer wrongfully, but all should be sensible, and endeavour his preservation . . .

and having some encouragement by my wife, from what my Lord General Cromwell should say of the injustice of the Parliament's proceedings, and of their (pretended) Act, I cast my self upon my native country, with resolutions of all peaceable demeanour towards all men; but how I have been used thereupon, and since, the Lord of heaven be judge between those in power and me; It being a cruelty beyond example, that I should be so violently hurried to Newgate, and most unjustly put upon my trial for my life as a Felon, upon so groundless a mere supposed Act, notwithstanding so many petitions to the contrary.

And now, that all men see the grossness of their cruelty and bloody intentions towards me, and having not consciences to go back, they now fill all men's mouths, whom they have power to deceive, that I am of so turbulent a spirit, that there will be no quietness in England exept I be taken off.

But dear Country-men, friends, and Christians, ask them what evil I have done, and they can show you none; no, my great and only fault is, that (as they conceive) I will never brook whilst I live to see (and be silent) the laws and rights of the Nation trod under foot by themselves, who have all the obligations of men and Christians to revive and restore them. They imagine, whilst I have breath, the old law of the land will be pleaded and upheld against the new, against all innovated law or practice whatsoever. And because I am, and continue constant to my principles upon which I first engaged for the common liberty, and will no more bear in these the violation of them, than I did in the King, Bishops, Lords, or Commons, but cry aloud many times of their abominable unworthiness in their so doing; therefore to stop my mouth, and take away my life, they cry out I never will be quiet, I never will be content with any power; but the just God here in heaven, and those who are his true servants will hear and consider upon earth, and I trust will not judge according to the voice of self-seeking ambitious men, their creatures and relations, but will judge righteous judgement, and then I doubt not all their aspersions of me will appear most false and causeless, when the worst I have said or written of them and their ways, will prove less than they have deserved.

Another stratagem they have upon me, is, to possess all men, that all the soldiers in the Army are against me; but they know the contrary, otherwise why do they so carefully suppress all petitions which the soldiers have been handing in my behalf? indeed those of the soldiers that hear nothing but what they please of me, either by their scandalous tongues or books, may through misinformation be against me; but would they permit them to hear or read what is extant to my vindication, I would wish no better friends than the soldiers of the Army; for I am certain I never wronged one of them, nor are they apt to wrong any man, except upon a misinformation.

But I hope this discourse will be satisfactory both to them and all other men, that I am no such Wolf, Bear, or Lion, that right or wrong deserves to be destroyed; and through the truth herein appearing, will strongly persuade for a more gentle construction of my intentions and conversation, and be an effectual Antidote against such poisonous asps who endeavour to kill me with the bitterness of their envenomed tongues, that they shall not be able to prevail against me, to sway the consciences of any to my prejudice in the day of my trial.

Frailties and infirmities I have, and thick and threefold have been my provocations; he that hath not failed in his tongue, is perfect, so am not I. I dare not say, Lord I am not as other men; but, Lord be merciful to me a sinner; But I have been hunted like a Partridge upon the mountains: My words and actions in the times of my trials and deepest distress and danger have been scanned with the spirit of Job's comforters; but yet I know I have to do with a gracious God, I know that my redeemer liveth, and that he will bring light out of his darkness, and clear my innocency to all the world.

Finis

5
John Milton, *Areopagitica* (1644)

Source: John Milton, *Areopagitica*, The Portable Milton, edited by D. Bush, Penguin, Harmondsworth, 1976, pp.169–70, 189–90.

John Milton (1608–74) was the son of a London scrivener. His precocious scholarship and love of classical literature earned him a place at Christ's College, Cambridge as a pensioner. He became increasingly alienated from Laudian Anglicanism and abandoned an original intention to be ordained. His unhappy first marriage may have been the reason for his publication of several pamphlets on divorce. The stir these caused, including threats from the Stationers' Company, may have led him to write the *Areopagitica* in 1644, attacking the practice of licensing printed works. The title refers to Areopagus, the hill in Athens where, in classical times, the aristocratic council met to safeguard the ancient laws of the city. Milton's support of the army earned him the post of Latin secretary to the Council of State, immediately after the execution of Charles I. He occupied the post throughout the Commonwealth and Protectorate, although deteriorating eyesight prevented his regular attendance at the Council. He was arrested for a brief period at the Restoration but soon set free and excused any financial penalties. The remainder of his life was lived in impecunious obscurity. It was, however, the period when he completed *Paradise Lost* and wrote *Paradise Regained* and *Samson Agonistes*.

. . . that infection which is from books of controversy in religion is more doubtful and dangerous to the learned than to the ignorant; and yet those books must by permitted untouched by the licenser. It will be hard to instance where any ignorant man hath been ever seduced by papistical book in English, unless it were commended and expounded to him by some of that clergy; and indeed all such tractates, whether false or true, are as the prophecy of Isaiah was to the eunuch, not to be 'understood without a guide.' But of our priests and doctors how many have been corrupted by studying the comments of Jesuits and Sorbonists,[1] and how fast they could transfuse that corruption into the people, our experience is both late and sad. It is not forgot, since the acute and distinct Arminius was perverted merely by the perusing of a nameless discourse written at Delft, which at first he took in hand to confute.

Seeing therefore that those books, and those in great abundance, which are likeliest to taint both life and doctrine, cannot be suppressed without the fall of learning, and of all ability in disputation; and that these books of either sort are most and soonest catching to the learned (from whom to the common people whatever is heretical or dissolute may quickly be conveyed); and that evil manners are as perfectly learnt without books a thousand other ways which cannot be stopped; and evil doctrine not with books can propagate, except a teacher guide, which he might also do without writing, and so beyond prohibiting; I am not able to unfold how this cautelous [cautious] enterprise of licensing can be exempted from the number of vain and impossible attempts. And he who were pleasantly disposed could not well avoid to liken it to the exploit of that gallant man who thought to pound up the crows by shutting his park gate.

Besides another inconvenience, if learned men be the first receivers out of books and dispreaders both of vice and error, how shall the licensers themselves be confided in, unless we can confer upon them, or they assume to themselves above all others in the land, the grace of infallibility and uncorruptedness? And again, if it be true that a wise man, like a good refiner, can gather gold out of the drossiest volume, and that a fool will be a fool with the best book, yea, or without book, there is no reason that we should deprive a wise man of any advantage to his wisdom, while we seek to restrain from a fool that which, being restrained, will be no hindrance to his folly. For if there should be so much exactness always used to keep that from him which is unfit for his reading, we should, in the judgment of Aristotle not only, but of Solomon and of our Saviour, not vouchsafe him good precepts, and by consequence not willingly admit him to good books; as being certain that a wise man will make better use of an idle pamphlet than a fool will do of sacred Scripture.

... we are hindered and disinured [unaccustomed to acquire] by this course of licensing toward the true knowledge of what we seem to know. For how much it hurts and hinders the licensers themselves in the calling of their ministry, more than any secular employment, if they will discharge that office as they ought, so that of necessity they must neglect either the one duty or the other, I insist not, because it is a particular, but leave it to their own conscience how they will decide it there.

There is yet behind of what I purposed to lay open, the incredible loss and detriment that this plot of licensing puts us to. More than if some enemy at sea should stop up all our havens and ports and creeks, it hinders and retards the importation of our richest merchandise, truth. Nay, it was first established and put in practice by antichristian malice and mystery, on set purpose to extinguish, if it were possible, the light of reformation, and to settle falsehood; little differing from that policy wherewith the Turk upholds his Alcoran, by the prohibition of printing. 'Tis not denied, but gladly confessed, we are to send our thanks and vows to Heaven, louder than most of nations, for that great measure of truth which we enjoy, especially in those main points between us and the pope, with his appurtenances the prelates; but he who thinks we are to pitch our tent here, and have attained the utmost prospect of reformation that the mortal glass wherein we contemplate can show us, till we come to beatific vision, that man by this very opinion declares that he is yet far short of truth.

¹ Academics from the Sorbonne, the great university of Paris.

6

Pierre Bayle, *Concerning Obscenities* (1699)

Source: Pierre Bayle, *The Historical and Critical Dictionary*, 2nd edn, translated by Monsieur des Maizeaux, London, 1738, pp.837–8.

Pierre Bayle (1647–1706) was born in Carlat, in the county of Foix, France, the son of a Huguenot minister. After a brief conversion to Catholicism (whilst studying philosophy and history at Toulouse), he reverted to the Protestant faith and fled to Geneva. There he abandoned scholasticism, espousing instead the new methodology of Descartes. He returned to France hoping that his apostasy would pass unnoticed. In 1675 he became Professor of Philosophy at the Protestant academy at Sedan and remained there until it was suppressed by Louis XIV. He retired to Rotterdam where he published a series of books which were highly critical of established religious beliefs and traditional knowledge. His greatest work, *The Dictionary* was first produced in 1699: as Bayle himself said '. . . my talent is to raise doubts'.

That if there are some Obscenities in this book, they are such as cannot be justly censured.

I.   When people say that there are Obscenities in any book, they may understand,

I.   Either that the author gives the description of his debaucheries in lewd terms, applauds and congratulates himself for them, exhorts his readers to plunge themselves into all manner of lewdness, recommends it to them as the most effectual means of leading a sweet and happy life, and pretends, that the censures of the public are to be laughed at, and that the maxims of virtuous men ought to be slighted as old womens' tales.

II.   Or, that the author relates, in a free and gay style, some love-adventures, feigned as to the substance, or at least as to their circumstances, and embellishments; and introduces into his narrative several immodest incidents, which he dresses in all the charms imaginable, in order to make them diverting, and fitter to raise the desire for love-intrigues than any thing else.

III.   Or, that the author, in order to revenge himself on an unfaithful mistress, or to excuse the transports of his passion, or make invectives against an old courtezan, or celebrate his friend's marriage, or divert himself with merry thoughts, gives a free scope to his Muse, and writes Epigrams, Epithalamiums [nuptial poems], etc. full of impure and smutty expressions.

IV.   Or, that the author, inveighing against lewdness, describes it in too lively, naked and gross colours.

V.   Or, that the author in a tract of Physic, Natural Philosophy, or Civil-Law, expresses himself filthily on the subject of generation, or, causes and remedies of barrenness, or the motives of divorce, etc.

VI.   Or, that the author, commenting upon Catullus, Petronius, or Martial,[1] has inserted in his commentary several lewd discourses or expressions.

VII.   Or, that the author, giving the History of a sect, or person, whose actions were infamous, has related, in too open a manner, a great many things offensive to chaste ears.

VIII.   Or, that the author, treating of cases of conscience, and enumerating the different species of carnal sins, has said many things which modesty cannot easily digest.

IX.   Or, lastly, that the author relates Historical facts mentioned by other authors whom he carefully cites, which facts are filthy and immodest, and adds a commentary on his Historical narrations to illustrate them by testimonies, by reflexions, and by proofs, etc. in which he sometimes alleges the words of certain authors who have wrote freely, some of them, as Physicians, or Lawyers; others, as Gallants, or Poets; but he never says any thing containing either explicitly, or even implicitly, the approbation of impurity; that, on the contrary, he endeavours, upon many occasions, to expose it to our abhorrence, and to confute loose Morality.

These, I think, are the chief cases wherein a writer can be charged with venting obscenities.

In the first case, he deserves not only all the severest punishments of the Canon-Law, but ought also to be prosecuted by the Magistrate as a disturber of the public modesty, and a professed enemy to virtue.

As to those of the second, third, fourth and fifth, sixth, seventh, and eighth classes, let every one judge of them as he pleases: I am not concerned in them, mine being only the ninth case; and it is sufficient for me to examine what concerns that ninth kind of obscenity. However, I will make two or three general reflexions upon the rest.

II.   I say in the first place, that there are several degrees in the seven classes of writers whom I leave to the reader's judgement. A man may keep himself within certain bounds, or may exceed them: this prodigiously varies the differences and proportions; and it would be very unjust to pronounce the same sentence against all the writers of the second class. The hundred *Nouvelles nouvelles*, those of the Queen of Navarre, Boccace's Decameron, la Fontaine's Tales[2] do not deserve the same rigour as Aretin's Raggionamenti, and the Aloisia Sigrea Toletana.[3] The authors of these two last works deserve, as well as Ovid, to be placed in the first class of obscene authors.

Secondly I observe, that in all times a great number of men have agreed in condemning obscenities; and yet this never seemed to be a decision of equal force with the Civil Laws, a decision to which Poets, Commentators, etc. were obliged to conform on the penalty of being excluded the rank of honest men. The censurers of obscenities seem to be so much the more capable of terminating the question by a decisive and executive sentence, in the whole Republic of Letters, because they might make up a Senate out of all sorts of men. There would be in it not only persons venerable for the austerity of their lives, and sacred character, but also military men, and professed gallants, and, in a word, many who give offence by their voluptuous life. This is an authority of great weight; for the liberty of lewd verses must needs be an ill thing, since it is disliked by those very persons who live debauchery. But in vain have obscene writings been exclaimed against, it has had no effect to distinguish between honest and dishonest men. There has always been, in the Republic of Letters, a right or liberty of publishing writings of this nature. This right has never been liable to prescription; several persons of a distinguished merit have prevented it by the freedom they have allowed themselves in such sort of works; and this has brought no disgrace upon them, nor any ways incapacitated them for the enjoyment of all the honours and privileges belonging to their condition, nor prevented the preferments they might hope for from their fortune.

[1] Roman writers who included obscene material in their works.

[2] Marguerite de Valois, sister of François I of France, Giovanni Boccaccio and Jean de la Fontaine, a contemporary of Bayle.

[3] Pietro Arentino and *Aloisie ou les amours de Madame de M.T.P.*, a contemporary obscene book.

7
Mrs Manley, leaders in *The Examiner* (1712)

Source: Mrs Mary de la Riviere Manley, leaders in *The Examiner*, vol. II, nos 12 and 13, Thursday February 14 to Thursday February 28, 1712.

Mrs Mary de la Riviere Manley (1627–1724) made a bad start in life by contracting a marriage of dubious legality with John Manley of Truro. From the 1690s she seems to have lived by her pen and, since she had no reputation to lose, conducted liaisons with several prominent men including a fellow-journalist, Richard Steele. Her most famous works were a satire on the Duchess of Marlborough, *The Secret History of Queen Zarah* and the scandalous volumes *From the New Atlantis*. By 1711 her writings in support of the Tories won her the approbation of Jonathan Swift and the editorship of his journal, *The Examiner*. A series of her leaders, from which the extracts printed below were taken, violently attacked the Duke of Marlborough and the Whigs for continuing the war with France.

I.

I have laboured for some time past under an indisposition of mind and body, attended with the usual circumstances of loss of appetite and rest; my physician hath over-ruled my natural antipathy to opiates, and last night persuaded me to take what he called a 'quieting draught'; which soon took place, and began to give me a sort of pleasure I had never been acquainted with, that I knowing I slept, and yet seeing Elysian fields and delightful images dance before me . . .

I was carried away with great rapidity to a vast and magnificent circus or amphitheatre, . . . Patricians and senators in proper gowns were placed as guards or assistants to the throne, which was raised at the upper end under a canopy, where sat a lady in imperial robes [Queen Anne], of a graceful presence and majestic mien, her head adorned with a crown of gold, studded with jewels; of the diamonds set before, were these letters composed distinctly, *Mater Patriae Augusta* [Augusta, Mother of the Nation].

. . . There advanced from the other side of the circus an astonishing form [John Churchill, Duke of Marlborough]; the shape and features were partly human, but so altered by art, that they appeared much taller and larger than the life; they had suffered such a transmutation that the substance was entirely changed into solid gold . . . [The man of gold and his supporters, for their own selfish purposes, urged the Queen to continue the war, her good advisors wanted to conclude a peace].

II.

. . . On one side . . . Justice appeared, with the sword and weights; on the other, stood Resolution, godlike Fortitude, and Magnanimity, whom the Man of Gold beholding, he was seized with heart-sick qualms and despondency, asking all about him, as it was his custom on a day of battle, what he should do? For he was not by nature valiant; the ignorant vulgar had indeed extolled him for his constant success, they think a general does all himself, that is only done by his soldiers; and if the battle be gained by their means, though he never stirs from his post of safety, he must be courageous, in proportion to the victory that they have obtained.

Whilst the Man of Gold was in this uncertainty, Resolution animated the Empress [Queen Anne]. Fortitude stood forth and exhorted her to examine his crimes; Justice thrice brandished her awful sword before his eyes, and prepared her weights and scales: but before she could fix the balance, the Man of Gold fell all to pieces, by the touch of a rod[1] at the command of Augusta, which the Favourite Statesman held in his hand: his head immediately burst asunder, from whence rushed forth a monster called Faction, armed with stings and a forked tail . . . The body opened, and disclosed the Man of Gold's heart, where seemed to brood the genuine seeds of Ingratitude and Avarice. His paunch was filled with mouldy crusts, and biscuit full of maggots, of which he had cheated the needy soldiers. Avarice seeing him fall, would have fled, but was seized by Justice, who emptied his store before the assembly: those who had lent their money, with a good intent, in the exigency of the State, were repaid from hence, with interest and thanks . . . Ceres,[2] accompanied with the seasons, offered their cornucopias to Augusta; there were seen blooming Spring, delighful Summer, and yellow Autumn, each bringing so prodigious a supply, that no year had ever been so fruitful as that in which Peace was renewed in the Empire, and the Empress restored to the full enjoyment of her undoubted prerogative. Faction was crushed, or fled the land: all mankind beheld with acclamations the prodigious advantages Peace had over War, and resolved from that time forth to do all that was in their power towards perpetuating so great a happiness.

[1] A reference to the rod of office of Lord Treasurer recently assumed by the Tory Robert Harley.

[2] Roman goddess of the fertility of the earth.

8

The Anglican Canons of 1640

Source: J.P. Kenyon (ed.), *The Stuart Constitution 1603–1688: Documents and Commentary*, 2nd edn, Cambridge University Press, Cambridge, 1986, pp.149–51.

Promulgated by Convocation, which continued to sit after the Dissolution of the Short Parliament, and issued under the Great Seal, the Canons embodied many of the Laudian innovations of the 1630s in addition to the articles published here.

Constitutions and canons ecclesiastical, treated upon by the ... convocations ... of Canterbury and York, ... and now published for the due observation of them by his Majesty's authority under the great seal of England

[*16 June 1640*]

Charles, by the Grace of God king of England, Scotland, France and Ireland, Defender of the Faith, etc., to all whom these presents shall come, greeting ... Forasmuch as we are given to understand that many of our subjects, being misled against the rites and ceremonies now used in the Church of England, have lately taken offence at the same, upon an unjust supposal that they are not only contrary to our laws but also introductive unto popish superstitions; ... yet, as we have cause to fear, aim at our own royal person, and would fain have our good subjects imagine that we ourselves are perverted, and do worship God in a superstitious way, and that we intend to bring in some alteration of the religion here established. Now, how far we are from that, and how utterly we detest every thought thereof, we have by many public declarations and otherwise upon sundry occasions given such assurance to the world, as that from thence we also assure ourself, that no man of wisdom and discretion could ever be so beguiled as to give any serious entertainment to such brainsick jealousies; ...

We therefore, out of our princely inclination to uniformity and peace, in matters especially that concern the holy worship of God, ... and ..., having fully advised herein with our metropolitan, and with the commissioners authorised under our Great Seal for causes ecclesiastical, have thought good to give them free leave to treat in Convocation, and agree upon certain other canons necessary for the advancement of God's glory, the edifying of his Holy Church, and the due reverence of his blessed Mysteries and Sacraments; that, as we have ever been and by God's assistance (by whom alone we reign) shall ever so continue, careful and ready to cut off superstition with one hand, so we may no less expel irreverence and profaneness with the other ...

Concerning the regal power

Whereas sundry laws, ordinances and constitutions have been formerly made for the acknowledgment and profession of the most lawful and independent authority of our dread sovereign lord the king's most excellent Majesty, over the state ecclesiastical and civil ... for the fuller and clear instruction and information of all Christian people within this realm in their duties in this particular we do further ordain and decree that every parson, vicar, curate or preacher upon some one Sunday in every quarter of the year, at morning prayer, shall, in the place where he serves, treatably and audibly read these explanations of the regal power here inserted:

The most high and sacred Order of Kings is of Divine Right, being the ordinance of God himself, founded in the prime laws of nature, and clearly established by express texts both of the Old and New Testaments. A supreme power is given to this most excellent Order by God himself in the Scriptures, which is, that kings should rule and command in their several dominions all persons of what rank or estate soever, whether ecclesiastical or civil, and that they should restrain and punish with the temporal sword all stubborn and wicked doers.

The care of God's Church is so committed to kings in the Scripture that they are commended when the Church keeps the right way, and taxed when it runs amiss, and therefore her government belongs in chief unto kings; for otherwise one man would be commended for another's care, and taxed but for another's negligence, which is not God's way.

The power to call and dissolve Councils, both national and provincial, is the true right of all Christian kings within their own realms and territories; and when in the first times of Christ's Church prelates used this power, it was therefore only because in those days they had no Christian kings; and it was then so only used as in times of persecution, that is, with supposition (in case it were required) of submitting their very lives unto the very laws and commands even of those pagan princes that they might not so much as seem to disturb their civil government, which Christ came to confirm, but by no means to undermine.

For any person or persons to set up, maintain or avow in any their said realms or territories respectively, under any pretence whatsoever, any independent coactive power, either papal or popular (whether directly or indirectly), is to undermine their great royal office, and cunningly to over-throw that most sacred ordinance which God himself hath established, and so is treasonable against God as well as against the king.

For subjects to bear arms against their kings, offensive or defensive, upon any pretence whatsoever, is at least to resist the powers which are ordained of God; and though they do not invade but only resist, St Paul tells them plainly they shall receive to themselves damnation. [This was followed by an oath to resist 'all innovations in doctrine and government' of the church, which was to be administered to all the clergy.]

9

Richard Baxter's Account of his Ministry (1647–60)

Source: R. Baxter, *The Autobiography of Richard Baxter: Being the Reliquae Baxterianae Abridged*, edited by J.H. Lloyd Thomas, Everyman, Dent, London, New York, 1931, pp.77–9.

Richard Baxter (1615–91) became lecturer (or preacher) at Kidderminster in 1641 and sided with parliament on the outbreak of war. He was one of the ministers who accompanied Charles II back to England, was offered and declined a bishopric, and was removed from the ministry in 1662. Thereafter, despite suffering bouts of imprisonment, he remained influential among both Anglicans and dissenters through his sermons and books. His account of his ministry is a classic statement of godly aspiration and achievement.

I shall next record, to the praise of my Redeemer, the comfortable employment and successes which he vouchsafed me during my abode at Kidderminster, . . .

(1) I preached before the wars twice each Lord's-day; but after the war but once, and once every Thursday, besides occasional sermons. Every Thursday evening my neighbours that were most desirous and had opportunity met at my house, and there one of them repeated the sermon, and afterwards they proposed what doubts any of them had about the sermon, or any other case of conscience, and I resolved their doubts; and last of all I caused sometimes one and sometimes another of them to pray (to exercise them); and sometimes I prayed with them myself, which (beside singing a psalm) was all they did. And once a week also some of the younger sort, who were not fit to pray in so great an assembly, met among a few, more privately, where they spent three hours in prayer together; every Saturday night they met at some of their houses to repeat the sermon of the last Lord's-day, and to pray and prepare themselves for the following day . . . Two days every week my assistant and I myself took fourteen families between us for private catechising and conference (he going through the parish, and the town coming to me) . . .

Besides all this I was forced five or six years, by the people's necessity, to practice physic. A common pleurisy happening one year, and no physician being near, I was forced to advise them, to save their lives; and I could not afterwards avoid the importunity of the town and country round about. And because I never once took a penny of anyone, I was crowded with patients, so that almost twenty would be at my door at once; and though God by more success than I expected so long encouraged me, yet at last I could endure it no longer, . . . So that after some years' practice I procured a godly, diligent physician to come and live in the town. . . .

But all these my labours (except my private conferences with the families), even preaching and preparing for it, were but my recreations and, as it were, the work of my spare hours. For my writings were my chiefest daily labour, . . .

(2) I have mentioned my sweet and acceptable employment; let me, to the praise of my gracious Lord, acquaint you with some of my success. And I will not suppress it, though I foreknow that the malignant will impute the mention of it to pride and ostentation . . .

My public preaching met with an attentive diligent auditory . . .

The congregation was usually full, so that we were fain to build five galleries after my coming thither, the church itself being very capacious, and the most commodious and convenient that ever I was in. Our private meetings also were full. On the Lord's-days there was no disorder to be seen in the streets, but you might hear an hundred families singing psalms and repeating sermons as you passed through the streets. In a word, when I came thither first there was about one family in a street that worshipped God and called on his name, and when I came away there were some streets where there was not passed one family in the side of a street that did not so, and that did not, by professing serious godliness, give us hopes of their sincerity. And those families which were the worst, being inns and alehouses, usually *some persons* in each house did seem to be religious . . .

And in my poor endeavours with my brethren in the ministry my labours were not lost . . . Yea, the mercy was yet greater in that it was of farther public benefit. For some Independents and Anabaptists that had before conceited that parish churches were the great obstruction of all true Church order and discipline, and that it was impossible to bring them to any good consistency, did quite change their minds when they saw what was done at Kidderminster . . .

(3) Having related my comfortable successes in this place, I shall next tell you by what and how many advantages this much was effected . . .

One advantage was that I came to a people that never had any awakening ministry before (but a few formal cold sermons of the curate); for if they had been hardened under a powerful ministry and been sermon-proof I should have expected less . . .

Another, and the greatest advantage, was the change that was made in the public affairs by the success of the wars . . .

For my part, I bless God who gave me, even under an usurper whom I opposed, such liberty and advantage to preach his Gospel with success, which I cannot have under a king to whom I have sworn and performed true subjection and obedience . . .

And our unity and concord was a great advantage to us, and our freedom from those sects and heresies which many other places were infected with. We had no private church, though we had private meetings; we had not pastor against pastor, nor church against church, nor sect against sect, nor Christian against Christian . . . But we were all of one mind, and mouth and way. Not a Separatist, Anabaptist, Antinomian [extreme Protestant sects], etc., in the town! . . .

And it was a great advantage to me that my neighbours were of such a trade as allowed them time enough to read or talk of holy things; for the town liveth upon the weaving of Kidderminster stuffs, and as they stand in their loom they can set a book before them or edify one another . . .

10
Blaise Pascal: *Ninth letter written to a provincial by one of his friends* (1656)

Source: B. Pascal, *Provincial Letters*, translated and introduced by A.J. Krailsheimer, Penguin, Harmondsworth, 1967, pp.132–4. Translation from French.

This extract from a series of satirical anti-Jesuit tracts, published anonymously by the mathematician Blaise Pascal (1623–62) in 1656, lampoons the emphasis placed on 'pious practices'. The tracts were acclaimed in France and gave some support for the Jansenist position with its emphasis on moral discipline. They were also quickly translated into English.

Paris, 3 July 1656

Sir,

I will spend no more time on courtesies than the good Father did last time I saw him. As soon as he caught sight of me he came up and said, looking at a book he was holding; 'If someone opened up Paradise to you would he not be rendering you the highest service imaginable? Would you not give millions in gold to have a key and go inside whenever you felt like it? There is no need to incur such vast expense; here is a key, indeed a hundred, at much lower cost.' I did not know whether the good Father was reading, or speaking on his own account, but he saved me the trouble by saying:

'These are the opening words of a fine book by Fr. Barry of our Society; for I never say anything on my own account.'

'What book, Father?' I said.

'Here is the title,' he said; '*Paradise opened to Philagie by means of a hundred easily performed devotions to the Mother of God.*'

'What, Father? each of these easy devotions is enough to open heaven's gates?'

'Yes,' he said; 'have a look at the words following those you have just heard: "The devotions to the Mother of God which you will find in this book are all so many keys to heaven, which will open up the whole of Paradise to you if you only perform them;" and that is why he says in the conclusion: "that he is happy if you perform just one of them." '

'Tell me one of the simpler ones then, Father.'

'They are all simple,' he replied: 'for instance; "salute the Holy Virgin when you come upon images of her; recite the little rosary of the ten pleasures of the Virgin; frequently utter the name of Mary; charge the angels with paying her our respects; desire to build more churches to her name than all the monarchs of the world put together have done; greet her every morning and

93

evening; say the *Ave Maria* [Hail Mary] every day in honour of the heart of Mary." And he says that with that one you can moreover be assured of winning the Virgin's heart.'

'But Father,' I said, 'always provided you give her yours too?'

'That is not necessary,' he said, 'when you are too closely attached to the world. Listen: "An exchange of hearts would indeed be right; but yours is a little too dependent and sets too much store on creatures. Therefore I dare not invite you today to present the little slave you call your heart." And he is satisfied with the *Ave Maria* he had asked for.'

'That is very convenient,' I said, 'and I do not think there will be any more people damned after that.'

'Alas!' said the Father, 'I can see that you have no idea how hard-hearted cetain people can be! There are some who would never undertake to say daily the two words "good morning, good evening" because it demands some effort of memory. And so Fr. Barry has had to provide them with still easier practices "like wearing night and day beads round the arm in the form of a bracelet, or carrying a rosary or an image of the Virgin. And now say that I do not provide you with easy devotions for winning the favours of Mary," as Fr. Barry says on p.106.'

'That, Father,' I said, 'is the ultimate in simplicity.'

'And,' he said, 'that is the best that could be done, and I think it will suffice; for only an utter wretch would refuse to take up one moment of his whole life to put beads round his arm, or a rosary in his pocket, thus making so certain of salvation that those who have tried have never been disappointed, whatever their way of life, although we advise people to lead a good life all the same. I will only quote you the example on p.34 of a woman who daily performed the devotion of saluting images of the Virgin, lived all her life in mortal sin, finally died in that state and was yet saved by the merits of this devotion.'

'How so?' I cried.

'Our Lord brought her back to life specially,' he said, 'so certain it is that no one can perish who performs one of these devotions.'

'Indeed, Father, I know that devotions to the Virgin are a powerful means of winning salvation, and that the least of them are very meritorious when motivated by faith and charity, as with the saints who have practised them. But if you convince those who use them without changing their evil life that they will be converted on their deathbed, or that God will restore them to life, it seems to me much more likely to keep sinners in their evil ways, lulled into a false security by such rash confidence, than to draw them away by a genuine conversion which only grace can effect.'

' "What does it matter," ' said the Father, ' "how we enter Paradise so long as we enter?" ' . . .

'I confess,' I said, 'that it does not matter; but the question is whether one will enter.'

11
Bishop Burnet's Account of his Episcopal Responsibilities (1689–1715)

Source: N. Williams, *The 18th Century Constitution*, Cambridge University Press, Cambridge, 1960, pp.364–6.

Gilbert Burnet (1643–1715) was a Scot who, having been Professor of Divinity at Glasgow, played an important part in the Glorious Revolution and was appointed Bishop of Salisbury in 1689. His sympathies were with the Latitudinarian wing of the Established Church. He sought to use his office to improve the quality of the parochial clergy and to raise levels of understanding among the laity.

I Went to my Diocese to do my duty there

But now I was to go into my Diocese, and for that end I formed my designs thus; I resolved to preach constantly every Lord's day and also to preach the weekly lecture at Salisbury. I resolved to go round my Diocese about three weeks or a month once a year, preaching and confirming every day from Church to Church. I resolved thus once in three years besides the formality of the Triennial Visitation to go round to all the chief parts of my Diocese and to hold conferences with my Clergy upon the chief heads of Divinity, in which in a discourse of about two hours length I opened all that related to the head proposed, and encouraged them to object or propose questions relating to the subject . . . I found the Clergy were not much the better for them, and false stories were made and believed of what I delivered in those conferences; and though as I went round I kept an open table to all the Clergy, yet nothing could mollify their aversion to a man that was for toleration and for treating the Dissenters with gentleness. I continued still to go about preaching and confirming, so that I have confirmed and preached in 275 Churches of my Diocese, and 10 or 12 times in all the market towns and considerable places. I look upon confirmation if rightly managed as the most effectual means possible for reviving Christianity, but I could never prevail with the greater part of my Clergy to think of any other way of preparing their youth to it but to hear them repeat their catechism, they did not study to make them consider it as the becoming a Christian by an act of their own. I have now settled upon a method in which I intend to continue as long as God continues my strength to execute it. I stay a week in a place where every morning I go and preach and confirm in some Church within 6 or 7 miles of the place, and then at 5 a clock after evening prayer I catechise some children and explain the whole Catechism to them, so that I go through it all in six days and confirm there next Lord's day, and make presents to the value of about a crown a child to all whom I catechised, and I have them all to dine with me on the Lord's day.

This seems to be the most profitable method I can devise both for instructing as well as provoking the Clergy to catechise much, and for setting a good emulation among the younger sort to be well instructed. I have likewise set up a school for 50 poor children at Salisbury who are taught and clothed at my charge, and to whom I go once a month and hear 10 of them repeat such Psalms and parts of the New Testament as I prescribe, and give them 18 pence a piece for reward, this is a mean to keep them in good order. I set my self to encourage my Clergy not only by my going often about among them and by assisting them kindly in all their concerns, but by a large share of my income with which I have relieved their necessities. . . .

I looked on Ordinations as the most important part of a Bishop's care and that on which the law had laid no restraints, for it was absolutely in the Bishop's power to ordain or not as he judged a person qualified for it, and so I resolved to take that matter to heart. I never turned over the examining those who came to me for orders to a Chaplain or an Archdeacon, I examined them very carefully my self. I began always to examine them concerning the proof of the Christian religion and the authority of the Scriptures and the nature of the Gospel Covenant in Christ; . . .

One defect run through them all, even those who could not be called ignorant, they read the Scriptures so little that they scarce knew the most common things in them, but when I was satisfied that they had a competent measure of knowledge, I directed the rest of my discourse to their consciences and went through all the parts of the Pastoral Care to give them good directions and to awaken in them a right sense of things. I pressed them to employ their time in prayer, fasting and meditation and in reading carefully the Epistles to Timothy and Titus. . .

As for their morals we were forced to take that implicitly from the Testimonials signed by the Clergy in whose neighbourhood they had lived, in which I have found such an easyness of signing these, that unless I knew the men I grew to regard them very little. This was the best method that in the present state of our affairs I could take, yet I found it so defective and so far short of a due exactness that I must confess the Ordination weeks were much dreaded by me and were the most afflicting part of the whole year and of the whole Episcopal duty.

12
A Letter Concerning Toleration by John Locke (1685)

Source: John Locke, *A Letter Concerning Toleration,* edited by M. Montuori, Martinez Nijhoss, The Hague, 1963, pp.7–9, 16–19.

This was written by the philosopher John Locke (1632–1704), originally in Latin, in the Netherlands in the autumn of 1685, just after the Revocation of the Edict of Nantes by Louis XIV. The English version was an important intellectual influence on the Revolution Settlement of 1688 and the Act of Toleration which followed.

Honoured Sir

Since you are pleased to inquire what are my thoughts about the mutual toleration of Christians in their different professions of religion, I must needs answer you freely, that I esteem that toleration to be the chief characteristic mark of the true church. For whatsoever some people boast of the antiquity of places and names, or of the pomp of their outward worship; others, of the reformation of their discipline; all, of the orthodoxy of their faith (for every one is orthodox to himself): these things, and all others of this nature, are much rather marks of men striving for power and empire over one another, than of the church of Christ. Let any one have never so true a claim to all these things, yet if he be destitute of charity, meekness, and good-will in general towards all mankind, even to those that are not Christians, he is certainly yet short of being a true Christian himself. . . . The business of true religion is quite another thing. It is not instituted in order to the erecting of an external pomp, nor to the obtaining of ecclesiastical dominion, nor to the exercising of compulsive force, but to the regulating of men's lives, according to the rules of virtue and piety. . . . If the Gospel and the apostles may be credited, no man can be a Christian without *charity,* and without *that faith which works,* not by force, but by *love.* Now, I appeal to the consciences of those that persecute, torment, destroy, and kill other men upon pretence of religion, whether they do it out of friendship and kindness towards them or no? And I shall then indeed, and not until then, believe they do so, when I shall see those fiery zealots correcting, in the same manner, their friends and familiar acquaintance for the manifest sins they commit against the precepts of the Gospel; . . .

The toleration of those that differ from others in matters of religion, is so agreeable to the Gospel of Jesus Christ, and to the genuine reason of mankind, that it seems monstrous for men to be so blind as not to perceive the necessity and advantage of it in so clear a light. . . . But, however, that some may not colour their spirit of persecution and unchristian cruelty with a pretence of care of the public weal and observation of the laws; and that others, under pretence of religion, may not seek impunity for their libertinism and licentiousness; in a word, that none may impose either upon himself or others, by the pretences of loyalty and obedience to the prince, or of tenderness and sincerity in the worship of God I esteem it above all things necessary to distinguish exactly the business of civil government from that of religion, and to settle the just bounds that lie between the one and the other. If this be not done, there can be no end put to the controversies that will be always arising between those that have, or at least pretend to have, on the one side, a concernment for the interest of men's souls, and, on the other side, a care of the commonwealth.

The commonwealth seems to me to be a society of men constituted only for the procuring, preserving, and advancing of their own *civil interests*.

Civil interests I call life, liberty, health, and indolency of body; and the possession of outward things, such as money, lands, houses, furniture, and the like.

It is the duty of the civil magistrate, by the impartial execution of equal laws, to secure unto all the people in general, and to every one of his subjects in particular, the just possession of these things belonging to this life. . . .

Now that the whole jurisdiction of the magistrate reaches only to these civil concernments, and that all civil power, right, and dominion, is bounded and confined to the only care of promoting these things; and that it neither can nor ought in any manner to be extended to the salvation of souls, these following considerations seem unto me abundantly to demonstrate.

First. Because the care of souls is not committed to the civil magistrate, any more than to other men. It is not committed unto him, I say, by God; because it appears not that God has ever given any such authority to one man over another, as to compel any one to his religion. Nor can any such power be vested in the magistrate by the *consent of the people*, because no man can so far abandon the care of his own salvation as blindly to leave to the choice of any other, whether prince or subject, to prescribe to him what faith or worship he shall embrace. For no man can, if he would, conform his faith to the dictates of another. All the life and power of true religion consist in the inward and full persuasion of the mind; and faith is not faith without believing. Whatever profession we make, to whatever outward worship we conform, if we are not fully satisfied in our own mind that the one is true, and the other well pleasing unto God, such profession and such practice, far from being any furtherance, are indeed great obstacles to our salvation. For in this manner, instead of expiating other sins by the exercise of religion, I say, in offering thus unto God Almighty such a worship as we esteem to be displeasing unto him, we add unto the number of our other sins those also of hypocrisy, and contempt of his Divine Majesty.

In the second place. The care of souls cannot belong to the civil magistrate, because his power consists only in outward force; but true and saving religion consists in the inward persuasion of the mind, without which nothing can be acceptable to God. And such is the nature of the understanding, that it cannot be compelled to the belief of anything by outward force.

13
Sexual offences before the ecclesiastical courts at Stratford-upon-Avon (1622)

Source: E.R.C. Brinkworth, *Shakespeare and the Bawdy Court*, Phillimore, Chichester, 1979, pp.148–51.

This extract from the court records demonstrates the types of offences which came before the church courts and the penalties, excommunication and fines, which the officers imposed on the transgressors. Though the vicar held this court, they were more usually presided over by the officials appointed by the bishop or archdeacon, men who often had little social contact with the parishes.

Acts before Thomas Wilson, Vicar, in the parish church on Tuesday, 28 May 1622, in the presence of Thomas Fisher, notary public and scribe of the acts.

George Brown, junior and Joan Browne his sister: for not attending the church and for not receiving the sacrament.

Eleanor Badger, daughter of George Badger, for the same.

William Davis: for fishing on the Sabbath day; 19 May, pardoned with monition.

John Gibbins: for the same: let him be cited anew for the next court: pardoned.

Thomas Kymble: for profaning the Sabbath day: 'in durance at Warrwick jail'.

William Buck alias Smith: for the same: cited by Coates: he did not appear: excommunicated; pardoned.

Vincent Byddle: for the same: he admitted and promised that in the future he would desist from the like fault.

Richard Toovie, weaver: for the same: he denied: ordered 'that he bring a certificate from the churchwardens,' on pain of excommunication, 'that he did not play'.

Thomas Canning: for the same: admitted 'that he did play at ball on the sabbath day, and that it was the first time he so did, and doth promise that it shalbe the last' and he submitted himself to the correction of the judge.

Elizabeth Mills; for incontinence: 'for having a child unlawfully begotten': admitted 'and saith that Arthur Layton of Potters Hanly was the father of the child': she is enjoined to perform public penance in a white sheet' on the next Sunday, on pain of excommunication.

Edward Samon: 'for a common swearer': let him not be cited: 'he is the hayward at Loxly'.

William Heminge: for the same: cited by Coates: he did not appear: excommunicated.

Thomas Wilkins and Margaret his wife: they did not receive the sacrament: they appeared: ordered 'that they frequent the church hereafter and that they receive the sacrament at Whitsuntide and to certify' on pain of excommunication.

Margin he is pardoned the fee.

Edward Rogers: 'for striking the servant of William Castle, glover, in the church in sermon time': he appeared: admitted 'that he did swing the boy by the ear because the said boy did fight and jostle with another boy and did disturb the congregation': ordered as above with Richard Baker.

Thomas Loach, junior: he did not receive the sacrament: he appeared: ordered to receive and to certify before the last day of June on pain of excommunication.

Thomas Woodward: 'for keeping company with William Bramly who standeth aggravated, and the said Thomas hath been heretofore admonished in court several times to desist from the same': he appeared and admitted: ordered 'that upon the next Sabbath day he confess his fault in the time of divine service in the parish church of Stratford before the whole congregation and there to promise amendment' on pain of excommunication.

Eleanor Brockhurst: 'for fornication': she went away.

Joan Mathewes: for the same: she went away.

John Allen: 'for dancing the morris in evening prayer time on the feast day of Philip and Jacob': he appeared: admitted 'and saith that he will never commit the like': ordered 'that the next Sabbath day he does publicly confess his fault in the church of Stratford before the whole congregation and promise there amendment for henceforth' on pain of excommunication.

John Rickittes: for the same: cited by Coates: he did not appear: excommunicated: absolved.

William Plymmer: for the same: appeared: admitted: 'and is enjoined as above with John Allen' on pain of excommunication.

Humphrey Browne: for the same: he appeared: ordered as above with Allen.

Francis Palmer, servant to John Hobbins of Shatterlie: 'for being the Maid Marrian': not to be cited anew for the next court: pardoned.

Margaret Sargen: 'for not coming to the catechism': she did not appear: to be cited anew for the next court: pardoned.

Anne Brookes: for the same: 'she was mistaken by the churchwardens' and therefore is dismissed.

Mary Napton: for the same: she did not appear: penalty was reserved.

Joyce Bumpas: for the same: she appeared: admitted: ordered 'that she shall come to be publicly catechised the next Sabbath day, and also to pay the fees of the court' on pain of excommunication: afterwards decreed to be excommunicated in writing.

Thomas Fauxe: 'for scandalous speeches and slandering of Alice Brunt, calling her filthy whore and said that he would prove her to be a whore': he appeared: admitted 'that he called her whore but saith that it was in his passion being moved and abused by her, but denieth that he can prove her to be a whore, neither did he say so as he affirmeth': in the meantime the lord adjourned the cause.

Elizabeth Wotton: to give reason why she stands excommunicated: excommunication was aggravated.

Judith Sadler:[1] for incontinence; she went away.

Edward Ingram: for committing adultery with a certain Joan Clemson: 'he is enjoined to take out a proclamation of purgation before the next Sabbath day to be published' on pain of excommunication.

Joan Clemson: *no entry.*

[1] Judith, bastard to Judith Sadler, baptised 19 January 1621/2.

14
Visitation articles of the Diocese of Hereford (1662)

Source: Bodleian B 7 9 Linc. (21), pp.1–3.

In 1662 all bishops in the Church of England were ordered to conduct visitations of their dioceses. This meant that for each parish a questionnaire had to be returned answering queries about the church buildings and furnishings, the tithes and the vicarage, the minister, the parishioners, parish clerks, sextons, churchwardens, schools and schoolmasters, physicians, surgeons and midwives. Each bishop compiled his own articles of visitation, so there are differences in the information collected in the different dioceses.

Articles of Visitation and Enquiry concerning Matters Ecclesiastical exhibited to the Ministers, Churchwardens, and Sidesmen of every Parish within the Diocese of Hereford in the first Episcopal Visitation of the Right Reverend Father in God, Herbert by Divine Providence, Lord Bishop of Hereford, London, 1662.

Concerning Churches and Chapels, with the Ornaments and Furniture thereunto belonging.

I Is your parish church or chapel kept in good and sufficient repair? Are the roofs thereof well covered with lead, tile or slate; the windows well glazed; the floors well paved; the seats well fastened and conveniently placed; and all things so decently ordered as becometh the house of the Lord?

II Hath the steeple or tower of your church or chapel or any part thereof been pulled down, or any of the lead or bells formerly belonging thereunto been embezzled, sold or made away? In whose hands or custody doth the same, or any part thereof remain? Declare what you know or have heard therein.

III Is there a font of stone, with a good cover thereunto, standing in a convenient place towards the lower part of your church, for the administration of baptism? And is there in your chancel a decent communion table for the administration of the Lord's supper; with a carpet of silk, stuff or fine woollen cloth; and another covering of white and pure linen, to spread thereupon? And have you a fair communion cup or chalice with a cover of silver, and one or more flagons of silver, or pewter thereunto belonging?

IV Have you in your said church or chapel a convenient seat, or pew, for your minister to read Divine Service in; a pulpit with a comely cloth or cushion for the same; a Bible, of the late translation, in a large volume, and the Book of Common Prayer, both well and substantially bound? Have you likewise the Book of Homilies set forth by authority, a book of canons and constitutions ecclesiastical, and a printed table of the degrees wherein marriage is prohibited?

V Have you a comely surplice for the minister to wear at all times of his public ministration in the church provided, and to be duly washed at the charge of the parish?

VI Have you a register book of parchment wherein to register the names and surnames of all such persons as are married, christened or buried within your parish, together with the names and surnames of both parents of the children so christened expressing the day, month and year of all such christenings, marriages and burials? And is the transcript thereof yearly within one month after the 25 March brought in to the bishop's registry?

VII Have you likewise another book of paper wherein to record the names and licences of all such strangers as are admitted at any time to preach in your church or chapel? As also a third book wherein to write down the church-wardens' accounts; together with a strong chest with locks and keys wherein to keep the aforesaid books and all other the aforementioned furniture in safe custody? And, lastly, have you a bier, with a black hearse cloth, for the burial of the dead?

15
A Magistrate at work in Restoration England
(1663–88)

Source: J.A. Sharpe (ed.), *William Holcroft His Booke: Local Office Holding in late Stuart Essex*, Essex Records Office, Chelmsford, 1986, pp.32–3, 54, 56.

William Holcroft was a verderer, or magistrate, in Epping Forest and these extracts from a diary, or commonplace book, kept by him, show the everyday activities of the magistracy, Little is known of Holcroft beyond the material in the book and, as such, his record is probably typical of the minor landholding gentry which shouldered much of the burden of local government.

William Holcroft his Booke
[*f.4*] Stratford. Friday the 18 March 1663.
George Ruston of Barking made oath that he was in danger of being killed or wounded or hurt by Wm. Griffin of Barking, butcher. Wm Griffin was brought before me the same day and has entered into a recognizance of £10 for his appearance at the next general sessions of the peace for this county, and for keeping the peace . . .
1664
April 8. Sent John Borehan to the house of correction at Barking for abusing his master Peter Barrett and released him in 4 days . . .
13 Sent Lawrence Davis a glass-mender to the cage for one night for misdemeaning himself – he pretended he lived at the Blue Boar at Walee in Surrey.
1664 Thursday the 28th July An Taylor of Woodford Bridge complained that she had lost a good quantity of green wood and had two men and an old woman in suspicion, and brought one Richard Price and Sibell Jenninges before me. The other, whose name was Richard Flanson, got away. I committed Price and Jenninges to the constable's care who put them into the cage at Stratford. The same night they made their escapes out of the cage. Upon Monday the 1 day of August Sibell Jenninges was apprehended in Southwark and brought to me for whom I took bail to appear at the next quarter sessions . . .
[*f.4v*] Essex. Barking, 13th day of September 1664.
James Grigson junior of Uphall informed upon oath that Lenard Lee of Barking, tanner, upon Thursday the 8th of this instant did in the ground of James Grigson senior take one partridge with a long net about eight o'clock at night. Leonard Lee did not deny the fact, but produced the net before Colonel Mildmay and myself.

103

16 September. Lee entered into a recognizance of £40 with sureties. Rich. Mander of Barking, yeoman, Thomas Aderly of the same, yeoman, in £20 a piece.

Condition: that Leonard Lee shall not at any time hereafter kill or take any pheasants or partridges again with unlawful nets or otherways unlawfully.

The said Leo. Lee paid to Richard Mander (being an overseer for the poor) for the use of the poor of Barking 20s according to the statutes of 1 Jacobii 27 and 7 Jacobii 11 cap.

The 25th October 1664. Thomas Davis of Stratford Langthorne informed upon oath that there was stolen from the Crown at Stratford one pair of sheets marked J.S. and one flaxen napkin with the same mark, and 3 other sheets, one holland apron, a woman's shift and three linen foothose, all which linen was found the 24th of October in the possession of one Bartholomew Williams, as he called himself.

Information. Thomas Langborne said that the pair of sheets and the flaxen napkin marked J.S. are his goods.

Examination. Batholomew Williams, who was taken by Rich. Swift, constable of Stratford, upon suspicion with the linen about him the 24 October 1664 confesses that he had the formentioned linen about him, but said that he found the linen in a lane near a field near the 'Crown' in Stratford.

Upon information I bound Thomas Langburne and Thomas Davis in £10 apiece to prosecute Batholomew Williams at the next assizes.

I gave a warrant to the constables of Stratford the same day to carry the said Williams to the Gaol at Colchester.

Thursday the 27th October the prisoner broke the cage at Stratford and he made his escape . . .

Wednesday the 28th December 1664, Mr Wm White made a complaint that John Tinson being then his hired servant did in the house of one Thomas Jackson kick him about a month since. Upon his complaint I bound over John Tinson in £10, Thomas Batten and William Fuller in £5 apiece, for Tinsons appearing at the quarter sessions and to the good behaviour all of the persons being parishioners of West Ham.

Thursday the 16th February 1664, James Guy of Plaistow, carpenter, made complaint upon oath that coming along Churchstreet Lane the night before twelfth night he saw Abell Bono and William Crouch strike Thomas Miles of the same parish. And as the informant was a headborough [minor official] in the same parish he commanded them in the king's name to keep the peace. But instead of obeying, the said Abell Bono and William Crouch did both of them strike the said headborough, and Bono called him beggarly rogue. Upon which I bound over Abell Bono in £20 . . .

[*f.5v*] Essex. Saturday, being the 22nd day of April 1665. Jeane Norris, servant to Mr. Royston of Plaistow informed me upon oath that John Knight of Plaistow did by violence drag the informant down a lane to a well and threatened to throw her into the well if she would not let him lie with her, and took up her coats, which made her cry out for help and then he stopped her mouth with his hand. She then struggling with him got from him, &c. Upon which complaint I bound over to the next sessions John Knight in £20 . . .

Thursday being the 7 June 1666. Francis Cankin of Walthamstow came and informed me that his wife Mary Cankin had a former husband, one John Burr, that lived at Dunmow, and that he was come into these parts to harvest work. Upon which complaint John Burr and Mary Burr alias Cankin were brought before me, and upon examination John Burr confesses he was married to Martha his wife at Tilton [*sic*] in Essex, and to Mary his wife at a church in the Minoris, and that at the time of examination they were both living.

Mary Burr alias Cankin confessed that she was married to John Burr and to Francis Cankin. At a church in the Minoris, London to Jo. Burr about the 2 June 1660, and to Francis Cankin alias Burr acknowledged her confession before me. But Jo. Burr denied that ever he was married to Mary Ram alias Burr alias Cankin.

[*f*.22] 1685 June 15. I received orders from the Earl of Oxford to raise my company, and then to give notice to him or some of the deputy lieutenants at Chelmsford, and from thence to receive further orders.

Upon the receipt of the orders I showed out my warrants to the high constables for the meeting of my company at Great Ilford on Wednesday the 17th present, each soldier to bring with him 14 days' pay and the muster master's pay. And every fire arms to bring with them one pound of powder, and one pound of ball.

The day above written I received of Mr. Brett of Rumford by order of three deputy lieutenants twenty three pounds of powder, and one pound of ball.

The day above written I received of Mr. Brett of Rumford by order of three deputy lieutenants twenty three pounds for trophy money, having not had any for that use since 1661.

My company returned from Colchester by Colonel Turner's order the 11th July 1685. And I disbanded them at Ilford on Tuesday the 14th of July, they having been abroad then one month.

Moneys due to the officers of my company for 28 days service (for Wednesday the 17 June to Tuesday the 14th July 1685).

	£	s	d
To my self as a major and captain at 13s. per diem	£18:	4:	0
To my lieutenant [*sic*] Rich. Upphill at 4s. per diem	£ 5.	12:	—
To my ensign Walther Corbett, 3s. per diem	£ 4:	4:	—
To my four sergeants at 10s. per diem	£14:	—:	—

. . .

1687. 18th June. George Day and Rich. Osmon, both of Great Ilford ward were brought before me this day upon the complaint of the honourable Rob. Bartie, esq., for removing and carry [*sic*] away one of the king's timber trees. I bound them to the next Court of Attachment . . .

1687 8th September. Henry Tibballs of Stratford Langthorn, collarmaker, was brought before me by virtue of a warrant from captain Wroth, to be bound to give evidence at the Swaine Mote Court against John Stephens of Wansted for killing two of his majesty's deer.

October. I sent a certificate to my lord Huntingdon at the request of the vicar and other inhabitants of the parish of Low Layton to inclose a piece of ground between Wall Wood and Mr. Hubland's house, containing about 6 acres, and also another piece between Mr. Hubland's house and Whip's Cross, containing about 4 acres . . .

[December] I sent a certificate to my lord Huntingdon at the request of Rich. Hutchinson, esq., for a licence to build a brick wall in his own ditch, near his garden pales, in the parish of Low Layton.

[*f.21v*] 1688 4th June. The confession of John Smith, the apprentice of Benjam. Warder of Colledge Hill, London, watchmaker, as follows, &c.

The said John Smith was walking in the Forest of Waltham in Layton Walk, and in a wood behind the keeper's house there he met with some boys, who told him they could show him a faun and they did, and the [*sic*] took the same faun, and brought it to Stratford town, where he was stopped and brought before me, as one of the verderers of the said forest. I bound Rich. Alford for Stratford aforesaid, blacksmith, sureties for the said John Smith for his appearance in the next Forty Day Court for the said forest in £10 . . .

16th July. One Tho. Gray, a lodger of Paul Loggins in Goodman's Fields was this day brought before me by Thom. Jury, being taken by him upon the forest with a short bullet gun, the said Gray being not able to give any good account of himself nor to find any good sureties for his appearance at the next Court of Attachments, I committed him to the Round House at Stratford . . .

16
Objections to ship money in Kent (1637)

Source: J.S. Morrill, *The Revolt of the Provinces: Conservatives and Radicals in the English Civil War, 1630–1650*, Allen and Unwin, London, Historical Documents and Problems, no. 26, 1976, pp.145–6.

The imposition of ship money during the Personal Rule was objected to on administrative grounds in the first instance. Not only were the sums levied high, equivalent to two parliamentary subsidies, but they were based on out-of-date rate books. The sheriffs of the county were given wide discretionary powers to rectify this which added further to per- ceived inequities which led to delays and violence. The objections raised below were made by Sir Anthony Waldon to the levying of ship money in Kent. (See above, I.12, Speech of Oliver St John.)

The way to remedy this abuse by which neither sheriff nor high constable shall be left to their discretions.

There is in every County a Rate, which is called the great composition of his majesties most honourable household And this is yearly gathered by the high constables in money and paid into the hands of some one gentleman, nominated for Treasurer in that service for one year.

This was imposed on every parish by themselves, two of every parish being summoned in the behalf of the parish. And hath continued without either murmuring or alteration in most counties above 60 years. This composition is the best guide for the imposing of ship money . . . The only objection can be made against this, is that at the first settling the Composition great men favoured their parishes. The answer [is] that it is impossible to have anything so exact but something may be said against it, but 60 years continuance without either murmuring or alteration pleads sufficiently for it. And better any Rule, than the discretion of one man, and yet I dare say, whoever make this objection if his payment be looked upon, shall find the sheriff hath been favourable to him.

But this must be a guide only to the hundreds [adminstrative districts] not parishes but when it comes to be rated by every several parish then the poors assessment is the best guide. In which every man is charged by ability as well as land. And if any great man in a parish do favour himself it is the Fault of the Parish who by the Law may have Remedy either at Sessions, or by the Judge of Assizes . . .

The very same Liberty taken by the sheriff of Imposing upon the hundreds is used by the high constables upon the several parishes within his division. So that the sheriff and High Constables, do trample on all men and their estate which causeth much murmuring. And the reason gentlemen do not complain to the Lords of his majesties most honourable privy council is that they are unwilling to stand in competition with so mean fellows as High Constables now are. For it is not in their powers to be dishonest, but only partial. For what is imposed by superiors we take patiently, but if by equals or Inferiors It cannot be so well digested.

17

Avoidance of the *taille* at Lyon (1634)

Source: R. Bonney, *Society and Government in France under Richelieu and Mazarin*, Macmillan, London, Basingstoke, 1988, p.164. Translated from French.

False claims to nobility were often used by landholders to avoid liability to pay the *taille* (tax on property and/or possessions). This not only made collection difficult for the commissioners, but also led to greater burdens being placed on the poor, with predictable consequences for unrest. Pierre Séguier (1588–1672), to whom this report was addressed, was Chancellor for many years.

The power which the King has given us by his letters patent and separate instructions sent to us has obliged us to order the investigation of noble titles, to distinguish between the true nobles, exempted persons and privileged persons, and those who usurp these titles or have lost this status. We find plenty of people in this *généralité*,[1] my lord, who usurp the title of noble, baron, viscount, count and marquis without any basis whatsoever, and who have no letters patent duly verified in the sovereign courts . . . Such usurpers of nobility nearly all have ancestors who were in the third estate and they have never carried arms for the King's service. Others have farmed land, or continue to farm land directly or indirectly. The wealth of others is ignoble, arising from the sale of goods and mercantile activities at fairs and markets. They carry out ignoble acts which diminishes the dignity of nobility and oppresses the other subjects of the King who pay taxes. A good number of these usurpers have been found to have either changed their names or coats of arms, and claim to be members of families who are truly noble. Others call themselves chevaliers of the order of St. Michel, although many of them have been in trade or mechanic and unworthy activities, and have not carried arms for the King. Several of them present collated copies of their alleged titles, claiming that the originals were burnt or have been lost in the past disorders. On the basis of such collated copies or the testimony of gentlemen who are their friends, they have obtained sentences from the *élus*[2] which declare them noble. We wish to deal with these abuses, from which the third estate is greatly oppressed . . . The usurpation of the title of noble has been carried to such an extreme in this *généralité* that it is only little people in the towns that do not assume a noble title or that of *écuyer* [squire] with heraldic arms.

[1] Adminstrative areas, later replaced by 'departments'.
[2] Venal officials concerned with levying taxes.

18
A peasant revolt of Saintonge and Angoumois (1636)

Source: R. Bonney, *Society and Government in France under Richelieu and Mazarin*, Macmillan, London, Basingstoke, 1988, pp.207–8. Translated from French.

The peasants in the provinces declared their loyalty to the crown, which they believed to be deceived by evil ministers. The chief focuses of discontent were the central and local officers of the fiscal system, who were seen to have imposed new taxes on the people without the consent of the Estates General.

They [the peasants] protest that they are good Frenchmen who would rather die than continue under the tyranny of the Parisians and the financiers, who have reduced them to the despair and extreme poverty under which their province labours presently as a result of new and heavy taxes invented during the course of this reign. These burdens have forced many to abandon their landholdings in order to beg for bread, leaving the land uncultivated, the draught animals unable to live off the saffron crop, abandoning clothes and farm implements to be seized by the bailiffs. These seizures do not reduce their debts to the receiver, but merely cover the costs of collection. The peasants have made their complaints known on numerous occasions, but the gentlemen of Paris and the Council have ridiculed their sufferings, levying new taxes every year under the fine pretext of necessity of state. The aim of these gentlemen is to increase the personal wealth of a few individuals and the clients of the ruler of the state by extracting all the money from the province – thus they will achieve the ruin of the kingdom. The peasants have been forced to go to these extremes in order to gain redress of their grievances and to ensure that their complaints may be heard by the king and not just by his ministers who counsel him so badly . . . The people have paid more taxes in two years of this reign than in the whole of the reign of the king his father, and all the reigns of his predecessors since the beginning of the monarchy . . . All new taxes apart from the *taille* should be abolished as being for the ruin of the people. Properly spent, the *taille, taillon* [small tax] and traditional levies are sufficient for the upkeep of any army necessary for the protection of the realm against enemies. If these taxes should prove insufficient, the peasants are willing to contribute wholeheartedly provided that they are not taxed by the present ministers, who must no longer be allowed the power to impose arbitrarily new taxes and exactions upon the people. Such taxes should be levied only in times of national crisis, after a vote of the Estates General as has been the custom since time immemorial.

19
The duties of the *Intendants*, Colbert's instructions
(1680)

Source: Roger Mettam, *Government and Society in Louis XIV's France*, Macmillan, London, Basingstoke, 1977, pp.18–21. Translated from French.

Instructions were issued annually from central government, the wording varying little from year to year. These documents give arguably the best overall view of the public responsibilities of these officials, though further instructions on particular problems were also issued, especially if the matter invoked the undermining of local privileges and thus required secrecy.

Fontainebleau, 1 June 1680

The King has instructed me to repeat most strongly to you the orders which His Majesty has given you, in every preceding year, about the inspection of the generality in which you serve. He wants you to apply yourself to this task even more vigorously than you have in the past, because he wishes there to be equality in the allocation of taxes and a reduction in all kinds of abuses and expenses, thus bringing further relief to his peoples in addition to that which they have received from the lowering of taxation.

The King intends that, as soon as you have read this letter, you should begin your visit to each of the *élections* in your *generality* [administrative district]:

That, during this tour, you should examine with the utmost care the extent of landed wealth, the quality of livestock, the state of industries and in fact everything in each *élection* which helps to attract money there; that you should seek out, with the same diligence, anything which might help to increase animal foodstuffs, to expand industrial production or even to establish new manufactures. At the same time, His Majesty wants you to journey to three of four of the main towns in each election, excluding those which you have chosen in earlier years, and in these places to call before you a large number of the tax-collectors and leading inhabitants from the surrounding parishes; to take pains to find out all that has taken place concerning the receipt of the King's orders, the nomination of collectors, and the allocation and payment of the *taille*; to ferret out all the malpractices in these procedures; to try to remedy them yourself; and, in case you find some which can be treated only by a royal judgment or decree, to send me a report in order that I may inform His Majesty . . .

Listen to all the complaints which are brought to you about inequalities in allocation on the rolls of the *tailles*, and do everything which you consider appropriate to stamp out these iniquities and to make the allocation as fair as possible. Examine with the same thoroughness the expenses which are incurred, both by the receivers in relation to the collectors and by the collectors in relation to the taxpayers. As this is something which has always been open to endless trickery, you cannot show too much determination in trying to expose it. One of the most effective methods which His Majesty wishes you to use in repressing these abuses is to suspend the receiver of the *tailles* who seems the most culpable in your *generality*, and to entrust his duties to someone else for the next year. This punishment will assuredly cause the disappearance of many of these evil practices. His Majesty will also offer a reward to the receiver who has run his *élection* the most effectively, and who has incurred the least expenses.

His Majesty likewise requires that you should report every three months, without fail, on the number of prisoners who have been arrested concerning the *taille* or the various indirect taxes.

He further wishes you to prevent, in so far as this is possible, the receivers general of the finances, and the receivers and collectors of the *tailles* from impounding livestock; because on the multiplying of their numbers depends a large part of the kingdom's prosperity, not to mention the ability of the people to make a living and to pay their taxes . . .

You must also inspect in each *élection* the amount of the taxes collected to date, both for last year and for this, giving all the necessary orders for hurrying up the whole process, and must join the receivers of the *tailles* in searching for means of regulating collection so that the taxes are paid during the current year or within the first three months of the following one at the very latest.

With regard to the nomination of collectors, see that the rotas of collectors have been properly drawn up, and that they are implemented promptly. Check that there is no corruption involved in this method of naming collectors, and if there is you must decide how to remedy it. . . .

Having explained to you His Majesty's intentions concerning the *taille*, I am further instructed to tell you that he wishes you to investigate, at the same time, all the disorders which have arisen in collecting the indirect taxes; to which end he requires that, as soon as you become acquainted with some abuse, you should report it to the agents who have been appointed in each *generality* or *élection* to collect these dues; that you should listen to their explanations, and should send me an exact account of all you have discovered together with your views on the most suitable remedies which should be applied.

He further tells me to inform you that he will be able to see, from the places and dates at the head of your letters, whether or not you have carried out his orders promptly.

His Majesty has already made known to you at such length his intentions for the liquidation and repayment of the debts of the communities, that it is enough for me to say simply that he wishes you to devote adequate attention to this task, which you must undertake for each *élection* as you have been told to do. He also requires you to keep watch over everything involving the coinage throughout your *generality*, which is to say that only coins authorised by royal edict and decree may be in circulation. On this same subject, His Majesty wants you continually to ascertain that there are no mints producing false coins; and, if you should find one, to send word immediately, so that His Majesty may issue the necessary orders for bringing the culprits to trial without delay, because there is no crime which is more prejudicial to the interests of the people than this one.

20
The Clubmen of Dorset and Wiltshire (1645)

Source: J.S. Morrill, *The Revolt of the Provinces: Conservatives and Radicals in the English Civil War, 1630–1650*, Allen and Unwin, London, Historical Problems and Documents, no. 26, 1976, pp.199–200.

By 1645 associations of individuals in the south-western and south midland counties represented popular expressions of local resentment at the intrusion of warfare into their localities. Whether their ambitions were essentially to protect their locality or whether each county association was in touch with others remains a matter of debate.

The Desires and Resolutions of the Clubmen of the Counties of Dorset and Wilts: with articles of their Covenant and Certain Directions for present behaviour, made and agreed on at a meeting at Gorehedge-Corner on 25 May 1645, and read at Badbury in Dorset by Mr Thomas Young a lawyer; when there were present near 4000 armed with clubs, swords, bills, pitchforks and other several weapons . . .

[Their propositions for peace follow, and then their Articles of Association]

Whereas by articles of Association we belong unto an Association we challenge unto ourselves no other freedom for the present from the burthen of the War than to preserve ourselves from plunder and all other unlawful violence. It is therefore advised by the Generality that until such time as we receive answers to our petitions from the King and the two Houses of Parliament:

(1) Every town, tithing [administrative area], parish, and great hamlet, make present choice of three or more of the ablest men for wisdom, valour, and estate, inhabitants of the same, unto whom at all times they may repair for assistance and direction.

(2) That the Constable, Tithingman and other officers of the town etc. in pursuance of the Statute in that case provided, set a constant watch of two at the least, and they every night well-armed and if required by day also; the number of watchmen to be increased according to the direction of the chosen able men and officers.

[(3) and (4) govern the behaviour of the watchmen.]

(5) That all such as pretend themselves soldiers, and are taken plundering or doing any other unlawful violence, be presently disarmed and after examination (having confessed into which army he doth belong) to be safely guarded thither (together with sufficient witness to prove the offence) . . .

(6) That to avoid false alarms no man shall rise into arms but such as are summoned by the watchmen, unless they see apparent violence, or in case the watchmen be defective or surprised.

(7) That all men furnish themselves sufficiently with as many and good arms and ammunition as they can procure: and the rich out of a good conscience to relieve the poor herein, as also in their labours of watching, and other assistance in some proportionable measure:

(8) That the weekly contribution money and all other provision and necessary maintenance for armies, if it be demanded by a lawful warrant directed to an officer of the place, be not denied, but every man as he is able in some reasonable proportion forthwith to contribute: and for those truly unable, a certificate of inability to be made by the said officer with the advice of the said chosen able men of the place, unto their Commander in Chief from whom the warrant issued, with petition for respite and mitigation of the proportion of the warrant required, until they shall be better enabled.

(9) That if quarter be demanded according to Order Martial,[1] the soldier is to be friendly entertained behaving himself fairly in his quarters, but if he plunder or offer any other violence then he is to be restrained and delivered up unto the Commander in Chief to be by him corrected.

(10) That whatsoever person, though seemingly associated himself, shall be found to occasion any outcry or by any means to assemble any in favour or opposition to either party, King or Parliament, or on behalf of any person not associated, or in any way contrary to the articles of our Association: he shall be accounted unworthy of our protection as dissembling his inclination to our party in frustrating according to his power our real intentions for the Counties good.

(11) That no person or persons upon any pretext whatsoever presume to search a house or seize the person or goods of any of the Associated in inhabitants of the County but only Constables, Tithingmen and other sworn officers of the county for that place and upon lawful warrant.

(12) Not to admit any man to subscribe to the Articles of Association with you who is in arms for either party, or is known to be no Protestant, neither are you to protect any man who doth not associate.

---

[1] Martial or military law which applies within England in times of emergency.

21
The articles of the *Ormée* of Bordeaux (1651)

Source: S.A. Westrich, *The Ormée of Bordeaux: A Revolution During the Fronde*, Johns Hopkins University Studies in historical and political science, 89th series, 2, Johns Hopkins University Press, Baltimore, 1972, pp.50–1, 67. Translated from French.

In 1651, the citizens of Bordeaux joned together in a defensive alliance to protect their local privileges, when it was rumoured that the king wished to reappoint the duc d'Épernon as governor of Guyenne. The *Ormée* had contacts with English merchants and agents, which may have contributed to the radical nature of some of the ideas which circulated among its members. The extracts below are taken from 'The Articles of the Union of the *Ormée*'.

Should anyone of the Company be threatened, whether legally or otherwise, he will be protected in every possible and reasonable way. Should he be burdened with debt, we shall lend him money free of interest for a stated period of time.

As soon as one of the Company falls ill, his neighbors will exhort him to take care of his conscience and to arrange his affairs so that his heirs will not be troubled. And when he dies, his widow and orphans will be protected as if he were still living.

Should a member of the Company become impoverished, he will be provided with work. And if this is not possible, he will be given all the necessities of life, and this without the public's knowledge . . .

We, the bourgeois, peasants, and inhabitants of Bordeaux, cognizant of the high marks of favor and assistance obtained from God during the recent and still continuing troubles, have resolved to express our profound gratitude so that we may continue to enjoy God's benign grace. Accordingly, we shall strive to better love our neighbors and particularly those who are on our side. Toward this end we declare the following articles and invite all Christians to do likewise or more, if God so inspires them. . . .

We solemnly swear to love and protect each other as brothers and establish between us the peace and concordat of Jesus Christ . . .

In the eventuality that an individual is leading a scandalous and incorrigible life which is contrary to God's teachings, he shall be banished as unworthy of our society and shall be proclaimed a traitor to his honor and to the public good.

22
Recommendations for sustaining peace of the Highlands (1684)

Source: Acts of the Privy Council of Scotland, H.M. Stationery Office, 1924, vol. 9, pp.198–9.

The Highlands had been the scene of bitter clan warfare at the end of the 1670s followed by repressive action by the government. A separate commission was set up for the Highlands to combat the influence of the Campbells, and the following recommendations were designed to reduce the endemic violence of the region.

'Concerning the Commissioners of the division of Aberdeen, etc., their diligence and the present state of that country or what proposals they have to make, since none of them come to this meeting, we can give no further information than is contained in a paper subscribed and sent to us by their convenor herewith produced, only we think it very imperfect and that the Commissioners of that jurisdiction have not unanimously concurred for using their utmost care and diligence in execution of the Kings commission entrusted to them.'

'The Commissioners, having laid before your Lordships how that by their indefatigable pains the frequent thieving and robbing usually committed heretofore in the Highlands is now so happily suppressed and the peace thereof brought to such a perfection, they humbly crave leave to represent that now, after they had employed themselves above two years in that service with great labour, toil and expense, and by constant attendance have been withdrawn from their own necessary affairs to their great prejudice, the inferior members of their courts such as clerks fiscals, officers, officials and others have deserted them for want of means whereupon to subsist, they may be now relieved of the great burden of that commission, which they are not able longer to undergo and that your Lordships will consider to employ others in the commission for relieving of them, or think upon what other course your Lordships shall judge expedient for continuing the peace of the Highlands now so well established. And, to the end your Lordships may have the more time for deliberation; they offer to continue in their care and diligence to secure the country and keep it in the present quiet by all possible endeavours for this season which is the principal time of thieving until the winter draw on. And, for your Lordships further information what are the properest means for making the present peace of the Highlands durable, in whose hands soever your Lordships shall think fit to settle that power, they offer their opinion in the particulars following:—

'First. They judge it absolute necessary that a garrison be settled at Innerlochie.'

'Second, that the noblemen be required to give in their bands to the Council for the men, tenants and servants upon their properties, as the other heretours, chiefs and heads of clans have done, so that all persons may be alike bound and none exempted for securing the peace.'

'Third. If your Lordships judge it convenient to appoint some of the Kings forces to countenance the poyndings [confiscations as surety] upon decreits [judgements] for restitution of stolen goods, lest some unruly persons presume to make deforcements [unlawful seizures], whereby insolences may be committed.'

'Fourth, that such as have been declared and denounced fugitives from the King's laws and now have suplicat to be received in upon the kings mercy, giving sufficient bond and security to appear whenever called for peaceable and honest deportment hereafter and restitution of such damages as shall be proven they have done, the particular names whereof shall be given in, that these may have relaxations *gratis*, and that such others contumacious in their villainies, who have been often cited and contemptuously decline to compeir before our courts as executions thereof will make appear, that such persons, whose names shall also be presented, may by the interposition of your Lordships authority be printed and published as outlaws and intercomoned persons for terror and example to others.'

'Fifth. We having fined several heretours and others for not comparing before us for giving their bonds for securing the peace in common form and caused our clerks extract the decreits, we desire that letters of horneing [outlawry] may be given us *gratis* against such persons for payment of their fines and compelling them to come in and subscribe their bonds as others have done.'

'Sixth, that the Lords of his Majesties Council would consider how such heretours shall be assisted as are not able of themselves to order and command their unruly tenants such as the Laird of McIntosh for his lands in Brae of Lochaber, Weyme and Strowan Robertsone for their lands in Ranoch, as also how to bind the Laird of Keppoch, McMartine and others that depend on their families, to good behaviour and the securing of the peace.'

'And, lastly, the Commissioners offer their hunble opinion that, if it seem good to the Lords of his Majesties Privy Council, the King's indemnity may be procured as to personal punishment only for thefts committed before the [ ] day of [ ] providing restitution be made or satisfaction given for all that shall be proven to have been stolen before that time, providing also that every clan who shall have the benefit of this indemnity shall be obliged to bring in and present to justice such a number of the broken [unruly] men of their name (not exceeding three or four of the greatest clan), as shall be named to their respective heads or chiefs privily by the Commissioners, and that the King would allow to such persons as would undertake the bringing in dead or alive

116

some of the most notorious thieves, a reward competent to their service, which would prove of great consequence to the rooting out of the trade of thieving out of all the Highlands.'

23
A Charge to Quarter Sessions (1692)

Source: Surrey Archaeological Collections, vol. 12 (ii), Surrey Archaeological Society, Kingston-on-Thames, 1895, pp. 109–30.

This extract illustrates the extent to which the magistracy in the 1690s was concerned with moral regulation, and demonstrates the fact that, with the decline of the disciplinary powers of the ecclesiastical courts, the gentry, through quarter sessions, had assumed the initiative in this area.

Gentlemen of the Jury,

   As the Necessity of Government flows from the corruption of Human Nature, so the Strength, the Glory, and the Honour of it consist in the regular Administration of Justice; and as without the one, Societies cannot be upheld, so without the other, all Communities would be but little better than well-modelled Combinations to oppress, cheat, and ruin the weaker and submitting part of Mankind. Not but that the advantages of a Political Union are so considerable, that it may be doubted whether Tyranny it self, though as execrable as that formerly practised by the *Roman Nero*, and in these our Days, revived with many Additions by the *French Louis*, be not rather to be chosen than a wild and confused Anarchy. . . .

   And I am sure they serve the Government best, who though they may want Eloquence to give it its due Praises, yet have Courage enough to defend and preserve it when disturbed by any of its Enemies, in which number are to be reckon'd, not only that Ambitious, Bloody, and Perfidious Prince (that *Ishmael* of our Age, *whose Hand is against every Man, and every Man's Hand against Him*) with whom we are at this time necessarily engaged in a just and honourable War, for the common Safety, Liberty, and Repose of *Europe*; but also those more dangerous Enemies, our Domestic Ones: I mean all Profane, Lewd, Debauched, Traitorous, Seditious, Lawless and Disorderly Persons, who Blaspheme God, and Dishonour themselves; who conspire the Ruin of the Government, under whose Protection they live, and censure all its Proceedings; who Rob, Murder, and Oppress the Innocent, and, in a Word, disturb the Public Peace. Of all which sorts of People I may truly say, that as they are a Scandal and Reproach to Human Nature, so do they naturally

117

weaken the Foundations of any Constitution, and must in time, if not duly repressed and punished, occasion its Overthrow.

. . . Gentlemen, The Offenders against Moral Justice are those who are guilty of profane Cursing and Swearing, of Perjury and Subornation, of the Profanation of the Lord's Day, of Drunkenness, Adultery, Fornication, and such other dissolute Practices, as do still abound in this Kingdom, notwithstanding the many good Laws in force against them; which Laws if they were duly and impartially Executed, Vice and Debauchery would be much less Impudent, Scandalous, and Contagious than now they are; and consequently the Guilt of National Impiety would not so loudly call for Vengeance. Gentlemen, we neither want good Laws, nor due encouragement from our Superiors, nor yet good Magistrates of the higher Rank; but the Constables, Headboroughs, and other under Officers, have so little Religion or Honesty in them, that their negligence in Informing and Prosecuting, renders our pains as it were ineffectual for the promoting a general Reformation of Manners. . . .

And first, Gentlemen, the daily increase of profane Cursing and Swearing is a thing seriously and sadly to be considered. Men are now grown so hardened and riveted in this Blasphemous Custom, that one may justly wonder at the Merciful forbearance of Almighty God, in not punishing those impious Wretches by an immediate stroke of his Almighty Vengeance; in not consigning them, in the very instant of their Wickedness, to that Devil whose Protection they so often invoke, in not sinking them quick into that irrecoverable State of Damnation they so zealously imprecate upon themselves, for the confirmation of some trifling matter, not worthy a wise Man's Notice, and perhaps sometimes of a downright falsehood? This is an Immorality so unworthy of any one who professeth himself a Christian, that even an honest Heathen would have blushed to be suprised in it; for tho' their Religion was false, and their Gods were fictitious, yet they were rather guilty of an immoderate Superstition, than of any thing that so much as bordered upon Profaneness, which of the two Errors in Worshipping the Deity, is far the more inexcusable.

. . . and to which our Laws have affixed the following Penalty; namely, *Twelve Pence for every profane Oath and Curse.* The Forfeitures fall to the Poor of the Parish where the Offence is committed, and the Offender is to be prosecuted within twenty days after; . . .

Next to Profane Swearing and Cursing, we must consider the Sin of Perjury and Subornation, which, as I before observed, does in a great Measure deduce its Original from, and owe its increase to the impious Custom Men have taken up of interlarding their careless Talk, and even the common Civilities of Conversation with rash and vain Oaths. But, Gentlemen, as the sin of this is much greater, so are the Consequences of it much more Pernicious to private Persons, Families and Societies than those of the other. It is an offence both against Moral and Civil Justice; being a willful and deliberate Breach not only

118

of the third Commandment, (*Thou shalt not take the name of the Lord thy God in vain,*) but also of the Ninth: (*Thou shalt not bear false Witness against thy Neighbour;*) . . .

The third Immorality which is to be corrected, is the Profanation of the Lord's Day; and this is as notorious a Breach of the Fourth Commandment, as rash and vain Oaths and Curses are of the Third, and as Perjury and Subornation are both of that and of the Ninth; yet how generally this Sin also is practised, I am ashamed to think. *Remember thou keep Holy the Sabbath Day*, were it not (as it most certainly is) a Divine Command; yet it is one of the most prudent and useful Constitutions that ever was made. . . .

Thus Scripture and Reason teach us, and this likewise do the Laws of *England* permit; though at the same time, they are very strict against all those Profanations of the Lord's Day, which proceed either from Mens Covetousness, or their Licentiousness.

Thus all Carriers, Waggoners, Carters, Wain-men and Drovers are prohibited to Travel with any Horse, Wagons, Carts, or Cattle on the Lord's Day, under the Penalty of forfeiting Twenty Shillings to the Poor of the Parish where the Offence shall be Committed: All Butchers that Kill or Sell, or cause to be Killed or Sold, any Meat on the Lord's Day, or are Privy or Consenting to such Slaughter or Sale, forfeit in like manner Six Shillings and Eight Pence for every Offence. The Offence must be proved before any one Justice of the Peace, by the Oaths of two Witnesses, or by the Confession of the Party, . . .

Nor, Gentlemen, are these the only Profanations of the Lord's Day, that our Laws take Cognizance of, but by a Statute of a latter Date: All Persons that shall on the Lord's Day, or any part thereof, Sell or expose any thing to Sale, shall forfeit the Goods so sold or exposed to Sale, to the Poor of the Parish where the Offence is Committed. . . .

The Fourth Immorality which our Laws endeavour to suppress, is Drunkenness: A Vice on which one of our Statutes fixes this infamous Character; That it is Odious and Loathsome, that it is the Root and Foundation of Blood-shed, Stabbing, Murder, Swearing, Fornication, Adultery and such like enormous Sins, to the dishonour of God, and of our Nation, the overthrow of many good Arts, and Manual Trades, the disabling of divers Workmen, and the general Impoverishment of many good Subjects, abusively wasting the good Creatures of God. . . .

Gentlemen, in the next place, all notorious Adulterers, and Fornicators, Bawds, and Whores, and all Masters, and Mistresses of those infamous Houses, that Harbour and Encourage them, fall under the Cognizance and Censure of the Law. And since I cannot say there is already so sufficient a provision made for the punishing and preventing the increase of so scandalous a Debauchery, which is a (deliberate and presumptuous Violation of the 7th Commandment) as all good Men wish to see; yet (besides the Censures of the Spiritual Courts, which are very seldom exerted on these Occasions, unless they have the Prospect of a tedious and expensive Suit) we can inflict some Punishments upon them. For Bawdry is an offence Temporal, as well as Spiritual, and is against the Peace of the Land; therefore, Gentlemen, you are to take care to enquire and present all such Persons, who being duly convicted before us, shall suffer the utmost Severities the Law will allow of. . . .

You are also to enquire and present all Persons that have depraved the Sacrament of the Body and Blood of our Blessed Lord and Saviour, either by word of Mouth, or otherwise; who being convicted shall suffer Imprisonment, and make Fine and Ransom at the King's Will and Pleasure if they be prosecuted within three Months after the Offence is committed.

You are also to enquire if any Person hath Depraved, Despised, or Derogated from the book of Common-Prayer, by any Interludes, Plays, Songs, Rhymes or other open Words; or hath compelled any Minister to use any other form of Worship; for in this Case the Offender that is guilty of so great an Irreverence to God, and disrespect to the Government, both in Church and State, shall for the first Offence forfeit to their Majesties 100 Marks, for the second Offence 400 Marks, and for the third Offence, all his Goods and Chattels, and shall suffer Imprisonment during Life. . . .

I have now, Gentlemen, gone through the first part of my Charge, I have not knowingly omitted any point that is Material, and as for smaller Defects, I doubt not but your Experience in the Proceedings of this Court will fully supply them.

24
Instructions for building houses in the Grande Rue at Richelieu (1633)

Source: Jean-Claude Aubineau, *Richelieu: par Ordre du Cardinal*, J.-C. Aubin Imprimeur, Liguge, Poitiers, 1980, p.52. Translated by A. Laurence.

Instructions for building houses in the Grande Rue in Richelieu, from the contract between Jean Barbet *entrepreneur* and the future owners of the hôtels [mansions]. Barbet's contract was based upon a previous one with the cardinal dated 2 March 1633 in which he undertook to build 28 small houses and 4 larger ones.

Each of the smaller houses must look both on to the street and on to the courtyard behind, have a frontage on to the street of about 10 toises [20 metres], by a depth of 4 toises, one and a half feet [8.5 metres] from front to back. There will in addition be domestic offices in the re-entrant angle . . . In the main body of the house there will be an eight foot passage for access to the courtyard and, alongside the passage, a large room with a fireplace at one end; a staircase, beside which will be the kitchen; then a pantry, and underneath the kitchen a cellar. Beyond the pantry and incorporated into the main building will be stables, fourteen feet [4.66 metres] in width and running the length of the courtyard. Between the said stables and the pantry will be placed the privies. The courtyard will be 8 toises in length and in it there will be a well. The cess-pit will be a vaulted chamber 12 feet square and six feet deep.

Above the main room, the kitchen and the pantry, there will be two bed-rooms with fireplaces, each of them with a dressing-room, in one of which there will also be a fireplace . . . Above the bed-rooms and the dressing-rooms there will be an attic; in addition, the staircase will be constructed of dressed bond-stones, as also will be the steps and the landings, which will be cut and finished on the underside, too, up to the first floor. Between the first and second floors the staircase will be of wood and the steps will be paved with terracotta treads set into a mortar of lime and sand . . . The garden will be 28 toises [56 metres] in depth. Its boundary walls, like those the courtyard, will be 9 feet in height and well-buttressed, as is appropriate.

25
Extracts from the Register of Passports for Vagrants in Salisbury (1620–38)

Source: Paul Slack (ed.), *Poverty in Early Stuart Salisbury*, Wiltshire Record Society, 31, Devizes, 1975, pp.52–64.

The register was kept in accordance with the legislation of 1598 which laid down that any rogues, vagabonds or sturdy beggars over the age of seven found begging, vagrant or misbehaving were to be whipped and sent back to the parish of their birth. Such people had no claim on local parish relief. The normal administration of the statute on vagrancy was through the parish, with the minister empowered to keep a register of passports issued. In Salisbury, however, the administration of the three city centre parishes was combined.

25 March 1620

Margaret Cheeke, wandering with a lewd fellow named Martin Drake, was punished. Assigned 6 days to go to Banwell, Somerset, where she says she was born.

Martin Drake, wandering as a vagrant with Margaret Cheeke, is assigned 14 days to go to Truro, Cornwall, where he says his dwelling is. They confessed they lived together lewdly for about 3 years.

2 March 1621

Elizabeth Griffen, petty chapwoman, and Anne Griffen her daughter, wandering, having other idle persons accompanying them and using shifts by wandering away and cozening his Majesty's subjects with counterfeit pieces or slips, were punished. Assigned 4 days to go to Faringdon, Berks, where they say they dwell.

23 May 1624

Thomas Coxe, tinker, Ellen his wife, Thomas Barnes his apprentice, and two children, wandering and vagrant, were punished. Assigned 13 days to go to Gaddesden, Herts, where he was born and dwells.

16 April 1629

An obstinate Irishman, begging and refusing to tell his name. Passport to Bristol and from there to Ireland.

28 November 1635

Nathaniel Leache, a poor child, about 9 or 10 years of age, likely to perish and die in the streets with cold, was taken begging and crying. Passport to Lyndhurst, Hants, where he says he was born.

27 February 1638

Richard Flower, apprentice of John Joyner of Devizes, found wandering, confessed that he unlawfully ran away from his master. He was punished. Passport to return to his master in St Mary's parish, Devizes.

26
Regulations for the Hungerford Almshouses at Corsham, Wiltshire (1668)

Source: Wiltshire Record Office, WRO 490/11.

Lady Margaret Hungerford was widow of Sir Edward Hungerford, and daughter and co-heiress of William Halliday, alderman of the City of London. In 1668 she endowed at Corsham, Wiltshire, a free school and an almshouse for six poor people. She laid down the rules for the conduct of the almshouse.

1. First I ordain that the plot of ground lying at Corsham aforesaid at the town's end there abutting on the king's highway or common road leading from London to the city of Bath by me lately purchased containing by estimation about four acres of ground be it more or less shall be and remain to and for the only use and benefit of the schoolmaster which shall be of the aforesaid school and schoolhouse and of the six poor people (man or woman) for ever . . .

2. Item I ordain that the said schoolhouse with the chapel adjoining and also the kitchen or brewhouse, the stable and all other housing and buildings by me lately built upon the said parcel of ground for the use of the said schoolmaster, and the use of the well and pump and also the orchard, gardens, bartons [farmyard] and backside to the said schoolhouse by me set out and allotted shall be and remain to the use of such person as shall be schoolmaster of the said school for ever.

3. Item that the almshouse with all such housing, buildings, backsides, bartons, gardens, and orchards to the said almshouse (with the needful use of the well or pump there) by me assigned and allotted shall be and remain to the use of six poor people (men or women) for ever and everyone to have and enjoy a several part according as the said [housing] is set out and divided.

5. Item and that (for the support and maintenance of the aforesaid poor people) I allow £30 of the like lawful money of England to be forever yearly paid unto them (that is to say) to every of them £5. The same to be paid unto them at the foresaid several feasts yearly of the Annunciation of the blessed Virgin Mary, St John the Baptist, St Michael the Archangel and St Thomas the Apostle by equal portions or within 6 days at the most after the said several feasts.

6. I do order and appoint that every of the said poor people shall every year before Michaelmas buy and bestow in wood and coal the sum of 20s. And every of them lay the same in her or his own woodyard there publicly to be seen to the end that no one of them may be put upon stealing wood and breaking of hedges . . . And that if any of the said poor people shall be found stealing of wood or breaking of hedges, then that person shall be forfeit and lose for the first offence therein 2s 6d; for the second offence 5s; and for the third offence 10s; and for the fourth offence to be expelled.

9. Item my will further is that every of the said poor people shall every third year have three yards of broad cloth at the price of 7s the yard at the least to make them every one a gown against Christmas. The same gowns to be made plain only edged black at the seams and a silver badge of my crest to be fastened and sewn on the left arm of every of the same gowns . . .

10. Item my will is that if any of the said poor people die before the three years of keeping her or his gown be expired, then such party's gown to go to the next successor and the badge whensoever she or he die however is to go to the use of such person as shall be chosen in his or her place.

11. And as for the persons that shall be chosen my will is that they shall be single poor people as are of an honest life and conversation and have been industrious in their youth and who have now need of relief (man or woman).

12. And that for the avoiding of strife and contention which usually ariseth where children of divers parents are, my will is that such poor persons be chosen as be single and unmarried if such conveniently may be had. But for defect of such then aged married folk (having no children) fittest for relief.

13. And that none be chose but such as fear God and are of honest

conversation not any such as are not able to rehearse the Lord's prayer, the articles of their faith and ten commandments, not such as have not carefully frequented the church to hear God's word read and preached, nor yet such as have any infectious disease or loathsome to others.

14. And my will is that when any of the foresaid poor people shall be sick or diseased then the others of them shall do their best endeavour (in their several turns) to keep and attend such person or persons which if any shall refuse to do then to be removed and if need be to desire the help of any skilful neighbour to aid them in the time of such their sickness.

16. And for the better ordering of the foresaid poor people that they may behave themselves like Christians my will is that every of them (being able) shall constantly come to church twice every Lord's day and likewise on the weekday when there is a lecture and upon other occasions when there is public prayer or preaching at the church and shall be in the church at the very beginning of divine service and diligently attend there till the end thereof and shall likewise receive the holy communion three times in the year at the least (the minister first to examine their knowledge) and if any person fail therein (unless hindered by sickness or some other lawful cause) that person shall forfeit for every such default 12*d* to be deducted out of his stipend at the quarter's end. And for the manner of their coming to church, they shall come together in their gowns and sit together in the place appointed for them. And I do likewise appoint that every one of the said poor people shall constantly be present every weekday at the prayers twice in a day at the schoolhouse and likewise at the repetition of the sermon every Sunday in the evening either at the schoolhouse or at the great mansion house in Corsham aforesaid upon pain of forfeit for every default therein 12*d*.

17. And because it may be pretended by the said poor people that they are not able to come to church when in truth they are well able . . . therefore I do appoint that whensoever any of them is or are so well as to stir out of his or her house upon their own occasions either for provision or otherwise such one shall be adjudged able to come to church . . .

18. Item I do ordain that none of the said poor people shall offend by swearing or ungodly talking under pain of forfeiting for the first offence 4*d*, for the second offence 8*d*, and for the third offence 12*d*, to be deducted as before and not to be continued if swearers or drunkards.

19. Item my will is that none of the said poor people shall give any reproachful words against their fellows or any of their neighbours under pain to forfeit for the first offence 4*d*, for the second offence 8*d*, and for the third offence 12*d* to be deducted as before.

21. Item I order and ordain that (for the avoiding of idleness) the said poor people shall all arise betimes in the morning every day and on the working days give themselves to some honest labour and on the sabbath day (for their souls' health and happiness) prepare for their going to church.

22. Item that none of the said poor people shall frequent alehouses or

places of unlawful gaming otherwise than about their necessary business and occasions neither shall they play at any unlawful games themselves or keep evil company upon pain to forfeit for every such offence 6*d*.

23. Item that none of the said poor people shall live upon begging or go to any house to beggar alms or crave an alms of any traveller upon pain of forfeit for every offence 6*d*.

26. Item I order and ordain that none of the said poor people shall commit fornication, adultery, drunkenness, or any horrible sin (which God forbid), or shall fall into any gross heresy (denying any the articles of Christian faith) and that in case any of them shall in any such way offend then ever such person so offending shall be expelled the house forever and never to be received in again.

32. Item I ordain and my will is that once in every year the said poor people shall (at their own several charge) empty their privy-house and repair what shall be amiss in the inside thereof and scour and keep sufficiently cleansed that ditch which carrieth away the draft thereof . . . and shall (at their like charge) keep well repaired the windows at the end of the penthouse walk [verandah] eastward.

37. And also that those two women who shall live at the east end of the said almshouse shall (as often as occasion is being required thereunto) attend any sick person (of what disease soever) which shall be brought or sent to their house either from Corsham house or from the schoolhouse being allowed all things necessary for lodging, diet and physic and being paid for their labour and for what they lay out for or about such sick person.

45. And to the end that ignorance may not excuse the said poor people or cause them to go awry that are willing to live in order my desire is that the said schoolmaster that now is and his successors after him would at two several times of the year (that is to say) at the feasts of the annunciation of the blessed Virgin Mary and St Michael the Archangel (being two days appointed for payment of their pensions as aforementioned) in the foresaid chapel or schoolhouse read over these ordinances plainly and distinctly in the presence and hearing of them.

27

Edict of Louis XIV for the founding of the first Hôpital Général in Paris (1656 and 1662)

Source: Michel Foucault, *Folie et Deraison: Histoire de la Folie à l'âge classique*, Librairie Plon, Paris, 1981, pp.646–51. Translated by Angela Scholar.

A. *Edict of 1656*

This edict created the first Hôpital Général in Paris at La Salpêtrière, and established the principal of creating enclosed communities of the poor.

Edict of the King for the Establishment of the Hôpital Général for Housing Poor Beggars of the City and Suburbs of Paris, given at Paris in the month of April 1656, registered by the Parlement on the 1 September following.

Louis, by the grace of God, King of France and of Navarre, to all present and to come, Greetings. During the last hundred years our royal forebears have introduced several public order regulations concerning the presence of poor people in our noble city of Paris and have striven, as much out of zeal as on their own authority, to eliminate begging and idleness, which are the sources of every disorder. And although our own Sovereign Companies[1] have made every effort to support the carrying out of these regulations, the latter have nevertheless become, during the course of time, unproductive and ineffectual, either because of lack of the funds necessary for the continuance of so large a scheme, or because of the departure of directors who were both well-established and well suited to the requirements of the work . . . The result is that licence prevails among the beggars to the point of excess, thanks to their unfortunate indulgence in all sorts of crimes which, if they are left unpunished, must bring down the curse of God upon everyone. It is the experience of people engaged in this charitable work that a number of the poor of both sexes and many of their children have not been baptized, and that almost all of them live in ignorance of religion and in contempt of the sacraments, habitually practising all kinds of vice. That is why, just as we ourselves are beholden to Divine Mercy for so many favours and for the protection He has shown us, which not only guided us at the time of our accession but has also throughout our felicitous reign manifested itself in the success of our armies and the happiness of our victories, so we believe ourselves to be the more obliged to show our gratitude by a royal and Christian regard for the things which concern His honour and His service; let us look upon these poor beggars as living members of Jesus Christ and not as useless members of the State; and ourselves as carrying out this great work, not on grounds of public order, but with Charity as our only motive . . .

We wish and command that poor beggars of both sexes, both able-bodied and disabled, be employed in a hospital engaged in works, manufacture and other employment, according to their capacities, as is amply set out in the order signed by our hand, and included under the counter seal of these present, and which we wish to be carried out in accordance with its terms and content.

[1] The Company of the Blessed Sacrament, an association of devout laypeople which ran much of the institutional relief in the early seventeenth century.

B.   *Edict of 1662*

This edict, following the success of the establishment of the Hôpital Général at La Salpêtrière, sought to ensure that similar institutions were set up in all French towns, whilst not providing any funds for so doing.

A proclamation by the King, regarding the establishment of an Hôpital Général in all the towns and principal boroughs of the Kingdom, in accordance with the decrees issued by the Kings Charles IX and Henry III.

In view of the [subsistence] with which we have always had to supply the needs of beggars, who are the most forsaken of human-beings, to work for their salvation by Christian instruction, and to abolish begging and idleness by educating their children in the trade to which they are best suited, we have established the Hôpital Général in our noble city of Paris . . .

However, the excessive number of beggars who have arrived from the various provinces of our Kingdom has reached such a point that, although the said Directors do not have half of the revenue which is necessary for the ordinary subsistence of four to five thousand poor people, they are in addition obliged to give out food in six places in the city to three thousand other poor married persons. In addition to whom one sees still a very great number of beggars in the said city . . .

We command, require and it pleases us that in all towns and principal boroughs in our Kingdom where no Hôpital Général is yet established, progress should forthwith be made towards the establishment of an Hôpital, towards the furnishing of the same, in order to lodge, confine and feed there the poor and invalid beggars who are natives of those places or born of beggar parents. All of which beggars shall be instructed in piety and in the Christian religion, and in trade to which they are best suited . . .

Issued in Saint-Germain-en-Laye, in the month of June 1662.

127

28
An Act Against Conjuration, Witchcraft etc. (1604)

Source: Barbara Rosen (ed.), *Witchcraft in England 1558–1618*, University of Massachusetts Press, Amherst, 1991, pp.57–8.

This English Act of 1604 owed a good deal to King James's interest in witchcraft, an interest which he had displayed in his previous writings about the subject whilst he was still in Scotland.

An Act against conjuration, witchcraft and dealing with evil and wicked spirits.

Be it enacted by the King our sovereign Lord the Lords spiritual and temporal and the Commons in this present Parliament assembled, and by the authority of the same, That the Statute made in the fifth year of the reign of our late sovereign lady of most famous and happy memory Queen Elizabeth, intituled An Act against conjurations, enchantments and witchcrafts, be from the Feast of St. Michael the Archangel next coming, for and concerning all offences to be committed after the same Feast, utterly repealed.

And for the better restraining the said offences, and more severe punishing the same, be it further enacted by the authority aforesaid, That if any person or persons, after the said Feast of St. Michael the Archangel next coming, shall use, practise or exercise any invocation or conjuration of any evil and wicked spirit, or shall consult, covenant with, entertain, employ, feed, or reward any evil and wicked spirit to or for any intent or purpose; or take up any dead man, woman, or child out of his, her, or their grave, or any other place where the dead body resteth, or the skin, bone, or any other part of any dead person, to be employed or used in any manner of witchcraft, sorcery, charm, or enchantment; or shall use, practise, or exercise any witchcraft, enchantment, charm, or sorcery, whereby any person shall be killed, destroyed, wasted, consumed, pined, or lamed in his or her body, or any part thereof; that then every such offender or offenders, their aiders, abetters and counsellors, being of any the said offences duly and lawfully convicted and attainted, shall suffer pains of death as a felon or felons, and shall lose the privilege and benefit of clergy and sanctuary.

And further, to the intent that all manner of practice, use, or exercise of witchcraft, enchantment, charm, or sorcery, should be from henceforth utterly avoided, abolished and taken away, Be it enacted by the authority of this present Parliament, That if any person or persons shall, from and after the said Feast of St. Michael the Archangel next coming, take upon him or them by witchcraft, enchantment, charm, or sorcery, to tell or declare in what place any treasure of gold or silver should or might be found or had, in the earth or other secret places, or where goods or things lost or stolen should be found or become; and to the intent to provoke any person to unlawful love, or where any chattel or goods of any person shall be destroyed, wasted or impaired, or to hurt or destroy any person in his or her body, although the same be not effected and done; that then all and every such person and persons so offending, and being thereof lawfully convicted, shall for the said offence suffer imprisonment by the space of one whole year, without bail or mainprise [surety], and once in every quarter of the said year, shall in some market town, upon the market day, or at such time as any fair shall be kept there, stand openly upon the pillory by the space of six hours, and there shall openly confess his or her error and offence; And if any person or persons being once convicted of the same offence as is aforesaid, do eftsoons [again] perpetrate and commit the like offence, that then every such offender, being of any the said offences the second time lawfully and duly convicted and attainted as is aforesaid, shall suffer pains of death as a felon or felons, and shall lose the benefit and privilege of clergy and sanctuary: Saving to the wife of such person as shall offend in any thing contrary to this Act, her title of dower; and also to the heir and successor of every such person, his or their titles of inheritance, succession and other rights, as though no such attainder of the ancestor or predecessor had been made; Provided always, That if the offender in any of the cases aforesaid shall happen to be a peer of the realm, then his trial therein to be had by his peers, as it is used in cases of felony or treason and not otherwise.

29
Account of the Expenses of Burning a Witch (1649)

Source: T.B. Howell, *A Complete Collection of State Trials*, vol. 4 (1640–49), London, 1816, pp.831–2.

The prosecution, conviction and execution of a witch could cost a small community a great deal of money. This is an account of the expenses of burning a witch in 1649, a voucher for the payment of Alexander Louddon, factor to the estate of Burncastle, Lylstoun, somewhere in Scotland.

More for Margarit Dunhome the time she was in prison,
and was put to death   65: 14: 4

Count given out by Alexander Louddon in Lylstoun in the year of God 1649 years, for Margaret Dollmoune in Burncastell.

Item, in the first, to Wm Currie and Andrew Gray for the watching of her the space of 30 days, inde [owed] ilke [each] day, xxx sh, inde	xlv lib Scot[1]
Item more to John Kinked for brodding [prodding] of her	vi lib Scot
More for meat and drink and wine to him and his man	iiij lib Scot
More for cloth to her	iij lib Scot
More for twa tare treis[2]	xi sh Scot
Item more for twa treis, and the making of them, to the workmen	iij lib Scot
Item, to the hangman in Hadingtoun, and fetching of him, three dollars [five shillings] for his expence, is	iiij lib xiiii sh
Item, more for meat and drink and wine for his intertigne [entertainment]	iij lib Scot
Item more for one man and two horses, for the fetching of him, and taking of him home again	xl sh Scot
More for her for meat and drink both one day, iiij sh the space of xxx days, is	vi lib Scot
Item, more to the two officers, for their fee ilk day six shilling eight pennies, is	x lib Scot
Summa is iiij scoir (score) 12 lib xiiij sh	

Ghilbert Laudar

Um Lauder Bilzuars

Taking of this above written sum twenty-seven pounds which said umql [late] Margrit Dinham had of her own

¹ A Scottish pound was a twelfth of an English pound.
² 'twa' – two; 'tare' – probably tar; 'treis' – probably barrels. (The staff of the Dictionary of the Older Scottish tongue are puzzled about 'tare treis'.) Tar barrels were used in burning witches.

30
Statement of Marie Nicaise

Source: R. Muchembled (ed.), *La Sorcière à Village XVe–XVIIe Siècle*, Julliard/Gallimard, Paris, 1979, pp.157–8. Translated by Anne Laurence.

French legal processes required that witnesses be interrogated by the prosecutor and that a conviction was secured by the confession of the accused.

Marie Nicaise, widow of Gabry Bernard, aged some 40 years. Under oath she said and affirmed that six or seven years previously, when she was selling faggots at the woodyard, Marie Lanenchin, widow of Jean de Vaulx, sometimes went to buy them. Seeing this, her late husband had said to her, 'If you sell faggots to this bitch I will beat you because she is a witch.' To which she replied, 'There's absolutely no need for you to tell me. I'm as afraid as you are.' And in fact, she refused her once. And being asked if her late husband had never described to her having once found the said Marie de Vaulx making rain at Saint Maurice, said that she had no recollection of this. But she said that for a long time past she had always heard it said, and it was common rumour, that the said Marie Lanenchin was a witch. It was even said that when Jean de Vaulx died, she was blamed. Furthermore, it was said that when the pastor of Basuyel gave him extreme unction, he said that the said de Vaulx was bewitched, to which the said Marie his wife said, 'Oh, goodness, who would have done that to him?'

Mark of Marie Nicaise (cross).

31
Several examinations and confessions of witches (1645)

Source: T.B. Howell, *A Complete Collection of State Trials*, vol. 4 (1640–49), London, 1816, pp. 832–6.

In England cases were normally brought by private individuals, often the injured party. In the 1640s Matthew Hopkins (d.1647) who may have trained as a lawyer, set himself up as a witchfinder, and was employed by various towns in East Anglia to seek out witches. This produced an unprecedented spate of prosecutions for witchcraft. Witnesses made their statements before magistrates.

Information of John Rivet, of Manningtree, tailor, taken before Sir Harbottle Grimstone, Knight and Baronet, one of the Members of the Honourable House of Commons; and Sir Thomas Bowes, Knight, another of his Majesty's Justices of the Peace for this county, the 21 March 1645.

This informant saith, That about Christmas last, his wife was taken sick and lame,[1] with such violent fits that this informant verily conceived that her sickness was something more than merely natural. Whereupon this informant, about a fortnight since, went to a cunning woman, the wife of one Hovye, at Hadleigh in Suffolk, who told this informant that his wife was cured by two women who were near neighbours to this informant, the one dwelling a little above his house and the other beneath the house, this informant's house standing on the side of an hill. Whereupon he believed his said wife was bewitched by one Elizabeth Clarke, alias Bedinfield, for that the said Elizabeth's mother and some other of her kinsfolk did suffer death for witchcraft and murder.

The information of Matthew Hopkins, of Manningtree, Gent, taken upon oath before us, 25 March 1645.

This informant saith, that the said Elizabeth Clarke (suspected for a witch as aforesaid) being by the appointment of the said justices watched certain nights, for the better discovery of her wicked practices, this informant came into the room where the said Elizabeth was watched, as aforesaid, the last night, being 24th of this instant March, but intended not to have stayed long there. But the said Elizabeth forthwith told this informant and one Master Sterne there present, if they would stay and do the said Elizabeth no harm, she would call one of her white imps, and play with it in her lap; but this informant told her, they would not allow of it: and that staying there a while longer, the said Elizabeth confessed she had had carnal copulation with the devil six or seven years; and that he would appear to her three or four times in a week at her bedside, and go to bed with her and lie with her half a night together in the shape of a proper gentleman, with a laced band, having the whole proportion of a man, and would say to her, 'Besse, I must lie with you'; and she did never deny him: and within a quarter of an hour after there appeared an imp like to a dog, which was white, with some sandy spots, and seemed to be very fat and plump, with very short legs, who forthwith vanished away: and the said Elizabeth said the name of that imp was Jarmana: and immediately there appeared another imp, which she called Vinegar Tom, in the shape of a greyhound with long legs: and the said Elizabeth then said that the next imp should be a black imp, and should come for the said Master Sterne, which appeared, but presently vanished: and the last that appeared was in the shape of a pole cat, but the head somewhat bigger. And the said Elizabeth then told this informant that she had five imps of her own, and two of the imps of the old beldame Weste (meaning one Anne Weste, widow) who is now suspected to be guilty of witchcraft; and said, sometimes the imps of the old beldame sucked on the said Elizabeth, and

132

sometimes her imps sucked on the old beldame Weste. And the said Elizabeth further told this informant, that Satan would never let her rest, or be quiet, until she did consent to the killing of the hogs of one Mr Edwards of Manningtree aforesaid, and the horse of one Robert Taylor of the same town.[2] . . .

The examination of the said Elizabeth Clarke, alias Bedinfield, taken before the said Justices the 25 March 1645.

This examinant saith, that about six months since she met with the said Anne Weste, widow, (who is now likewise apprehended) in the field near the house of the said Elizabeth, where the said Elizabeth was picking up a few sticks. The said Anne Weste seemed to pity this examinant for her lameness (having but one leg) and her poverty; and said to this examinant, 'That there was ways and means for her to live much better than now she did: and said, that she would send to this examinant a thing like a little kitlyn [kitten] which would fetch home some victuals for this examinant; and that it should do her no hurt. And this examinant saith, that within two or three nights after there came a white thing to her in the night, and the night after a grey one, which spake to this examinant, and told her they would do her no hurt, but would help her to an husband, who should maintain her ever after: and that these two things came unto this examinant's bed every night, or every other night, and sucked upon the lower parts of her body.

---

[1] The word 'lame' was often used of general maladies and did not refer to restricted mobility alone.

[2] Edwards complained that two of his cows died and Taylor complained that his horse went lame and two days later died after he had refused to let an associate of Elizabeth's have half a pound of cheese on credit.

32
The family troubles of William Stout (1691–1709)

Source: W.S. Stout of Lancaster, *Autobiography*, edited by J. Harland, London, Manchester, 1851, pp.32, 79.

William Stout (1665–175?) was a grocer and ironmonger who lived in Lancaster. He was a Quaker and a reasonably successful businessman. The printed edition of his autobiography is taken from a small book written in his own hand.

1691

And my mother, then sixty years of age, continued to keep my said brother's house with much industry and care, being my brother Josias did not seem inclined to marry . . .

1709

My dear mother was now about seventy six years of age, and dwelt with my brother Josias as his housekeeper, and was become very infirm and uneasy with the care of the house, and was urgent of him to marry, he not being willing to keep house with a servant. And thereupon, with his mother's consent and approbation, he married Sibill Green . . . My brother Josias was about forty eight years of age, and his wife about thirty years of age, and my mother seemed well satisfied with the marriage. But when the young wife came to housekeeping, my mother thought to have some direction in that, more than the young wife (who had been her father's housekeeper) would allow; which made their mother uneasy. And in a year's time my brother Josias desired me to entertain her, which I freely offered to do. So she came to me and my sister, and dwelt with us in much content and unity till the time of her death, which was about eight years, without any consideration except what my said brother Josias would freely offer; who was a quiet and easy man, his wife being of a resolute disposition, and he was very condescending for peace sake.

33

Bossuet and Beuvelet on marriage and the family

A. *Bossuet on marriage and the family (1687)*

Source: Bishop J.B. Bossuet, *Catéchisme du diocèse de Meaux*, Paris, 1687, pp.183–5. Translated and quoted in R. Briggs, *Communities of Belief*, Clarendon Press, Oxford, 1989, pp.239–40.

Bishop Bossuet was a moralist who exercised a considerable influence during the reign of Louis XIV. For futher details see above, I.19, and below, III.24.

Q. To what purpose should one make use of marriage?
A. For the purpose of multiplying the children of God.
Q. What other purpose can one have?
A. That of remedying the disorders of concupiscence.
Q. What are the obligations of marriage?
A. To unite with one another, and support one another through charity; to bear mutually with one another and all the pains of marriage with patience; and to obtain salvation by the holy education given to one's children.
  . . .
Q. Tell me the evil which must be avoided in the use of marriage?

A. It is to refuse conjugal rights unjustly; to make use of marriage to satisfy sensuality; to avoid having children, which is an abominable crime.

B. *Beuvelet on marriage and the family (1669)*

Source: M. Beuvelet, *Instruction sur le Manuel*, 7th edn, Paris, 1669, pt. i, pp.310–22. Translated and quoted in R. Briggs, *Communities of Belief*, Clarendon Press, Oxford, 1989, p.241.

Mathieu Beuvelet (*c*.1600–after 1663) was an ascetic writer who belonged to the congregation of the Priests of Saint Nicolas du Chardonnet, Paris. His *Instruction* was intended for seminarists and was very popular. The extract is taken from a model exhortation which parish priests could use during the marriage ceremony to 'encourage' the marriage partners.

. . . the grandeur and the dignity of marriage are not well understood by all Christians, and the dispositions in which most present themselves for it make all too clear to us the little esteem in which they hold it . . . but at the same time as we speak of happiness in marriage, we are astonished to see so much unhappiness there. Do you wish to know the reason? It is that most people do not receive the grace of marriage. It is an article of faith that there are particular helps attached to the state and condition of marriage, to live in a holy manner therein, to support its changes and burdens, and to bring up children according to God: but how many are there, who receive these graces? The person from whom one should expect them is banished from marriage [i.e. Christ] . . . Pay attention to this, for today once past, it will no longer be time, this grace is only given at the moment of marriage, and to those who come to it properly prepared. [i.e. through the sacrament of marriage which is accompanied by celebration of nuptial mass] This is what will decide all your happiness or your unhappiness.

34
Lordelot, *On the duties of domestic life* (1706)

Source: B. Lordelot, *Devoirs de la Vie Domestique par un père de famille*, Paris, 1706. Copied from a version printed in Brussels in 1707 'chez les Frères T Serstevens pres les Dominicains'. Translated by Angela Scholar.

Bénigne Lordelot (1639–1720) worked as a lawyer in Paris, enjoying the protection of Lamoignon, president of the *parlement* of Paris. He established a reputation as a moralist, publishing a number of works; the title

Figure 4 Frontispiece of *Les Devoirs de la vie domestique, par un père de famille*
[B. Lordelet], 1707.

of one of them, *On the Disorders of Carnival,* indicates that he was something of a kill-joy in his approach to life.

To the King

Sire

I could do no better than to address this work, whose aim is to establish good order within families, to Your Majesty, who is himself the august head and the benevolent master of his own. It is Your Majesty's paternal heart which prompts him to look upon his subjects as his children, whom he loves and by whom he is loved, and to be continually attentive to anything which can give them succour. The greatest blessing which they can enjoy is the continuance among them of that peace and harmony without which there can be nothing but trouble, civil strife and division. The most perfect example of how this may be preserved within families is offered for imitation by Your Majesty, who has maintained within the Royal Household a harmony so admirable that it should serve as model to all the monarchs in the world, and to every father. The fear of God is the solid foundation on which this concord must be established; it is this fear alone which guarantees its survival; and it is to this unshakeable support that Your Majesty has always held fast. Indeed, it is this salutary fear that we see every day made manifest in acts of religion and piety. Your Majesty's diligence in ensuring that in all his churches the worship which is God's due is rendered to Him is a certain sign of the return of those blessed times, and of the peace which Heaven allows to reign on earth only in so far as men show it reverence and submission . . .

Chapter IV On the duties of the husband towards his wife

The authority which God has conferred upon the husband over the person of his wife should not be a vile and tyrannical authority, but a mild and pleasant dominance: if he has gained power over her, this must only be to protect her; if he has entered into an association with her, it is as his faithful companion and not his slave. The glory of a man of honour lies in loving his wife, in showing consideration to her and in making her happy: the true mark of his love lies in maintaining towards her an inviolable fidelity; the consideration which he should show her consists in seeing to it that she enjoys respect; while he cannot make her happy without effort and application. If he fails in any one of his duties, he shows her neither love, nor consideration, nor tenderness.

It is because of some corruption in their hearts that a majority of husbands have blindly imagined that they are not under as much obligation to remain faithful to their wives as their wives are under a strict obligation to remain faithful to them; this duty is prescribed for the one no less than for the other, and the crime is equal. How curious that a husband should desire his wife to be chaste, while he is licentious; and that a sex which is weaker than his, although stronger in resisting the bad example which he gives, should remain within the bounds of duty.

137

It is true that there are Christian women who regard with compassion the aberrations of their husbands, who pray to God for their conversion and who try to win them back by gentleness and by an inviolable fidelity. It would be desirable that they should be generally imitated. But there are unfortunately others who, corrupted by the bad example of their husbands and led astray by their own passions, embark on a disorderly life . . .

Chapter V The duties of the wife towards her husband

If a woman is to be induced to perform her duties towards her husband, she must first be fully persuaded of her submission and her dependence; this is the first law which the Lord imposed on her, the first punishment for her rebellion. 'You will,' said the Lord, 'be subject to the power of your husband, and you will live under his rule'; therefore, she must submit to him.

A woman cannot be more powerfully persuaded of her submission than by being obliged to leave her parents in order to become attached to her husband, to follow him whatever his domicile and his fortune, to bear his name, to do nothing without his authority, to be dependent on him for her living. It is for the husband not to abuse this, it is for the wife to submit to it: when she tries to evade it, she becomes a baneful source of trouble and division; man was created to command, woman to obey. As long as she remains within the confines of a just dependence, she will live peacefully and happily; and as soon as, out of a spirit of vanity and pride, she tries to escape and to rule, she brings nothing but disorder and confusion.

If she wants to have a good understanding with her husband, she must add to her submissiveness an inviolable fidelity. An honest woman should seek to please only her husband; if she makes efforts to be pleasing to others, her chastity is endangered.

It is not enough for a woman to be good in her own heart, she must avoid occasions and appearances which could bring her conduct under suspicion. If she appears in public with an immodest air and dressed like a dissolute woman, she exposes her reputation to great risk. Goodness should not be displayed ostentatiously; but when it is genuine, some hint of its beauty is always discernible, and this makes it admirable in the eyes of the world.

35
Sir Robert Filmer, *In Praise of the Virtuous Wife* (n.d.)

Source: M. Eazell, *The Patriarch's Wife*, Johns Hopkins University Press, London, Baltimore, 1987, pp.169–90, taken from a manuscript in the possession of Peter Laslett.

Sir Robert Filmer (*c*.1585–1653) matriculated from Trinity College, Cambridge in 1604. He later inherited the manor of East Sutton, Kent. He was persecuted during the civil wars for his strong royalist views. He is best known for the *Patriarcha*, a book in which he argued that the royal power was derived directly from God and that it should not be subject to temporal restraint. He married Anne Heton, daughter of the Bishop of Ely, and they had six sons and two daughters; was it personal experience that had led him to write 'In Praise of the Virtuous Wife'?

Proverbs 12.4, *A virtuous woman is the Crown of her husband; But she that maket[h] him ashamed is as corruption to his bones.*
In the fifth commandment three duties are enjoine[d]
1. Between Superiors and inferiors. 2. Towar[ds] Equals.
3. Towards Our selves. of the first kind some are Private or Public. Private as [the] duty of the wife, of Parents and Children, or Serv[ants] and Masters. To these appertaineth the doctrin[e] of Chastisement, and the respect of Age. Publi[c] as the office of a King. To equals appertain[eth] the doctrine of Manners the contrary where of is Pride. To ourselves appertains the regard of our own good fame.

First of the wife as being the first estate. She [is] described 1. by Solomon. 2. by Bathsheba. By Solomon she is set out by the Effect and the Cause. The effect is threefold. 1. Honour in the verse. 2. Profit Chap: 14.1. 3. Pleasure whic[h] is expressed by the contrary Chap: 19:13. The cau[se] is gods favour, chap: 18.22 and 19.14 [References to Proverbs]

The honour is demonstrated by the Cause then amplifi[ed.] The cause in these words. *A virtuous woman* or according to the hebrew *A woman of strength or courage* as it is taken chap: 31.10. Ruth 3.11. Hence we learn that courage ought to be in women which is proved by *Scripture, Reason, example.* For scripture 1. Peter. 3.6 whose Daughters ye are whilst ye do well, not being afraid of any terror. For reason it thus is framed *Courage is true virtue*, and true virtue may be and ought to be in women. that Courage is true virtue it appeare[th] because true virtue is the moderation of the affections by faith and prudence the one showing what is lawful, the other what is *possible* and *Convenient*. now this moderation is nothing but courage. Besides that true virtue may be and ought to be in women is proved First by scriptures Gen:1.27. Ephes:4.24. out of these places it appears that women being made god's image ought to have Knowledge, holiness, and righteousness, now to have these is to have virtue. Again gen: 3.7 where (by eyes) are meant *consciences*, now if *conscience* do accuse, it was made to excuse, for god makes nothing evil. Besides in four commandments of the law *women* are named or implied viz: the *fourth, fifth, seventh* and *tenth*, the law therefore was given to women. Lastly these places are plain *not withstanding through bearing children she shall be saved if they continue in faith and love and holiness with modesty* or rather as our new translation hath it (she shall be saved in childbearing) 1, Tim.2 [15]. Likewise the husbands dwell with them according [to] knowledge giving honour unto the wife as [unto] the weaker vessel, and as being heirs together of th[e] grace of life that your prayers be not hindered. 1. Pet:3.7 Secondly that virtue may be [and] ought to be in women it appeareth by the fourt[h,] privileges of women, whereby they are not to b[e] puffed up, but to be made thankful and hopeful in regard of virtue. These privileges are eithe[r] in the *narration* or in the thing. The narration of womans Creation is thrice repeate[d] gen: 1.27. gen: 2.22 and 5.2. which is of creation else save man. In the thing are three privileges, first before the creation a double appr[o]bation of the woman 1. by god, gen.2.18 2ly by man the experimental feeling of his want *but for Adam there was not found a help meet for him* gen: 2.20. Secondly in the Creation for she was ma[de] last in order and so was added as a perfection to the best, she was created in *Paradise*, lastly out of man[s] *Rib* not out the earth. Thirdly after the creati[on] the privileges are in the law, or gospel. In the *Law* first *Angelical*, for the first angel was seen by *Hagar* I mean by the way of Comfort. Second Judicial: Deut. 20.14 *thou shalt smite every male thereof with the edge of the sword, but the women and the little ones etc.* In the gospel two ways[.] First as it was promised both by prophecy where in the woman is first named gen: 3.15. and also by Ceremony levit: 12.6. For a double purification for a double sin of eating and deceiving as it implied a double repentance, so a double pardon and honour. Secondly as it was performed, For the incarnation and resurrection of Christ were first revealed to woman, And they loved Christ best alive and dead. These privileges had not been granted if woman could not be virtuous.

This ought to be their Comfort in terror of Conscience and against the scoffs of the wicked.

It is objected. 1. *woman was the first sinner.*

Answer. 1. Not the cause (for that was mans will) but the occasion. 2. She was the occasion not by hateful knowledge (as Satan) but by *ignorant love.* 3. As she was the first in sinning so she was most grievously punished of all mankind, for Satan had three punishments; the woman two; the man but one. The woman did deceive out of error; the devil out of knowledge; the man did eat: so that she is to be pitied not hated. 4. She was the occasion though not the cause of our Salvation in Christ.

Objection. 2 Women have been most wicked.

Answer. If some women have been worst, then some women have been better than men, As devils are therefore worse because good angels are better then m[en.] The corruption of the best is worst, the best wine makes the strongest vinegar. The examples that prove that courage may be or [ought] to be in woman, are either *Direct* and commendable; or e[lse] *Indirect* and evil. The direct examples are twelve. Two in Exodus and 1.19. Four in the Judges, Debo[rah,] Jael, she that stoned Abmilech, and Manoahs wife w[ho] had stronger faith at the sight of an angel than Jac[ob,] Daniel, John. Two in the first of Samuel Mich[al] in dismissing David, and Abigail. Two in the second o[f] Samuel, the woman of Tekoah, of Abel. The eleventh in Esther. The last is in Hebrews. II.35. taken out of the 2. Mac: 7. These examples should ca[use] men to emulate even the courage of woman. The indirect examples are twelve in eight cases all e[vil.] First a woman had the Courage to abuse or deceive her lov[er] as Delilah did Sampson. Secondly her father as Rach[el] did Laban. Thirdly her King as Rachab. Fourthly h[er] husband as Eve, Jobs wife, Rebecca, Zippora: Fifthly her husband and King as Michal, Vashti. Sixthly he[r] children as Athalia, Seventhly her subjects as did Jezebel. Eighthly neighbours or strangers as Cozbi. If they be thus courageous in evil by nature why should we deny them good courage by grace.

Use. 1. Woman had need of patience against the day of *Sickness* and *Childbirth: widowhood* and *Martyrdom*. For Julietta said that the rib was as well bone as flesh. Use.2. The means to attain courage are three, First skill in Housewifery and religion to prevent bodily and ghostly terrors, secondly *Labour*. Thirdly *temperance*.

Objection. A woman is the weaker vessel. 1.Pet. 3.7

Answer. 1. That is in perseverance, but not in a sudden *act.* 2. her weakness is a fit middle term to combine the father to his tender children; again if both were equally strong neither should yield and so no concord. 3. Gods power is seen in our infirmity 2. Cor: 12.9.

Hitherto of the demonstration by the cause, now follows the amplification by a *similitude* and *Contrary*. For the Similitude *she is the crown of her husband or lord*. A crown is a lawful purchased golden ornament of a Kings head. Here the working cause is that it must come *lawfully*, As by *just war, Election, Donation of god or man, Entrance into vacuity, Succession not usurpation.* So is a woman given by god if she be virtuous and marry willingly, not for *lust, Beauty, honour, wealth,* else she is a hellish screetchowl not a heavenly nightingale. Secondly the matter of which a crown is made of gold a great enemy to the *consumption* and *plague*, so a good woman preserves a man from the consumption of melancholy and plague of *Adultery* which takes away the heart Hosea 4.II.

Objection: A Crown of gold is heavy so is a woman. I Corinth: 7.26.

Answer: It is better to have heavy persecution without than more heavy temptation within[.] In time of public troubles god many times gives the gift of continence, but if he deny it is better even then to marry than to burn with distracting lust. Again the matter about which a crown is employed is [the] head of a King, for jewels and earings are worn by other persons, but crowns only by Kings. that is absolute governors as the word is taken Gen: 36.31. Now a King may in sundry sorts dispose of his crown yet may he [not] give or sell it away as king *John of England* did. S[o] may not a man put away his wife neither for sickness [of] body; as *leprosy, Epilepsy,* unless it were fraudulent[ly] concealed before marriage: For after wedlock though separation be necessary in regard of *cohabitation,* yet [the] gift of continence may be hoped for in respect of the necessity. Neither yet for the sin of the mind, n[or] for false religion unless she willingly depart and will n[ot] return. Not for murder nor like *crying crimes* un[less] he be a magistrate, or complain to him. Not for Adultery, for if she repent the good Levite will receive her Judges 19.3. as Christ did his church, if she repent not, yet it is to be expected. And because of the outward *inconvenience* (though simply it be lawful) yet by our laws it is held unfit; and to live without her is dangerous because we have no necessity of calling hereunto. All which doubts would easily be dissolved if Adultery were death according to gods law which bound ev[en] the very *Pagans.* Ge[n]: 20.6. Jereme.29. 22. 23. Thirdly the form and end of a *Crown* is in this word *ornament,* For it is a sign of honour to a prince for his victories and authority, and is honoured itself for the *Princes sake*: So a good *woman* is given to a man as a reward and sign of his authority and victory over lust, and she is the more honoured for his sake, as being not the cause but the sign and image of his honour. 1.Corinth. II.7.

Thus much of the similitude, now follows the *Contrary* wherein we may consider the *working* and the *work*: the working in these words *she that shameth her husband.* This done through want of *Obedience* in three things. 1. *good;* 2.*Bad*: 3. *Indifferent.* In good things three ways, First if She do not that which is necessarily good unless her husband command it: For besides her obedience to her spiritual husband Christ (who is the husband of the *Church*) her own husband is also brought into Suspicion by choosing an unfit wife. Secondly when that she refuseth to do good things though he command it; herein she sinneth both against *god* and *man.* Thirdly when she doth not intreat, or persuade, but command her husband to do *good things.* In evil things there is a double error first on the left hand, namely when she forsakes not evil though he forbid it; or tempts him to the commiting of evil. Secondly on the right hand, when she will not endure his evil deeds, but reproveth him before others, or privately without leave: or speaketh of them to them to whom their knowledge pertains not.

Abigail is objected. 1.*Sam*: 25.25. *Answer* I. She was a prophetess, for she foretells the death of *Saul* and *Nabal,* the kingdom of *David,* and her own marriage to him. 2. She doth it not to accuse her husband but to save his life. 3.She discloseth no secret but acknowledgeth a known sin to the Lords anointed being now armed and in fury. In things indifferent this is done three ways. First when she commandeth him to do things indifferent. Secondly when she refuseth to do things indifferent at his charge. Thirdly when she doth th[em] upon her own head. 1. Tim: 2.12. *But I suffer not [a] woman to teach, nor to usurp authority over the ma[n] but to be in silence. Abigail is again objected. Answer.* her gifts are excused by the extremity of the necessity.

Hitherto of the working, there remaineth the work in the words she is as rotteness or consumption in his bones. here is an allusion to the disease too well known or some like, which make a man sad in his mind, namely full of fear, despair, suspicion for that which is to come; gr[ief,] disdain, anger for that which is passed. Also loathsome, for that he hath not found or made her good. we read not in scripture that a *good* man had a *wicked* wife.

Objection. I. *Adam was seduced by his wife.*

Answer. I. That Eve was a good woman appeareth because the promise was made to her Gen: 3.15. and received the same Gen: 4.25. which thing also is avouched wisdom 10.1.2 She was deceived but was first deceived herself 1. Tim: 2.14. 2. Corinth: 11.3. let none therefore with Adam lay the blame on her, but rather blame him that should have been the wiser of the two.

Object: 2. Jobs wife is objected. Job. 2.9. and 19.17.

Answ: In the first place she only biddeth him bless god and acknowledge his secret sin, which was also the error of his three friends, three as wise men as were then of the world, and one of them a prophet Job. 4.12. The other fact was but an error of human infirmity.

Object: 3. Zippora is pretended Exod. 4.25.

Answ: She was not yet fully instructed then as Ra[c]hel about images *Gen:* 31.19. Again she returned with her father to *Moses:* and her brother was good to the *Israelit[es]* in all their journeys, lastly god punished *Miriam* with leprosy that spake against her *Numb:* 12.2.

Object: 4. Michal is brought forth. 2. Sam: 6.23.

Answ. She thought *David* took upon him the levites office, or that his joy was too immoderate, or less beseeming princely gravity; For which error though she were justly punished with barrenness yet may we not count her a scoffer that saved the life of David against her fathers will.

Question: may not then a good man have a wicked wife?

Answer: He may, as shall be showed hereafter.

Thus far of the honour which a good woman bringeth, now follows the *Profit Chap* 14 V. I. Set out, First by the cause, Secondly by the work. Thirdly by the Contrary. The Cause in these words wise women. The wisdom of a woman is twofold. I. In spiritual things as she is a Christian. 2. In things for this life, and this is threefold. First for Pleasure as Music. secondly for Commodity as Housewifery. Thirdly for Credit which is twofold. 1. *Private As curious Arts.* 2. *Public, As Physic and Surgery.* These bring nobility to wom[en] as *Arms* and *Learning* do to men. In this place is only meant housewifery which must be attained, and kept Attained by three means. 1. If they be broken of the[ir] will when they are young. 2. If they be kept in service far from home. 3. If they be not marri[ed] until they be skilful in housewifery. It is kept also by three means. 1. If they marry husbands that be neither *Spendthrifts* nor meddlers within doors. 2. If they have no *concurrent mothers* or any other to command. 3. If they change not servants yearly wanting courage to correct, and so be put every year to instruct a *new servant* in a new manner. Thus much of the cause, the work follows, *shall build her house*, which is done three ways. First by saving. Secondly by increasing. Thirdly by *absolute raising of a mans estate*. This last is most noble to the woman but most dangerous to the man[.] The *Contrary* in these words *A foolish woman with her own hands destroyeth her house*. A similitude taken from them who pull down their own houses, in time of fire or when the enemy approacheth.

That much of the honour and *Profit* of a virtuous woman. now remains the Pleasure which is described by the *contrary*[,] namely the trouble of a *Contentious wife. Chap:* 19.V.13. The word *Contentious* cometh of a hebrew word that signifieth to judge. For strife ariseth when we judge others without *Knowledge, Vocations,* and *Charity*. These are amplified by a double comparison, First of the *unequal*, which is thus framed, *the foolish son is a heaviness to the father*, much more than *a contentious wife*. The son is not *equal* to his father, he is but a part of him he may be *restrained, disinherited, dismissed, Other sons* may be had; all these fail in wife. The second comparison is of the like, namely a *continual dropping* which eateth through the hardest stone, and being let in rotteth the strongest houses.

Use. I. Man must learn to prevent Contention in wives by two means. *Choosing* and *Using*. In choosing they must mark the *mind, body, estate*. In the mind her *understanding*, and *Affection*. For her understanding she must know thy *language and Religion*. For her affections, first in general she must not be greivously tainted with *Pride, Lust, covetousness*. the last is most tolerable; And in particular she must affect thy *Calling* and *Person*. For her body, avoid an eminent *contagious* disease lest it breed *separation* though not *perpetual divorce*. For her state either let thine answer hers, or attempt some heroical and public actions[.] So was the case of *Joseph* and *Mahomet*. In the using her after marriage. First abroad give her no *Rule* but moderate *liberty*. At home both *Rule* and *Liberty*, so that she be not tainted with idleness[,] covetousness, pride, or ignorance in extreme degree[.] Secondly communicate no secrets unto her above her capacity. Thirdly honour her in the presence of *Children, Servants, Strangers:* unless her vices be *open* and *outragous*: If these things be neglec[ted] thou shalt but blow the bellows of Contention. Use. 2.We must pray for *Constancy* for the drop[ings] of *temptation* may eat into us though not by force yet by often falling.

Use.3. If a contentious wife be such a purgatory what a paradise is a woman of meek spirit. 1.P[et] 3.5. Hitherto of the efforts of a good woman now followeth the Cause of a good woman. Namely gods favour, set out partly by the *Institution*. cap: 18.12. *He that findeth a wife* that is such a one as *Issa* was before her fall (who afterwards was termed Eve) or he that findeth a wife that is a *good wife* (as Esia.1.[27]. 18) . . . this man finds good and receives her as an argument of gods favour. And partly by Comparison cap: 19.14. The doctrine is plain that a good wife is a symbol of gods favour.

Object: Nabal a son of Belial had Abigail to wife. 1. Samuel.25.3 and 25.

Answ: he had her for his futher condemnation to make his impenitency inexcusable, and for the trial of her patience, for indeed she was reserved for *David. May not then a good man have a wicked wife?* Though we read no such example in scripture, yet this may fall out, either as a *Chastisement* for some sin past, or a preventing of some to come, or else for a *Domestical martyrdom.* Men therefore that do intend to marry 1. must repent them for the sins of their *youth* lest they find their *mirror* in their wives iniquities. 2. They must pray that they may enjoy this heaven upon earth if it be convenient trusting more to gods providence than to the experience of friends or to their own fancies. Thus far go the words of *Solomon.* Now we come to the song of *Bathsheba* cap: 31.10 and so to the end. This song is set down according to the order of the Hebrew *letters,* As we find seven Psalms so written the 25. 34. 37. 111. 112. 119. 145. and the four first chapters of the *Lamentations.* Now for as much as this was done to the aiding of *memory* we must endeavour to strengthen the same by all lawful means; And although we doubt of *artificial memory* by *places, images* and *actions* whether it be rather a *confusion* than a help: And although all men cannot attain to *Logic* which is the true *art of memory* yet there is none so rude, who by lading the same like a *Camel* may not make it stronger, provided always that he loads man by Judgement; for it is not an orderly but a barbarous memory which retaineth things not understood.

This song hath two parts. A *Proposition.* ver: 10. *An exposition* to the end. The proposition is set out by a *question* and *compariso[n.]* The question in these words *who shall find* etc. This is threefold. First *what kind of man shal[l] find such a woman?* The answer is given by Solom[on:]He that is in gods favour. Secondly *How hardly shall a man find?* Answer; very hardly: for where as there be but four ways to know her. First, the *Place,* . . . So large being the visible church, it is also most uncertain because many lambs are without and wolves within the fold, that the knowledge is difficult. Secondly *Company.* This is also uncertain, because a maid may have such company as she disliketh, though it be imposed by her friends. Thirdly *Report,* this may be *ignorant, Crafty, Partial.* Fourthly *trial of her virtues.* This [is] dangerous, and uncertain for as Locusts lie hid in a country till a year of dearth: so sundry sins which were smothered in time of youth, break forth in *marriage* and *government.* Again it is hard to obtain her, As either being *promised* before, or *not affected to thee* or *unfit for thy calling.* We must pray therefore that god will send his angel before us in this business. Thirdly *How happily is he that finds her? Answer:* He is happy in his family and neighbours[.] in his families, first in himself verse 23. *Her husband is known in the gates, when he sitteth with the Elders of the land*. Secondly in his Children, verse 28. *her children rise up and call her blessed*. Thirdly in his servants. verse 21. *She is not afraid of the snow for her household, for her household are clothed with scarlet.* In his neighbours. I. the Poor. vers: 20. *she stretcheth out her hand to the poor, yea she reacheth forth her hand to the needy*. 2. the Rich. *both the Judges of the land whom she honoureth*. verse 23. *and the merchant whom she pleaseth* verse 24. From the question we come to the comparison, Her *price is above pearls*. Pearls are esteemed not only for their rareness but for their virtues.

Use.1. Virtue is to be regarded in marriage.

Object.1. God *commands the brother to raise up seed without regard to the virtue of the woman* Deut: 25.5.

Answ: Some think that he was only to adventure the penalty as spitting in his face, plucking of his shoe and the like, But it is rather to be thought that he was absolutely bound to do it, for seeing he married her in faith and obedience to gods law he had probability of hope concerning her amendment. *Objects*. 2. *Hosea was commanded to marry two harlots*. Hos[ea] 1.2. and 3.1. *Answer:* we agree not to them that make this a vision or a parable but taking it to be a real stor[y] do think out of the 3. Chap: verse 2. that the prophe[cy] of harlots was to make them *chaste*. neither was this entering into temptation, seeing god commanded it for a typ[sic?trial.]

Objection: 3. *Isaac, Jacob, Joseph and Moses married Idolatrous women;* Gen: 31.19 and 41.45. Exod: 4:25.

Answ: It appears that *Rebecca* had true religion (thoug[h] somewhat confused) by the author of Laban, gen: 24.31. and 59. As for Joseph's wife she was given him by *Pharoah* and so might not be refused, besides how know we that she was not a virtuous proselyte. for Zipporah we did answer before. Here then; they first are condemned that will not marry where virtue is separated from *wealth*; the contrary we see in Jacob. gen: 29.17 *Booz Ruth:* 3.10[,] *Hosea*. 3.3. who bought his wife at gods commandment. Secondly those that are not regarding virtue marry in respect of honour as Solomon did. 1. Kings. II.I or of Beauty as Gen: 4.22 and 6.2 . . .

Thus much of the *proposition* now follows the *Exposition* women are two things. 1. the works of a good woman. verse II. to the 28.2 The *Testimony* given concening her verse 28. to the end. In the works two virtues are seen *faithfulness* and *providence*. The faithfulness is set down in *substance* vers: II. and in *circumstance* vers. 12. The substance is declard by a double event. The First is *The heart of her husband trusteth in her.* I. In respect of her *speech*. 2. of her *Deeds* he may trust her for speech or silence if he tell her no *secrets* which either go beyond her understanding as a matter of state, or may drive her into suspicion, grief, anger: or wherein she can give her council nor help . . .

Again for her deeds he may trust her three ways. 1. For her *Chastity*. 2. *Government*. 3. *Expenses*. For her *Chastity* if she be free from adultery and the reasonable suspicion thereof; if [he] Deny her not due benenvolence, if he restrain her not of moderate libertie, pe[rmitting] that she visit not too much the daughters of the land Gen: 34.1. Nor wander like a busy prattler 1. Tim. 5.13. For government he may trust her first in regard of *Daughters* and *maidservants:* Secondly even of sons when they be young. *Lastly* for expense which is here meant principally: if *prodigal pride* and *luxury* with *lust* and *vanity* be not found to exceed he may trust her, and by trusting make her trusty. The second event is he shall *have no need of spoil* the hebrew word signifieth *wealth or excellent things* so doth the greek word Heb: 7.4. For *Abram paid tithes of his own goods as well as of the warlike spoils.* Again these words may be thus expounded. *As a victorious army needs no booty: so the husband of a good woman needs no needy shift to get his living.* That these things may be so, it is requisite, First that the woman be void of ignorance in *housewifery* secondly of *idleness*, thirdly of *bellycheere*, [luxurious self-indulgence] fourthly of *lust*, fifthly of *vanity* in apparel and building (which frenzy doth possess even some women also) of all these caterpillars the most dangerous are *idleness* and *bellycheere*. Idleness are these kinds. First *Niceness* when woman will always be faining themselves sick (*this is a sumptuous sin.*) The second is *carelessness* when things are spoiled for lack of keeping and attendance. Thirdly slothfulness when in labour there is neither *earliness, vehemency, continuance,* nor *method:* sufficient *help,* or *alacrity.* Fourthly fearfulness when they will not *Chastise* their servants, being more ready to change than amend them, whereas by the first law *servants should not alter under 7 years.* Bellycheere hath these parts, First *Daintyness.* Secondly *love of company at home*, but especially abroad. he that [hath] a wife with this viperous disease shall have need of spoils. Thus much the substance, the *circumstances of her faithfulness* are two. 1. *Entireness* 2. *Perseverance.* Entireness in these words: *She shall recompense him good and not evil:* that is *she shall not show him a cruel, babbling, or lustful trick:* Here observe, *a good woman may do her husband good;* First in his understanding, if she teach him religion being more skilful than he; this must be done modestly and secretly. Secondly in his affection, for she may sanctify him 1. Cor: 7.15. In this kind she is most happy that can comfort her husband against fear and grief . . . The next to her is she [who] *preserves her husband from anger.* The last is she that *cures him of the remediless disease of Jealousy,* this is also rather a thing to be wished than hoped for. The *Perseverance of her faithfulness in these words, All the days of her life,* being more fruitful of good works in her old age. Psal: 92.14. whereof these may be t[he] causes I. If she have led her youth well, or have repented of the sins of her youth, which commonly are revenged with the sins of old age. 2. If she have used rather wisdom than vehemency in her love, for things violen[t] are not durable. 3. If she have prayed constantly for perseverance.

Thus much of he faithfulness, Now follows her *Providen[ce]* verse 13. set down in three things. I. *In getting* 2. *In employing* 3. *Preserving.* Getting is propounded verse 13. and expounded in the five next, It is propounded in two things. For first she seeks *wool* and *flax* as matter for her labour. Secondly she labours with the cheerfulness or willingness of her hands upon this matter so purchased. Here we see the difference of *God, Nature, Art*. For God worketh without *matter,* creating the world of nothing; Nature of one substance frameth another. *Art* only bringeth in new qualities: God having supplied all things to us if we can but use them well. The labour of a Mistress is more worth than that of a servant because it is with more cheerfulnes, not issuing from fear; but from love of virtue, the family, and the master. Let servants then which intend hereafter to rule begin betimes to put put away eyeservice, and think themselves to be masters not in surliness or commanding but in cheerfulness of working. Again, let not the husband kill the spirit of the wife with bitter looks, words, deeds; which make her of a rib to become an excrement.

The providence in getting is expounded and that in regard of both parts, before named, diligence in seeking, and labour. Seeking is set down verse 14. by a similitude of ships, whereby bread or food all things are meant which bring in food or profit as *wool, flax* and the like. In this seeking two things are to be remembered. I. That she be a *housekeeper* that is no gadder abroad, but a traveller for lawful business with unsuspected company. *Tit:* 2.5. 2. She must seek out such things as are profitable for her country. for in some places it is more available to buy cloth ready made than to make it. Use.I. we see the excellency of laborious industry which maketh even barren places to be fruitful of all things, though wool be not meant that may be fetched from Militus; for god hath made on[e] country need another to take away self love.

Use. 2. Of all callings that of the merchant is the most dangerous, and yet is imitable by a woman, though i[n] a weaker measure; so there is no virtue in men so differen[t] which women may not hope in some sort to attain, for e[ven] sailing and war and government of kingdoms have been often times well handled by women, *Queen Dido* may be example for all, or rather *Q Elizabeth* in whose tim[e] these things flourished.

Use. 3. The woman must be allowed by her husband, else how can she employ messengers and money in these matters; but in this allowanc[e] love and discretion must meet. The second part of getting which is Labour is set out by three times, t[he] *Beginning, Middle, End* of the day. In the beginning or morning she doth three things, *Riseth, Ordereth, meditateth:* firstly verse 15. Use.1. Here they are confuted who think the night to serve only for sleep, for she riseth while it is yet night if it may stand with her health: besides the *moon* and *stars* were not made to sleep by but to work by: neither indeed is the proportion between the times of the day and night at some seasons of the year; that it were strang[e] to sleep 16 hours together, much more strange to sleep 6 months, all which time the night endureth in some Countries. Use.2. Early rising is commende[d] both here and elsewhere as most natural to man . . . Use.3. we must learn in spiritual things also to rise early *Psalm:* 119.V: 147 and 148. *I prevented the morning light, and cried; for I waited on thy word, Mine eyes prevent the night watches to meditate on thy word,* The second work of the morning is to give food or portion to our Household, this word is Psal: III. vers: 3 Use.1. Order for meat and work in families is most [need]ful . . . Use.2. Government of maids is to be permitted to the w[ife] as is plain by the stories of *Abigail* and *Hester* . . . Use.3. we must be content with the portion that god gives, for the world is his family, so tha[t] we may not murmur to see fools have full cups. Use.4. If the wife have such authority in the family concerning things indifferent: why should we take away this power from the Church which is the Lambs wife. The third work of the morning is to meditate verse 16. wherein we may consider the art or deed, and the means. The deed, to purchase the field or vineyard. the means are two. I. wise consideration. 2. She purchaseth it with money lawfully gotten . . .

[there follows a passage discussing the permissibility of the sale and purchase of land]

Slips of this truth remain in our law, for if a man die intestate, t[he] eldest son by the common law is heir to the land, if a man make an executor he is heir to the goods but not t[o] the land, so that howsoever things have been corrupted by *tyranny* and *usurpation* yet the ordinary sale of land is not to be justified. *Objection:* sundry good deeds may be done by the selling of land. *Answer:* The temple was built and sundry synagogues when this sale was exhibit[ed] for in those days sundry men did combine their revenues for such public works. Here then the good women either buyeth a lease till the years of *Jubilee,* or buyet[h] right out a house in a *City,* yet cutteth off no inheritan[ce] from a family *Levit; 25.24.* Thus much of the morning works; *at Noon she girdeth her loins* vers: 17. that is, she sleepeth not at noon but armeth her self to labour: Use.I. hindrances of labour are to be avoided which are I. *lust.* 2. *surfeiting* and all *voluptousness* 3. *lewd company* at home and abroad. 4. *disuse of labour* whereby many enfeeble their bodies and disable their minds. *Lastly at Night she puts not out her candle.* vers: 18.19. whereof the causes are rendered, *she feeleth that her merchandise* <are> *is good:* she sits up late for profit not against health. Secondly by the effect, *she handles the wheel and spindle.* Examples we have in *Penelope Lucretia and others.* Use.1. *Example is of great force.* The mistress example is a precedent for her servants as *Esther* 4.16. Though she were a Courtier and lived among *pagans,* and fasting was a hard doctrine *Mat.* 9.16 yet she by her example moved her maids to do it . . . Use. 2. By the wheel and spindle are meant all labour not only of body but of mind: if any woman excel in *Surgery, Physic, government* of a commonwealth she shall be no more bound to the *wheel* than a prince is to the *Plough.* Those husbands therefore are to *froward* that hinder these eminent graces in their wives: provided always that the women neglect not housewifery nor be bodshers [sic].

Thus much of her providence in getting, now followeth that of *employment* vers: 20. which is threefold for the matter, besides the manner. The I. *matter* is Necessity. 2. *of ornament.* 3. *of Profit:* of necessity twofold. First to the *Poor,* vers: 20. Here by the word *stretching* and *sending* is meant that she helps the poor far off as well as near: likewise by the word *poor* or *afflicted*, and, *needy* or *craving* is meant, that she is aiding as well to those that ask not, as to those that ask: wherefore it is said, that it is *religion* to visi[t] *James* 1.27. that is rather to inquire out the necessities of men, than to be importuned by the clamours of the *wanderers*. *Use.* Hence Husbands may learn to give first a general then a special consent to their wives upon trial in regard of liberality. The second necessity is in respect of the family. *verse.* 21. where the word *scarlet* is rather to be turned *doubles or changes of garments,* not *double dyed scarlet* an attire not fit for servants, howsoever the word be so taken commonly *Gen:* 38.25. *Use. Handsomeness is greatly commended* in the changes of raiment; such as *Joseph* gave to *Benjamin, Sampson to his friends, Balthasar to Daniel* for filthiness in raiment is an argument of looseness in women[.] *Ornament* is twofold. First in herself, then in her husband. For herself she adorns the family and her person *vers.*22. for her house she makes *carpets,* for her . . . person she wears purple and silk: . . . *Again* she adorns her husband for he is *known in the gates sitting with the elders,* by the fine attire which she makes for him. *Use.* Garments are made not only for covering of shame, and health or safety whether in peace or war: but also for distinction of orders, which they that break do also break their works like the giants . . .

Hitherto of the providence of employment, their remain[eth] that of *Keeping* which is twofold *spiritual* and *temporal*. The spiritual being more noble and so first is in verse 26. *she openeth her mouth in wisdom, and the law of pity or mercy is under her tongue. Use.* I. Two things are required of them that speak of *Religion.* First for the matter, that they treat of gods pity to us, and our pity to our neighbour, [or?] else religion is but babbling. Secondly for the manner that they know the law, or *doctrinal method* as the word imports, not contenting themselves with fragment[s] of disjointed sentences. *Use.* 2. knowledge of religion and arts pertaining to pity: specially the art of *Surgery* and *Alms* are very convenient for women. The temporal means of keeping are set down verse 27. which are two I. *overseeing* 2. *labour.* namely overseeing that things be well done and in time, also that things be not spoiled nor spend in vain, for *she overseeth the way of her household. Labour* likewise not so much for personal toil as exemplary cheerfulness, for she *eateth not the bread of idleness. Use.* Here gentlemen and gentlewomen are condemned who live by their lands in sloth, not in public labour of profitable housewifery.

Hitherto of the works now follows the *witnesses* verse 28. There are two, First the *Children* who bless her, secondly her *husband who praiseth her* . . . *Use.*I. It is the mothers duty to bring up her children that they may bless her: that is to give them good example, and love them without partiality, a sin punished in *Jacob, Elias, David,* and why not in women? *Use.* 2. Children must obey their mothers and be thankful in their wants. *Use.* 3. Husbands must encourage their wives with seasonable praise, and yet retain their own gravity for it is said her *Lord shall praise her,* His praise is set down by a *prosopopoeia* or speech upon his death bed to his sons, containing a *Narration* and an *Exhortation* . . .

The exhortatio[n] is in ver: 31. which is double, First *give her of the fruit of her hands, my sons, what she hath gotten in my life time*, let her enjoy a convenient and honourable portion thereof after my death: though she marry again grudge not at that which she enjoys, And secondly let *her works praise her in the Gates*. If she be accused in the gates of *Judgement* either for *witchcraft* or *whoredom*, or be molested in suits of law defend her by declaring her former innocency. *Use*. I. *Deeds doubtful* are charitably to be interpreted according to the former integrity. *Use*. 2. Children must defend their parents in war, and law, As here, and *Psalm*. 127.5.

PART III

Parliaments and kings, 1660–1714

Introduction

The final part of this book commences with an examination of the tension between the centre and the periphery in both the French and British states which was one of the factors which determined the precise nature and extent of government authority. Louis XIV, through the agency of able and industrious ministers, was much more successful than any of the Stuarts in enforcing obedience to his will in most of his kingdom. The means by which this was done are demonstrated in three extracts from the correspondence of Jean-Baptiste Colbert (III.1). *Intendants* were threatened for allowing subordinates to exceed their authority and for having carried out instructions in a sketchy fashion. The governor of Brittany fared no better; although the pressure exerted on him to implement the royal will was more subtle, the implied danger existed of losing the regard of the king if he was too lenient with the Estates.

In the British Isles the greatest threat to royal authority in the 1680s and 1690s came, not from outlying parts of the kingdoms, but from differences between Charles II and James II and their subjects over religion. The Exclusion Bill (III.2) of 1680 was the culmination of an attempt by the Whigs, the party which had inherited many of the attitudes of the parliamentary side in the civil wars, to bar James from succeeding to his brother's throne on the grounds that he was a Catholic. The Whigs enjoyed massive popular support which had been drummed up by the Earl of Shaftesbury and his sympathizers in an effective campaign of anti-Catholic propaganda. The attempt failed after some skilful manoeuvring by Charles, but this did not solve the basic problem. James, Duke of Monmouth, faced a difficult but not impossible task in presenting himself to the English as an alternative heir in 1685. His proclamation (III.3) had to pick a careful path between various minefields: his illegitimacy, the fear that rebellion would lead to anarchy and the failure of the nobility to support him. These were probably the main reasons why he ended up on the scaffold rather than on the throne.

By the reign of Louis XIV the common people in France, when they rose in rebellion, were likely to find themselves in opposition to the nobility. The effective enforcement of his authority in the provinces, through such means as are demonstrated in document III.1, meant that, unlike James II in 1685 and again in 1688, he did not have to fear revolution from members of the aristocracy. When French peasants revolted, it was invariably in protest against heavy taxation. The Peasant Code (III.5), produced in 1675 by Breton insurgents, shows their resentment of the nobility, who enjoyed so many exemptions from taxation, and their consequent desire to break down social barriers by intermarriage.

By the early eighteenth century in Britain the securing of the Protestant succession had changed the political agenda: the Whigs were no longer the natural party of opposition and the Tories the party which supported the crown. The Whig administration under Queen Anne, in 1710, made the big mistake of impeaching Dr Henry Sacheverell (III.6), a high Anglican divine, who had preached a sermon in which he castigated them for their neglect of the interests of the church. The huge and unruly popular demonstrations in his favour contributed to the subsequent fall of the government; it also reminded the governing classes that, at least in the cities, the weight of popular, unenfranchised opinion was something which they were foolish to ignore.

Much has been said above about the 'absolute' rule of seventeenth-century monarchs in France and the British Isles. In recent decades English and French historians such as Roger Mettam (1988) and Roland Mousnier (1979) have questioned several of the assumptions which were to be found in most of the earlier works on the period. They have, in the process, earned for themselves the title of 'revisionists' since, like those who have re-thought the causes of the British civil wars, they look for their evidence in the details of fiscal administration and local government rather than for 'the big explanation'.

Such evidence is to be found in Jean-Baptiste Colbert's summary of the enormous amounts of money raised and spent by the government of Louis XIV in 1680 (III.7). The *Memoirs* of the duc de Saint-Simon (III.8) record another phenomenon of absolute rule: the system of favours and penalties, most of them inherently worthless, by which Louis XIV motivated the nobility of France to pay court to him at Versailles and his other regular retreats. The Revocation of the Edict of Nantes (III.9) in 1685, which deprived the Huguenots of the religious privileges in certain cities that they had enjoyed under the first two Bourbons, could be represented as absolutism red in tooth and claw: paradoxically it enjoyed the support of the great majority of the French who were observant members of the Catholic Church.

The Test Act (III.10), passed by the English parliament in 1673, makes pretty tame reading in comparison to the draconian Revocation of the Edict of Nantes. Like that measure, however, it underlines the difficulties encountered by anyone who tried to sustain a measure of toleration against the confessional certainties of the majority in a state. Charles II and, in 1687

(III.11), his brother James II attempted to do just that in favour of the Catholics and, incidentally, Protestant dissenters. The policy was harmful to Charles and, in conjunction with other unwise and authoritarian measures, fatal to James. Had he used the considerable powers he inherited in 1685 more judiciously, he might have survived as an absolute monarch of a not dissimilar stature to that of his cousin Louis XIV and remained a Catholic into the bargain. The birth of the son in 1688 who would be raised as a Catholic shortened the odds against his ability to do so.

The next document, extracts from the Bill of Rights (III.12) promulgated by the English parliament of 1689, which confirmed the terms under which William and Mary were to rule in England and Wales, has traditionally been hailed as marking the turning point when the rule of an absolute monarch became an impossibility. Yet some recent writers have suggested that the government of Charles II and James II was not so absolute in its direction, and that of William and Mary so limited, as had previously been believed.

The English might have achieved a viable settlement with William and Mary between 1688 and 1701, but what of the Scots and Irish, many of whom had fought valiantly for James II after his flight from England? The latter were simply subjugated, and the Protestants could at least comfort themselves that their separate parliament had survived. The Scots were aware of the dangers that England's Glorious Revolution presented to their nationhood and passed the Act Anent Peace and War, 1703, and the Act for the Security of the Kingdom, 1704, to try to safeguard it (III.13). The successful progress of the Act of Union (III.14) two years later recognized the reality of the situation and, for better or for worse, initiated a state which was to employ the energies of both nations to formidable effect during the next two centuries.

The next part of this collection begins with a review of the first half of the century, concentrating on the development of political ideas. Even in the early decades there was, both in France and the British Isles, a potential for conflict between the belief that the state should be organized in terms of patriarchal authority and the claim that political power was originally vested in a person or group of people by means of a contract. Those who held these beliefs did not necessarily fall neatly into the categories of subjects who supported the rule of an absolute or a limited monarchy. Many who opposed aspects of the government of the Bourbons and Stuarts did so because they subscribed to ideas founded on Christian morality or the ancient laws and customs of the realm. Conversely, thinkers like Thomas Hobbes, in his *Leviathan*, proposed a contract theory which could be used to justify the most authoritarian regime.

The poems produced by the *nu-pied* rebels in Normandy in 1639 (III.15) and the criticisms Mathieu de Morgues aimed at the government of Louis XIII and Richelieu (III.17) exemplify the traditionalist thinking of the opposition to royal government in France. Its supporters, writers such as Guez de

Balzac (III.16), were more inclined to base their apologies for the unlimited exercise of kingly power on the work of Renaissance thinkers, especially on *The Prince* of Niccolo Machiavelli; his French followers justified the exercise of the most arbitrary government on the grounds of 'reasons of state'. The speech of Charles I to the House of Commons in 1629 (III.18) encapsulates the view that the will of the prince had the force of law, not a good line to take with the most litigious people in the world.

Another impetus to innovation came from a small but distinguished band of women writers who began to question the right of men to have exclusive control over education, politics and the professions. Mary Astell's *A Serious Proposal to the Ladies*, 1697 (III.20), was one of the most persuasive contributions to the debate, seeing education as a means of admitting women to some kind of public life. Madame de Maintenon was no feminist, but it is arguable that her school at Saint-Cyr and the ideas about women's education which she aired in her letters gave a prominence and a status to the subject that it had lacked before (see above, II.1).

The civil wars and the Interregnum in Britain created the liberal atmosphere in which, by the end of the century, original thinkers like Mary Astell could get a hearing. The late 1640s were probably the years when the largest number of the English felt that they might actually have some voice in their government: *The Agreement of the People* articulates these aspirations (III.21). To some, the emergence of the Levellers threatened the end of civilization and the introduction of anarchy. Thomas Hobbes offered an antidote to these fears in his *Leviathan* (III.22) in which he envisaged just such a turbulent situation where men would make contracts with each other to surrender enough of their personal liberty to a ruler to ensure their physical protection, and the ability to guarantee this was sufficient authorization of the regime; no supernatural approval was required.

Just as Louis XIII had enjoyed the support of writers such as Guez de Balzac, his son, Louis XIV, was powerful enough to control the press within France. The king's *Mémoires* (III.23) contain uncompromising statements that he ruled by divine right, which allowed him to expect unquestioning obedience from his subjects. Jacques-Bénigne Bossuet, bishop of Meaux, was a loyal supporter of Louis, as emerges clearly from his letter to the king and the extract from the treatise that he wrote for the Dauphin (III.24). As a churchman, however, he did not accept that the king was absolutely free to exercise his own will; he should show compassion as a Christian monarch and always remember that he was a mortal man as well as God's representative on earth.

Other subjects of Louis XIV showed less restraint in criticizing their monarch: Jean de la Bruyère's *Characters* (III.25) purported to be a satire on court life, but he took the opportunity to censure the king's megalomania in allegorical language. François de Salignac de la Mothe-Fénelon's letter to Louis of 1694 (III.28) was much more outspoken on the subject of his vulnerability to flattery and the wickedness of his war policies. As an aristocratic prelate, Fénelon may have thought that he could get away with these strictures: he discovered his mistake five years later when the king confined him to his see of Cambrai. The *Memoirs* of Louis de Rouvroy, duc de Saint-Simon (III.26), were compiled after the death of Louis and were not generally available until the nineteenth century. He adopted the method of recording all the good points about a person followed by their failings: in the case of Louis XIV the latter far outweighed the former. Pierre Bayle was a Huguenot exile when he wrote his work on which the later *The Great Contest of Faith and Reason* (III.27) was based. In his work he strongly opposed the king's policy of forced conversions to the Catholic faith. None of these writers, even Bayle, queried the institution of absolute monarchy which perpetrated the abuses of power they complained of.

In England the stormy relationship between king and parliament during the second half of the reign of Charles II and the crises of that of James II, concentrated some minds again on the delights of republicanism. Pamphleteers like the Irishman John Toland and the Scot Andrew Fletcher of Saltoun found that the most effective way of attacking the institution of monarchy was by questioning the need for a standing army, which they saw as an essential attribute of despotic rule (III.29). *The Two Treatises on Civil Government* (III.30) by John Locke, written in a political climate of opposition where his confederates ranged from moderate Whigs to rabid republicans, did not urge the necessity of government without a king. The point was that the exercise of sovereignty was dependent on the ruler's ability to safeguard the lives and property of subjects: they would be justified in changing their sovereign if he or they failed to do so.

Louis XIV was not only successful in establishing a strong, centralized government in France; during his reign French culture and fashion were pre-eminent throughout much of Europe. It is, of course, debatable how far the king was personally responsible for this, but it is undeniable that his employment of artists and writers such as Molière, Mansart, Le Vau and Le Brun helped set standards of excellence which monarchs and the upper classes in other countries hastened to emulate. The great state that he kept at his court at Versailles and his various country retreats and hunting lodges, surrounded by large numbers of retainers and courtiers, dressed in the height of fashion, playing modish games, eating lavish, spectacular food, giving great balls graced by the latest dances and music, all had a powerful impact on foreign observers.

The majority of people in Britain had good reason to be chary of the 'Sun King' and all his works for the political and religious reasons which have been discussed above. This did not stop the upper classes from feeling a strong attraction to many aspects of French life. Charles II and James II had spent their formative years as the guests of Louis and seem to have felt the influence of his absolutist stance and of the Catholic religion for the rest of their lives. Even William III, the arch enemy of France, Antony Lentin tells us in Unit 14 of the course, ordered his luxury goods from Paris. Sir Christopher Wren's letter of 1665 (III.31) expresses admiration of French architecture which he later translated into the sincerest form of flattery: imitation. Ralph Montagu, Earl and later Duke of Montagu, was the English ambassador at the court of Louis XIV for some years. On his return to England he translated his liking for French art and architecture into a great house at Boughton, filled it with French furniture and surrounded it with an impressive garden (III.32). William III's most successful general, Marlborough, used French craftsmen for his palace of Blenheim, which marked his victories over the French.

French literature and drama was also influential on many people in Britain. Some authors even went to such lengths as 'improving' Shakespeare by substituting their own words for his language when it was thought to be too crude for refined tastes. William D'Avenant's adaptation of *Macbeth* (III.33) and Thomas Shadwell's staging of *The Tempest* (III.37) in the 1670s exemplified this vogue. John Dryden, a convert to Catholicism, expressed the ambivalence of the attitude that many of the élite had towards Louis XIV: he was their enemy but also a great patron of the arts (III.34). Others felt French influence to be harmful to the national character and moral fibre: William Wycherley ridiculed foppish francophiles in his play *The Gentleman Dancing-Master* (III.36). Joseph Addison waged war through the pages of *The Spectator* (III.35) against the gallicization of the English language: this seems ironical today when we are constantly hearing about the French academic abhorrence of 'le Franglais'.

Throughout most of his adult life Louis XIV was involved in warfare to strengthen and extend the frontiers of France and to safeguard what he perceived to be her economic, dynastic and religious interests. Apart from a commercial war with the Dutch, England remained at peace, at least externally, until after the Revolution of 1688. That drew her, as one of the states ruled by William of Orange, into over twenty years of almost constant war with France. There were dangers and opportunities for both monarchies in this situation: a successfully bellicose sovereign would be in a good position to cow his subjects into total obedience, one who failed might endanger his tenure of the throne.

The optimistic memorandum from Sebastien le Prestre, marquis de Vauban (III.38) of 1678 was written when Louis XIV was still waging victorious wars and envisaged a situation in which an expanded frontier with Holland and the Empire would need to be defended. Vauban was one of the leading exponents of the art of defence; a necessary skill at a time when the development of fire power had made full-scale battles too costly in life and injuries to be joined too frequently. In England the king faced the much harder task of ensuring the provision of adequate finance to support a viable army. The problem for James II when he asked parliament for supplies for his standing army in 1685 (III.39) was that the members were not at all sure for what purpose such an army might be used: it just could be a means of depriving the Anglican governing classes of their political independence (III.40). James was fortunate that the members were, after expressing severe reservations, prepared to support him: the uncertainties of the Exclusion Crisis and of Monmouth's rebellion encouraged them to be most unwisely sanguine about their king's intentions.

As the years went by, it became increasingly difficult for Louis XIV and his ministers to finance his wars and to convince his subjects that they were being waged in their best interests. Vauban's memorandum of 1695 (III.41) was starkly realistic: the best prospect of defeating the English and Dutch at sea, where they excelled, was by privateering. This would represent a virtual abdication of royal responsibility for the conduct of an important part of the war. The grievance aired by Saint-Simon in his *Memoirs* (III.42) identifies another problem faced by the government. Traditionally the higher posts in the French army had been filled by peers and princes, yet it had become increasingly clear that some of the high-ranking officers must be appointed according to talent if France was ever to defeat her enemies. This was bound to cause disaffection amongst the aristocracy and, if Saint-Simon is to be believed, some of the most talented nobles, such as himself, were passed over.

As the need for soldiers became more desperate, Louis increased the number of *milice*, militia men who had to be chosen from amongst those who were unmarried in every community. According to René Lehoreau the young men who were assembled were totally unsatisfactory, deserting or dying at the first opportunity (III.43). The final document points to a perennial problem for all governments: if you keep a large army what do you actually do with it when it is not on campaign? The lawless activities reported by M. de Radiolles (III.44) in 1711 demonstrate the dangers of both a bored soldiery during the winter months and a civilian population sufficiently disaffected to collude with them in breaking the hated law which enforced the collection of the *gabelle* tax on salt.

James II had lost his throne when he failed to lead his perfectly adequate army against William of Orange in 1688. Had he done so successfully the British Isles might have experienced, at least for a while, absolutist rule. Louis XIII and Louis XIV, with the help of a series of able ministers, established a strong, authoritarian and centralized government which enabled the latter to survive two decades of less than glorious warfare apparently unscathed. The harm that was inflicted was mainly social and economic, but that is a matter of concern to twentieth-century historians rather than one which troubled most of the contemporaries of 'the Sun King'.

References

Mettam, R. (1988), *Power and Faction in Louis XIV's France*, Basil Blackwell, Oxford.
Mousnier, R. (1979), *The Institutions of France under Absolute Monarchy, 1598–1789*, University of Chicago Press, Chicago.

1

Three Official Letters from Colbert

Source: Roger Mettam, *Government and Society in Louis XIV's France*, Macmillan, London, Basingstoke, 1977, pp.21–30. Translated from French.

These three letters, two to *intendants*, one to a provincial governor, demonstrate clearly the very tight control Colbert exercised on behalf of the king. Document A concerns a relatively minor official (a toll collector) who, though apparently acting in the interests of the crown, has exceeded his powers. With respect to B, we need to know that the edicts complained of imposed new levies, and that, at this stage, Brittany was the remaining province without an *indendant* (one was appointed in 1689, embodying, of course, even tighter central control). C is relatively routine, and a most revealing example of French central government at work. Jean-Baptiste Colbert (1619–83) was a Controller General of Finance (from 1665) and Secretary of State for the Navy (from 1669).

A.   To *Chamillart,* Intendant *at Caen*

Saint-Germain-en-Laye, 15 April 1672
I was very surprised to hear from your letter of 11 April, that the collector of tolls at Valognes has ordered the arrest of a Dutch vessel in the port of Cherbourg, on the grounds that war has been declared against the States of the United Provinces. It is not the place of these toll-collectors to meddle in such matters; but, seeing that the ship has been seized, the master must be permitted to ask that it be returned to his charge. However, it is now your task to inform the collector in private that I have pondered over this event and have decided that, for an action of this kind, I should put the culprit in a dungeon, with his feet in irons, for a period of six months, to teach him that it is not his privilege to use force in this way and on his own initiative, and that he should show greater wisdom in the future.

I ask you to tell him this in private because it is not appropriate for the people to believe that there is dissatisfaction with some of the men who collect taxes for His Majesty.

B.   To *the duc de Chaulnes, Governor of Brittany*

Saint-Germain-en-Laye, 10 December 1673
I hope that the bad humour in which you have found all the members of the Estates will be turned to your greater glory and will make even better known to the King the respect in which you are held in the province, and your hard

work to bring to a successful conclusion those things which are pleasing to him and are in his best interests . . . I feel I should tell you that the edicts which have given rise to these complaints in Brittany have been put into operation and are still in force in Languedoc and Provence, two provinces where other circumstances make them seem even more burdensome than they do in Brittany, among which is the fact that in those areas it is the *intendants*, whom the provinces regard as outsiders, who judge all matters arising from the execution of these edicts . . .

I have no doubt at all that Brittany will do the same, or even better; but I confess to you that, as I hope that this province will yet show, and more strongly than others, clear signs of its unlimited devotion to the wishes of His Majesty, I am a little concerned that I shall be obliged to tell him of such ill will in the minds of his subjects. As I am convinced that you can inspire other feelings in them, I am hoping that I shall soon have the satisfaction of hearing more agreeable news to His Majesty . . .

C.   *To Ménars*, Intendant *at Paris*

Versailles, 17 July 1682

I have received your letters and memoirs of 20, 23, 27 and 30 June, and 3 and 5 July, describing your visit to the *élections* of Nemours, Sens, Joigny, Saint-Florentin and Tonnerre. I am sure you would wish me to tell you that to visit five *élections* in fifteen days is no way to satisfy the King, for it is impossible to carry out in so short a time all that His Majesty requires of you, as contained in the orders and letters I have sent to you. You should not have led yourself to believe that His Majesty would put any faith in your memoirs, when it is obvious that they have been prepared so hastily. You were asked to examine so many problems that you would quite clearly have been unable to carry out unaided all the investigations which you have put in your reports, and it is almost impossible to believe that you have done any more than consult some local officials about these matters, and have based your conclusions on what they told you.

2

The Exclusion Bill (1680)

Source: Manuscripts of the House of Lords, 1678, pp.195–7, reprinted in A. Browning (ed.), *English Historical Documents 1660–1714,* Eyre and Spottiswoode, London, 1953, pp.113–14.

This is one of three Exclusion Bills introduced at the time of the Exclusion Crisis (1679–81), when the Whigs were trying to ensure that Charles II's Catholic brother, James, duke of York, would never succeed to the throne. None of them ever passed into law.

*An act for securing of the Protestant religion
by disabling James, duke of York,
to inherit the imperial crown of England and Ireland
and the dominions and territories thereunto belonging*

Whereas James, duke of York, is notoriously known to have been perverted from the Protestant to the popish religion, whereby not only great encouragement hath been given to the popish party to enter into and carry on most devilish and horrid plots and conspiracies for the destruction of his Majesty's sacred person and government, and for the extirpation of the true Protestant religion, but also, if the said duke should succeed to the imperial crown of this realm, nothing is more manifest than that a total change of religion within these kingdoms would ensue, for the prevention whereof be it therefore enacted . . . that the said James, duke of York, shall be and is by authority of this present Parliament excluded and made for ever incapable to inherit, possess or enjoy the imperial crown of this realm and of the kingdom of Ireland and the dominions and territories to them or either of them belonging, or to have, exercise or enjoy any dominion, power, jurisdiction or authority within the same kingdoms, dominions or any of them.

And be it further enacted . . . that if the said James, duke of York, shall at any time hereafter challenge, claim or attempt to possess or enjoy, or shall take upon him to use or exercise any dominion, power, authority or jurisdiction within the said kingdoms, dominions or any of them as king or chief magistrate of the same, that then he the said James, duke of York, for every such offence shall be deemed and adjudged guilty of high treason, and shall suffer the pains, penalties and forfeitures as in cases of high treason.

And further, that if any person or persons whatsoever shall assist, aid, maintain, abet or willingly adhere unto the said James, duke of York, in such his challenge, claim or attempt, or shall of themselves attempt or endeavour to put or bring the said James, duke of York, into the possession or exercise of any regal power, jurisdiction or authority within the kingdoms or dominions aforesaid, or shall by writing or preaching advisedly publish, maintain or declare that he hath any right, title or authority to exercise the office of king or chief magistrate of the kingdoms and dominions aforesaid, that then every such person shall be deemed and adjudged guilty of high treason, and shall suffer and undergo the pains, penalties and forfeitures aforesaid.

And be it further enacted . . . that if the said James, duke of York, shall at any time from and after the fifth day of November in the year of our Lord God one thousand six hundred and eighty return or come into or within any of the kingdoms or dominions aforesaid, that then he, the said James, duke of York, shall be deemed and adjudged guilty of high treason, and shall suffer the pains, penalties and forfeitures as in cases of high treason; and further, that if any person or persons whatsoever shall be aiding or assisting unto such return of the said James, duke of York, that then every such person shall be deemed and adjudged guilty of high treason, and shall suffer as in cases of high treason.

And be it further enacted . . . that the said James, duke of York, or any other person being guilty of any of the treasons aforesaid, shall not be capable of or receive benefit by any pardon otherwise than by Act of Parliament. . . .

And be it further enacted and declared, and it is hereby enacted and declared, that it shall and may be lawful to and for all magistrates, officers and other subjects whatsoever of the kingdoms and dominions aforesaid, and they are hereby enjoined and required, to apprehend and secure the said James, duke of York, and every other person offending in any of the premises, and with him or them in case of resistance to fight, and him or them by force to subdue, for all which actings and for so doing they are and shall be by virtue of this Act saved harmless and indemnified.

Provided, and be it hereby declared, that nothing in this Act contained shall be construed, deemed or adjudged to disable any person from inheriting or enjoying the imperial crown of the realms and dominions aforesaid (other than the said James, duke of York), but that in case the said James, duke of York, shall survive his now Majesty and the heirs of his Majesty's body, the said imperial crown shall descend to and be enjoyed by such person and persons successively during the lifetime of the said James, duke of York, as should have inherited and enjoyed the same in case the said James, duke of York, were naturally dead, anything in this Act contained to the contrary notwithstanding.

And be it enacted . . . that during the life of the said James, duke of York, this Act shall be given in charge at every assizes and general sessions of the peace within the kingdoms, dominions and territories aforesaid, and also shall be openly read in every cathedral, collegiate church, parish church and chapel within the aforesaid kingdoms, dominions and territories by the several and respective parsons, vicars, curates and readers thereof, who are hereby required, immediately after divine service in the forenoon, to read the same twice in every year, that is to say on the five and twentieth day of December and upon Easter Day, during the life of the said James, duke of York.

3
Proclamation of the Duke of Monmouth on taking the title of king (1685)

Source: Historical Manuscripts Commission, Bath MSS 2, pp.170–1, in A. Browning (ed.), *English Historical Documents 1660–1714*, Eyre and Spottiswoode, London, 1953, pp.119–20.

James, duke of Monmouth (1649–85), illegitimate son of Charles II, having been in exile in Brussels at the time of his father's death, landed at Lyme Regis on 11 June 1685. He presented himself as the Protestant claimant to the throne to which James II had peacefully succeeded. At Lyme Regis, Monmouth issued a first Declaration which many supporters considered too modest. After marching triumphantly to Taunton, Monmouth issued this second statement, a Proclamation in which he took the title of King.

JAMES R.

Whereas upon our first landing at Lyme in our county of Dorset on Thursday the 11th day of this instant month of June, we did publish a declaration in the name of ourself, by the name of James, duke of Monmouth, and the noblemen, gentlemen and others now in arms for defence and vindication of the Protestant religion, and of the laws, rights and privileges of England, from the invasion made upon them, and for delivering the kingdom from the usurpation and tyranny of James, duke of York: wherein amongst other things therein contained we did declare that out of the love we bear to the English nation, whose welfare and settlement we did infinitely prefer to whatever might concern ourselves, we would not at present insist upon our title, but leave the determination thereof to the authority of a Parliament legally chosen and acting with freedom; since which it hath pleased Almighty God to succeed and prosper us hitherto in a very eminent manner, and also disposed the hearts of our loving subjects that from all parts of the country they flock in unanimously for the defence of our person and of the righteous cause we are engaged in; by which we have been enabled to march from Lyme aforesaid unto our good town of Taunton to the terror and amazement of all our enemies round about us: and whereas as well during our said march as since our coming to Taunton aforesaid all our loving subjects have with warm and repeated solicitations importuned us to exert and take upon us our sovereign and royal authority of king as well as of the power of a general, that we might thereby be enabled to make use of the laws and statutes of the realm in conjunction with our arms for their safety and preservation; and have likewise earnestly implored us for their own sakes not to defer the execution of our kingly office to so late a period as is mentioned in the said declaration, for that it will in all probability render the progress of our arms more slow, and thereby give our enemies a longer season to harass and impoverish our kingdom: we could not but with great reluctancy incline to consent to anything that might seem to be a departure from our said declaration, and thereby raise any diffidence amongst the sober and virtuous, or give occasion to wicked and malicious men to arraign the sincerity of our intentions; but as the said clause in the said declaration was inserted under this prospect, to convince the world that we postponed all things to the safety and welfare of our people, and that we consulted not so much our own interest as their prosperity, being so convinced both from the circumstances of affairs and from united advice of all our loving people's petitions that it was absolutely necessary for their protection and defence that we should immediately insist upon our title to the crowns of England, Scotland, France and Ireland, and the dominions and territories thereunto belonging, as son and heir apparent to Charles the Second, king of England, our royal father lately deceased: we have therefore suffered ourselves to be prevailed upon, and have complied with the earnest importunities and necessities of our people, giving way to our being proclaimed king on the 20th day of this instant June at our town of Taunton aforesaid; which we hereby solemnly declare we have consented unto out of tenderness and for the interest of all our loving subjects, and not upon any motives arising from ourself.

And we do further declare and faithfully promise upon the word of a king that we will inviolably keep and perform all and every the articles, sentences and clauses specified and comprised in our said declaration for the good of our kingdom and benefit of all our loyal subjects; and that we will in our first Parliament pass into laws all methods therein contained for the relief, ease and safety of our people.

Given at our camp at Taunton,
the 21st day of June,
in the first year of our reign.

4
Scots Act of Security (1704)

Source: Acts of the Parliament of Scotland, xi, in A. Browning (ed.), English Historical Documents 1660–1714, Eyre and Spottiswoode, London, 1953, pp.677–80.

The Scottish political nation had, on the whole, welcomed the accession of William and Mary, and then of their successor Anne. But by 1704 a number of separate grievances against English behaviour had accumulated to the extent that the Scots parliament was threatening that they might choose a different monarch from the one in the line of succession envisaged by the English parliament. This threat is expressed in the Act of Security.

Our sovereign lady the queen's Majesty, with advice and consent of the Estates of Parliament, doth hereby statute and ordain, that in the event of her Majesty's death, or of the death of any of her Majesty's heirs or successors, kings or queens of this realm, this present Parliament or any other Parliament that shall be then in being shall not be dissolved by the said death, but shall and is hereby required and ordained if assembled to sit and act in manner aftermentioned notwithstanding of the said death; and if the said Parliament be under adjournment the time of the said death, it shall notwithstanding meet precisely at Edinburgh the twentieth day after the said death, excluding the day thereof, whether the day of the said adjournment be sooner or later. And it is further statute and ordained, that in case there shall be no Parliament in being at the time of the death aforesaid, then the Estates or members of the last preceding Parliament, without regard to any Parliament that may be indicated but never met nor constituted, shall meet at Edinburgh on the twentieth day after the said death, the day thereof excluded. . . .

And the said Estates of Parliament, appointed in case of the death aforesaid to continue or meet as above, are hereby authorized and empowered to act and administrate the government in manner aftermentioned, that is, that upon the death of her Majesty, leaving heirs of her own body or, failing thereof, lawful successors designed or appointed by her Majesty and the Estates of Parliament, or upon the death of any succeeding king or queen, leaving lawful heirs and successors as said is, the said Estates of Parliament are authorized and empowered, after having read to the said heir or successor the Claim of Right, and desired them to accept the government in the terms thereof, to require of and administrate to the said heir or lawful successors, by themselves or such as they shall commissionate, the coronation oath, and that with all convenient speed, not exceeding thirty days after the meeting of the said Estates, if the said heir or successor be within the isle of Britain, or, if without the same, not exceeding three months after the said meeting, in order to their exercising the regal power, conform to the declaration of the Estates containing the Claim of Right; and also in case of the said heir or successor their being under age, which as to the exercise of the government is hereby declared to be until their attaining to seventeen years complete, to provide for, order and settle, within the space of sixty days after the said meeting, a regency for the kingdom until the said heir or successor take the coronation oath, and do actually enter to the exercise of the government, the regent or regents to be so appointed always having the Claim of Right read to him or them as above, and he or they taking at his or their entry the coronation oath, and to continue for such space as the said Estates shall appoint. . . .

And further, upon the said death of her Majesty without heirs of her body or a successor lawfully designed and appointed as above, or in the case of any other king or queen thereafter succeeding and deceasing without lawful heir or successor, the aforesaid Estates of Parliament convened or meeting are hereby authorized and empowered to nominate and declare the successor to the imperial crown of this realm, and to settle the succession thereof upon the heirs of the said successor's body, the said successor and the heirs of the successor's body being always of the royal line of Scotland and of the true Protestant religion; providing always that the same be not successor to the crown of England, unless that in this present session of Parliament, or any other session of this or any ensuing Parliament during her Majesty's reign, there be such conditions of government settled and enacted as may secure the honour and sovereignty of this crown and kingdom, the freedom, frequency and power of Parliaments, the religion, liberty and trade of the nation from English or any foreign influence with power to the said meetings of Estates to add such further conditions of Government as they shall think necessary, the same being consistent with, and no way derogatory from those which shall be enacted in this and any other Session of Parliament during her Majesties Reign. And it is hereby declared, that the said meeting of Estates shall not have power to nominate the said Successor to the Crown of this Kingdom in the event above expressed during the first Twenty days after their meeting; Which Twenty days being elapsed, they shall proceed to make the said nomination with all convenient diligence.

And it is hereby expressly provided and declared, that it shall be high treason for any person or persons to administrate the coronation oath, or be witnesses to the administration thereof, but by the appointment of the Estates of Parliament in manner above mentioned, or to own or acknowledge any person as king or queen of this realm, in the event of her Majesty's decease leaving heirs of her own body, until they have sworn the coronation oath and accepted the crown in the terms of the Claim of Right, and in the event of her Majesty's decease without heirs of her body, until they swear the coronation oath and accept on the terms of the Claim of Right and of such other conditions of government as shall be settled in this or any ensuing Parliament, or added in the said meeting of Estates, and be thereupon declared and admitted as above, which crime shall be irremissible without consent of Parliament.

5
The *Code Paysan,* Brittany (1675)

Source: Louis Arthur de la Borderie, *La Révolte du papier timbré advenue en Bretagne en 1675,* Imprimerie Prud'homme, Saint Brieuc, 1884, pp.93–8. Translated by Arthur Marwick.

Already in 1673 there had been tension between the Breton Estates and the crown (see III.1(B)), which ended with the Estates making a large grant. The government introduced a new stamp tax on legal documents, riots broke out in Bordeaux, and when news of these reached Brittany the townsfolk of Rennes also took to the streets (women and children being actively involved). While the bourgeois militia refused to defend the tax offices, the Breton *parlement* actually condoned the demonstrations. Then some of the tax collectors, fearing they were about to lose what they had already paid to the crown, began to incite the rioters, hoping to stir the government into action. While the urban riots spread to other parts of Upper Brittany, in the agrarian west a rebellion began, with hordes of peasants attacking 'not only the royal officials, but the noble and ecclesiastical landlords as well' (Roger Mettam, *Power and Faction in Louis XIV's France* (1988), p.314). As has often been the way with popular revolts, the peasants created a mythical but terror-inspiring leader, Torrében, the Head-Smasher. In this document the Torrében rebels list their demands.

1. That the said fourteen parishes, united together for the liberty of the province, are deputing six of the most distinguished figures of their parishes to explain to the next meeting of the Estates the reasons for their rising . . .
2. That they [the inhabitants of the fourteen united parishes] will lay down their arms . . . until the stated time [Michaelmas day, 1675], by a special grace they are granting the gentlemen, by which they are summoned to return to their country houses as quickly as possible; failing which they will be deprived of the said grace.
3. That it shall be forbidden to sound the tocsin and to assemble armed men without the universal consent of the said union, on pain of the delinquents being hanged from the clock-towers . . .
4. That the rights of *champart* and *corveé* [i.e. labour services], claimed by the said gentlemen, shall be abolished, as a violation of Breton liberties.
5. That to confirm the peace and concord with the gentlemen and nobles living in the said parishes, there will be marriages with them, on condition that daughters of the nobility will choose husbands from the common people, so that their posterity shall be ennobled and thus able to

share equally in the benefits of their inheritance.

6. It is forbidden, on pain of being impaled on the fork, to give shelter to the *gabelle* and to her children, and to give them neither food nor any other commodity; but on the contrary to shoot her like a mad dog.

7. That there shall not be levied under all laws, more than one hundred sols per hogshead of non-Breton wine, and one écu for that made in the province, on the condition that landlords and pub-keepers cannot sell the former for more than five sols, and the latter for more than three sols, the pint.

8. That the money raised from the hearth tax will be used to buy tobacco, which will be distributed with the holy bread at the parish masses, for the satisfaction of the parishioners.

9. That the rectors, curates, and priests, being paid a stipend for serving their parishioners, shall not be able to claim any other tax or salary for their clerical functions.

10. That this justice will be exercised by competent people chosen by ourselves, who being paid, along with their officials, a stipend, shall not be able to claim attendance fees, on pain of punishment; – and that the stamp duty will be condemned by them and their successors, for which purpose all acts passed relating to the stamp duty will be written on separate paper and then burnt, in order to efface totally the memory of them.

11. That hunting shall be prohibited to all from the first day of March to mid-September . . .

12. That it will be lawful to go to whatever mill one wishes, and that the millers will be obliged to provide flour to the weight of the corn.

13. That the town of Quimper and others nearby shall be constrained by force of arms to approve and ratify these rules, on pain of being declared in violation of Breton liberty and their inhabitants punished wherever they are encountered; it is forbidden to furnish them with any commodity or merchandise until this point is fulfilled, on pain of *torrében* [i.e. of having your head smashed].

14. That these rules shall be read and published during sermons at the major masses and at all cross-roads and in the parishes, and affixed to special crosses which will be erected.

Signed TORRÉBEN and the inhabitants

6
Articles of Impeachment against Henry Sacheverell
(1710)

Source: Journals of the House of Commons, XVI, pp.257–8, reprinted in A. Browning (ed.), *English Historical Documents 1660–1714*, Eyre and Spottiswoode, London, 1953, pp.206–7.

In the reign of Queen Anne party politics took on a new dimension and, integrated with activists and their often rowdy followers in the towns, emerged as a potential threat to stability. The Whigs supported the Protestant succession, whilst the Tories tended to oppose it. Dr Henry Sacheverell (1674?–1724) was an Anglican, and strongly Tory, cleric. The Whig government considered his sermons seditious and, at the end of February 1710, he was put on trial in Westminster Hall. These Articles specify the charges against him.

First. He, the said Henry Sacheverell, in his said sermon preached at Saint Paul's, doth suggest and maintain that the necessary means used to bring about the said happy revolution were odious and unjustifiable, that his late Majesty in his declaration disclaimed the least imputation of resistance, and that to impute resistance to the said revolution is to cast black and odious colours upon his late Majesty and the said revolution.

Secondly. He, the said Henry Sacheverell, in his said sermon preached at Saint Paul's, doth suggest and maintain that the aforesaid toleration granted by law is unreasonable, and the allowance of it unwarrantable; and asserts that he is a false brother with relation to God, religion or the Church who defends toleration and liberty of conscience. . . .

Thirdly. He, the said Henry Sacheverell, in his said sermon preached at Saint Paul's, doth falsely and seditiously suggest and assert that the Church of England is in a condition of great peril and adversity under her Majesty's administration, and in order to arraign and blacken the said vote or resolution of both Houses of Parliament, approved by her Majesty as aforesaid, he, in opposition thereto, doth suggest the Church to be in danger, and as a parallel mentions a vote that the person of King Charles the First was voted to be out of danger at the same time that his murderers were conspiring his death, thereby wickedly and maliciously insinuating that the members of both Houses who passed the said vote were then conspiring the ruin of the Church.

Fourthly. He, the said Henry Sacheverell, in his said sermons and books, doth falsely and maliciously suggest that her Majesty's administration, both in ecclesiastical and civil affairs, tends to the destruction of the constitution, and that there are men of characters and stations in Church and State who are

171

false brethren, and do themselves weaken, undermine and betray, and do encourage and put it in the power of others, who are professed enemies, to overturn and destroy, the constitution and establishment; . . . and that his said malicious and seditious suggestions may make the stronger impression upon the minds of her Majesty's subjects, he, the said Henry Sacheverell, doth wickedly wrest and pervert divers texts and passages of Holy Scripture.

All which crimes and misdemeanours the Commons are ready to prove, not only by the general scope of the same sermons or books, but likewise by several clauses, sentences and expressions in the said sermons or books contained; and that he, the said Henry Sacheverell, by preaching the sermons and publishing the books aforesaid, did abuse his holy function, and hath most grievously offended against the peace of her Majesty, her crown and dignity, the rights and liberties of the subject, the laws and statutes of this kingdom, and the prosperity and good government of the same. And the said Commons by protestation, saving to themselves the liberty of exhibiting at any time hereafter any other article of impeachment against the said Henry Sacheverell, and also of replying to his answers or any of them, and of offering proofs of all the premises or any of them, or of any other article of impeachment that shall be exhibited by them, as the case, according to the course of Parliament, shall require, do pray that he, the said Henry Sacheverell, may be put to answer to all and every the premises, and that such proceeding, examination, trial, judgment and exemplary punishment may be thereupon had and executed as is agreeable to law and justice.

7
Colbert's Summary of royal finances (1680)

Source: R. Mettam, *Government and Society in Louis XIV's France*, Macmillan, London, Basingstoke, 1977, pp.90–1. Translated from French.

Some small inaccuracies have been identified in this list. It was not intended to be a working document but simply a brief digest of income and expenditure which Louis XIV could carry about in his pocket. (See also above III.1.)

V. Receipts and expenditure:

Receipts

1	Tax farms[1]	29,318,762
2	*Recettes générales*[2]	23,894,659
3	*Recettes générales* and free gifts from the *pays d'états*	7,369,411

4	Woods and forests	865,736
5	Extraordinary sums[3]	13,961,374
6	Anticipation of receipts for the year 1681	16,349,414

Total receipts for the year 1680 — 91,759,356

Expenditure

The King's household	763,338
Victualling account	1,917,413
Extraordinary household expenses	2,246,803
Butchery account	398,510
Royal mews	817,489
Purchase of horses	12,000
Treasurer of the Offertory	88,437
Justice of the household	61,050
Royal guard	187,335
Swiss guard	69,303
Hunting and falconry	342,044
Wolf hunting	34,293
The Queen's household	1,381,128
Madame la Dauphine's household	867,498
Monsieur's household[4]	1,198,000
Madame's household	252,000
Favours and rewards	193,366
Ready cash for the King's personal use	2,030,092
Building and maintenance of royal houses	8,513,804
Swiss regiment	262,000
Garrisons	2,345,269
Military supplies	1,509,502
Bread ration	86,571
Extraordinary military expenses	31,233,986
Bounties to commanders of troops	825,616
Navy	4,928,773
Galleys	2,869,223
Fortifications	1,603,386
Embassies	810,100
The Bastille	189,330
Salaries	1,215,700
Emoluments of officials	2,302,427
Emoluments of marshals of France	276,150
Ordonnances de comptant for rewards	2,176,988
Ordonnances de comptant for secret business	2,224,969

Other emoluments	491,400
Roads and bridges	300,364
Paving of Paris	58,258
Payments of back-interest on government	
bonds (*rentes*)	1,182,013
Reimbursements	10,792,927
Commerce	324,281
Interest on loans and expenses of	
tax-collection	2,389,200
Small gifts paid by ordinance	784,813
Travel	406,892

Total 96,318,016

Deficit for the year 1680   4,558,660

¹ This includes the salt tax and customs dues.
² Direct taxes from the *pays d'élections*.
³ A variety of miscellaneous debts from individuals and official bodies, and the income from the sale of the newly created *rentes* of 1679.
⁴ 'Monsieur' was the courtesy title of the king's brother, the duc d'Orléans.

8
Saint-Simon describes Louis XIV and his court

Source: O. and P. Ranum (eds), *The Century of Louis XIV: Selected Documents*, Macmillan, London and Basingstoke, 1972, pp.81–3. Translated from French.

Louis de Rouvroy, duc de Saint-Simon (1675–1755) wrote what was to become one of the most famous records of the court of Louis XIV. His *Memoirs*, completed long after Louis' death, were first published in the nineteenth century. Though Saint-Simon was an eyewitness of much that he describes with colour and flamboyance, the *Memoirs* are a conscious literary work and not without bias. His usual technique was to state all a character's good points first and then the bad. The latter often outweighed the former.

Frequent fetes, private walks at Versailles, and excursions were means which the King seized upon in order to single out or to mortify [individuals] by naming the persons who should be there each time, and in order to keep each person assiduous and attentive to pleasing him. He sensed that he lacked by far enough favors to distribute in order to create a continuous effect. Therefore he substituted imaginary favors for real ones, through jealousy – little

174

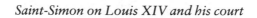

Figure 5 Print of Louis XIV in masque costume as Le Roi Soleil.

preferences which were shown daily, and one might say at each moment – [and] through his artfulness. The hopes to which these little preferences and these honors gave birth, and the deference which resulted from them – no one was more ingenious than he in unceasingly inventing these sorts of things. Marly, eventually, was of great use to him in this respect; and Trianon, where everyone, as a matter of fact, could go pay court to him, but where ladies had the honor of eating with him and where they were chosen at each meal; the candlestick which he had held for him each evening at bedtime by a courtier whom he wished to honor, and always from among the most worthy of those present, whom he named aloud upon coming out from saying his prayers. The official jerkin was another of these inventions; it was blue, lined with red, with red cuffs and vest, embroidered with a magnificent golden design with a bit of silver, reserved for these clothes. There was only a fixed number of them, which included the King, his family, and the princes of the blood: but the latter, like the rest of the courtiers, obtained one only when one fell vacant. The most distinguished persons at court by themselves or through an influential courtier asked the King for them, and it was an honor to receive one. The secretary of state for the King's household would send a commission for one, and none of them [the secretaries of state] was entitled to have one.[1] They were conceived for those, a very small number, who were entitled to follow the King on excursions from Saint-Germain to Versailles without being named [on a list], and when that practice ceased, these clothes also ceased to confer any privileges, except that of being worn even when in mourning at court or for one's family, provided the mourning was not deep or that it was near its end, and also at times when it was forbidden to wear gold and silver. I never saw it worn by the King, Monseigneur [the Dauphin], or Monsieur [the King's brother], but very often by the three sons of Monseigneur and by all the other princes; and until the King's death, as soon as one fell vacant, the question arose who among the most notable persons at court would have it, and if a young lord obtained it, it was a great honor. One could never finish enumerating the attention he paid in order to have a great many persons at court, and the various devices of this sort which followed one upon the other as the King advanced in age and as the fêtes changed or decreased in number.

Not only was he sensitive to the continual presence of the distinguished, but he was also so for those on lesser levels. He would look to the right and to the left upon rising, upon going to bed, during his meals, while passing through apartments, and in his gardens of Versailles, where only courtiers had the right to follow him; he saw and noticed everyone; no one escaped him, even those who did not even hope to be seen. He very clearly observed to himself the absences of those who were always at court, those of passersby who came there more or less often; he pieced together the general or personal causes of these absences and did not lose the slightest opportunity to act accordingly toward them. It was a demerit for some, and for all those who were the most distinguished, not to make the court their habitual residence, [a demerit] for others to come there rarely, and a sure disgrace for those who never, or almost never, came. When it was a question of something for them: 'I do not know him,' he would reply proudly; about those who rarely appeared: 'He is a man whom I never see,' and those sentences were irrevocable. It was another crime not to go to Fontainebleau, which he considered like Versailles, and for certain people not to make a request to go to Marly, some each time, others often, although he did not plan to take them there, some always or others often;[2] but, if one were in a position to go there at all times, one needed a valid reason to be excused, men and women alike. Above all he could not stand people who enjoyed being in Paris. He could rather easily bear those who liked their country estates; yet even there one had to restrain oneself or to have taken precautions before going to spend more than a short time there.

[1] That is, they were reserved for nobles, and no man of the robe, even at the highest level, was eligible for one.

[2] That is, he never intended to invite some of these suppliants; the others rarely were invited.

9
The Revocation of the Edict of Nantes (1685)

Source: O. and P. Ranum (eds), *The Century of Louis XIV: Selected Documents*, Macmillan, London and Basingstoke, 1972, pp.359–63. Translated from French.

French Protestants (Huguenots) had been allowed to practise their religion freely in many parts of France under Henri IV and Louis XIII. Louis XIV had subjected them to increasing harassment before 1685. The references to quartering soldiers in clause V describe one of the means he used to browbeat Protestants. The Revocation was generally welcomed by Catholic powers but it confirmed Protestant nations, such as the Dutch and English, in their hostility to France. The implicit threat it posed assisted William of Orange in maintaining an anti-French war coalition.

Edict of the King
Prohibiting any further public exercise of the Pretended Reformed Religion [P.R.R.] in his kingdom. Registered in the Chamber of the *Vacations*,[1] Oct. 22, 1685.
Louis, by the Grace of God, King of France and Navarre; to all present and to come, greeting. King Henry the Great, our grandfather of glorious memory,

being desirous that the peace which he had procured for his subjects after the grievous losses they had sustained in the course of domestic and foreign wars, should not be troubled on account of the P.R.R. as had happened in the reigns of the kings his predecessors, by his edict granted at Nantes in the month of April 1598, regulated the procedure to be adopted with regard to those of the said religion and the places in which they might meet for public worship, established extraordinary judges to administer justice to them, and, in fine, even provided by particular articles, for whatever could be thought necessary for maintaining the tranquillity of his kingdom and for diminishing mutual aversion between the members of the two religions, so as to put himself in a better condition to labour, as he had resolved to do, for the reunion to the Church of those who had so lightly withdrawn from it. And as the intention of the king, our grandfather, was frustrated by his sudden death, and as even the execution of the said edict was interrupted during the minority of the late king, our most honoured lord and father of glorious memory, by new enterprises on the part of the said persons of the P.R.R. who gave occasion to their being deprived of divers advantages accorded to them by the said edict: Nevertheless the king, our said late lord and father, in the exercise of his usual clemency, granted them yet another edict at Nîmes in July 1629, by means of which tranquillity being established anew, the said late king, animated with the same spirit and the same zeal for religion as the king our said grandfather, had resolved to take advantage of this repose for attempting to put his said pious design into execution, but foreign wars having supervened soon after, so that the kingdom being seldom tranquil, from 1635 to the truce concluded in 1684, with the powers of Europe, nothing more could be done for the advantage of religion beyond diminishing the number of places for the public exercise of the P.R.R. by interdicting such as were found established to the prejudice of the dispositions made by the edicts, and by the suppression of the *Chambres mi-partie*, these having been appointed provisionally only. God having at last permitted that our people should enjoy perfect repose, and that we, no longer occupied in protecting them from our enemies, should be able to profit by this truce, which we have ourselves facilitated, by applying our whole endeavours to the discovery of the means of accomplishing the designs of our said grandfather and father, adopted as these have been by ourselves since our succession to the crown. And now we see with the thankful acknowledgement we justly owe to God, that our endeavours have reached their proposed end, inasmuch as the better and the greater part of our subjects of the said P.R.R. have embraced the Catholic. And inasmuch as by this the execution of the Edict of Nantes and of all that has ever been ordained in favour of the said P.R.R. remains useless, we have determined that we can do nothing better in order wholly to obliterate the memory of the troubles, the confusion, and the evils which the progress of this false religion has caused in this kingdom, and which furnished occasion for the said edict and to so many previous and subsequent edicts and declarations, than entirely to revoke the said Edict of Nantes, with the particular articles accorded as a sequel to it, and all that has since been done in favour of the said religion.

I. We give you to wit that for these causes and others us thereto moving, and of our certain knowledge, full power, and royal authority, we have by this present perpetual and irrevocable edict, suppressed and revoked, suppress and revoke, the edict of our said grandfather, given at Nantes in April 1598, in its whole extent, together with the particular articles agreed upon in the month of May following, and the letters patent expedited upon the same; and the edict given at Nîmes in July 1629; we declare them null and void, together with all concessions made by them as well as by other edicts, declarations, and *arrêts* [rulings], in favour of the said persons of the P.R.R. of whatever nature they may be, the which shall remain in like manner as if they had never been granted, and in consequence we desire and it is our pleasure that all the temples of those of the said P.R.R. situate in our kingdom, countries, territories and lordships under our crown, shall be demolished without delay.

II. We forbid our subjects of the P.R.R. to meet any more for the exercise of the said religion in any place or private house under any pretext whatever, even of *exercices réels* [royal business], or of *bailliages* [organization of bailiwicks], although the said exercises may have been maintained hitherto in virtue of orders of our council.

III. We likewise forbid all noblemen of what condition soever, to have the religious exercises in their houses and feudalities, the whole under penalty, to be exacted of all our said subjects who shall engage in the said exercise, of confiscation of body and goods.

IV. We enjoin all ministers of the said P.R.R. who do not choose to become converts and to embrace the Catholic, Apostolic, and Roman religion, to leave our kingdom and the territories subject to us within fifteen days from the publication of our present edict, without leave to reside therein beyond that period, or during the said fifteen days, to engage in any preaching, exhortation, or any other function, on pain of being sent to the galleys.

V. We desire that such of the said ministers as shall convert themselves, continue to enjoy during their lives, and their widows after their decease, during their viduity [widowhood], the same exemptions from taxes, and from giving quarters to soldiers, which they enjoyed during the exercise of their functions as ministers; and, moreover, we shall cause to be paid to the said ministers a life annuity of one-third greater amount than they had as ministers, half of which annuity shall be continued to their wives after their death, as long as they shall remain in viduity.

VI. That if any of the said ministers wish to become advocates, or to take the degree of Doctor of Laws, it is our will and pleasure that they enjoy dispensation from three years of the studies prescribed by our declarations, and that after having undergone the ordinary examinations, and been found to have the requisite capacity, they be admitted as doctors, on payment of the half only of the usual dues received on that occasion at each of the universities.

VII. We forbid private schools for the instruction of the children of the said P.R.R. and in general all things whatever which can be regarded as a concession of whatever kind in favour of the said religion.

VIII. As for children who may be born of persons of the said P.R.R. we desire that from henceforth they be baptised by the parish priests. We enjoin parents to send them to the churches for that purpose, under penalty of five hundred livres of fine, to be increased as the case shall happen; and thereafter the children shall be brought up in the Catholic, Apostolic, and Roman religion, which we expressly enjoin the local magistrates to see being done.

IX. And in the exercise of our clemency towards our subjects of the said P.R.R. who have emigrated from our kingdoms, lands, and territories subject to us, previous to the publication of our present edict, it is our will and pleasure that in case of their returning within the period of four months from the day of the said publication, they may, and it shall be lawful for them to reenter into possession of their property, and to enjoy the same, as if they had all along remained there; on the contrary, that the property of those who during that space of four months shall not have returned into our kingdom, lands, and territories subject to us, and which property they shall have abandoned, shall remain and be confiscated in consequence of our declaration of the 20th of August last.

X. We repeat our most express prohibitions to all our subjects of the said P.R.R. against them, their wives and children, leaving our said kingdom, lands, and territories subject to us, or transporting their goods and effects, therefrom under penalty, as respects the men, of being sent to the galleys, and as respects the women, of confiscation of body and goods.

XI. It is our will and intention that the declarations rendered against the relapsed, shall be executed according to their form and tenor.

XII. As for the rest, liberty is granted to the said persons of the P.R.R. while waiting until it shall please God to enlighten them as well as others, to remain in the cities and places of our kingdom, lands, and territories subject to us, and there to continue their commerce, and to enjoy their possessions, without being subjected to molestation or hindrance, under pretext of the said P.R.R. on condition, as said is, of not engaging in the exercise, or of meeting under pretext of prayers, or of the religious services of the said religion, of whatever nature these may be, under the penalties above mentioned of confiscation of body and goods: Thus do we give in charge to our trusty and well-beloved counsellors, &c. Given at Fontainebleau in the month of October, the year of grace one thousand six hundred and eighty-five and of our reign the forty-third.

Signed "LOUIS *visa* LE TELLIER," and further down, "By the King, COLBERT." And sealed with the great seal, on green wax, with red and green strings.

Registered, heard, &c. at Paris, in the Chamber of Vacations, the 22d of October, 1685   Signed DE LA BAUNE

---

[1] Used when the *parlement* was not sitting.

10
The Test Act (1673)

Source: D. Oswald Dykes (ed.), *Source Book of Constitutional History from 1660*, Longmans, Green and Co., London, New York, Toronto, 1930, pp.247–50.

This act was passed in 1672 and came into operation in 1673. Parliament extracted this harsh measure, which prevented Catholics from taking any part in public life, from Charles II in return for a vote of supply for the Dutch war. The immediate consequence was that the Catholic heir to the throne, James, Duke of York, resigned his post as Lord High Admiral. Charles, who was sympathetic to Catholicism and had recently concluded the Treaty of Dover with Louis XIV, had attempted to alleviate the disabilities of all non-Anglicans by a Declaration of Indulgence. The Test Act represented a direct reversal of that policy and a defiance of the king's wishes.

An Act for preventing Dangers which may happen from Popish Recusants.

For preventing Dangers which may happen from Popish Recusants, and Quieting the Minds of his Majesty's good Subjects; Be it enacted by the King's most excellent Majesty, by and with the Advice and Consent of the Lords Spiritual and Temporal, and the Commons, in this present Parliament assembled, and by Authority of the same, That all and every Person or Persons, as well Peers as Commoners, that shall bear any Office or Offices Civil or Military, or shall receive any Pay, Salary, Fee, or Wages, by reason of any Patent or Grant from his Majesty, or shall have Command or Place of Trust from or under his Majesty, or from any of his Majesty's Predecessors, or by his or their Authority, or by Authority derived from him or them, within the Realm of England, Dominion of Wales, or Town of Berwick upon Tweed, or in his Majesty's Navy, or in the several Islands of Jersey and Guernsey, or shall be of the Household, or in the Service or Employment of his Majesty, or of his Royal Highness the Duke of York, who shall inhabit, reside, or be within the City of London or Westminster, or within Thirty miles distant from the same, at the First day of Easter Term that shall be in the year of our Lord One thousand six hundred seventy-three, or at any time during the said Term, all and every the said Person and Persons shall personally appear before the end of the said Term, or of Trinity Term next following, in his Majesty's High Court of Chancery, or in his Majesty's Court of King's Bench, and there in public and open Court, between the Hours of Nine of the Clock and Twelve in the forenoon, take the several Oaths of Supremacy and Allegiance (which Oath of Allegiance is contained in the Statute made in the

Third year of King James [I]), by Law established; and during the time of the taking thereof by the said Person and Persons, all Pleas and Proceedings in the said respective Courts shall cease; and that all and every of the said respective Persons and Officers, not having taken the said Oaths in the said respective Courts aforesaid, shall, on or before the First day of August, One thousand six hundred seventy-three, at the Quarter Sessions for that County or Place where he or they shall be, inhabit, or reside on the Twentieth day of May, take the said Oaths in open Court between the said hours of Nine and Twelve of the Clock in the forenoon; and the said respective Officers aforesaid shall also receive the Sacrament of the Lord's Supper, according to the Usage of the Church of England, at or before the First day of August in the year of our Lord One thousand six hundred and seventy-three, in some Parish Church, upon some Lord's Day, commonly called Sunday, immediately after Divine Service and Sermon. . . .

III. And every of the said Persons in the respective Court where he takes the said Oaths shall first deliver a Certificate of such his receiving the said Sacrament as aforesaid, under the Hands of the respective Minister and Churchwarden, and shall then make Proof of the Truth thereof by two credible witnesses at the least, upon oath; all which shall be inquired of, and put upon record in the respective Courts.

IV. And be it further enacted by the Authority aforesaid, That all and every the Person or Persons aforesaid, that do or shall neglect or refuse to take the said Oaths and Sacrament in the said Courts and Places, and at the respective times aforesaid, shall be *ipso facto* adjudged uncapable and disabled in Law, to all intents and purposes whatsoever, to have, occupy, or enjoy the said Office or Offices, Employment or Employments, or any part of them, or any matter or thing aforesaid, or any profit or advantage appertaining to them, or any of them; and every such Office and Place, Employment and Employments, shall be void, and is hereby adjudged void.

V. And be it further enacted, That all and every such Person or Persons that shall neglect or refuse to take the said Oaths or the Sacrament as aforesaid, within the times, and in the places aforesaid and in the manner aforesaid, and yet after such neglect or refusal shall execute any of the said Offices or Employments after the said times expired, wherein he or they ought to have taken the same, and being thereupon lawfully convicted, in or upon any Information, Presentment or Indictment, in any of the King's Courts at Westminster, or at the Assizes, every such Person and Persons shall be disabled from thenceforth to sue or use any Action, Bill, Plaint, or Information in course of Law, or to prosecute any Suit in any Court of Equity, or to be Guardian of any Child, or Executor or Administrator of any person, or capable of any Legacy or Deed of Gift, or to bear any Office within this Realm of England, Dominion of Wales, or Town of Berwick upon Tweed; and shall forfeit the sum of Five hundred Pounds, to be recovered by him or them that shall sue for the same, to be prosecuted by any Action of Debt, Suit, Bill,

Plaint, or Information, in any of his Majesty's Courts at Westminster, wherein no Essoin [excuse for absence], Protection, or Wager of Law, shall lie.

VIII. And be it further enacted, That if any Person or Persons, not bred up by his or their Parent or Parents from their Infancy in the Popish Religion, and professing themselves to be Popish Recusants, shall breed up, instruct or educate his or their Child or Children, or suffer them to be instructed or educated in the Popish Religion, every such Person being thereof convicted, shall be from thenceforth disabled of bearing any Office or Place of Trust or Profit in Church or State: And all such Children as shall be so brought up, instructed or educated, are and shall be hereby disabled of bearing any such Office or Place of Trust or Profit, until he and they shall be perfectly reconciled and converted to the Church of England, and shall take the Oaths of Supremacy and Allegiance aforesaid before the Justices of the Peace in the open Quarter Sessions of the Country or Place where they shall inhabit, and thereupon receive the Sacrament of the Lord's Supper after the Usage of the Church of England, and obtain a Certificate thereof under the Hands of two or more of the said Justices of the Peace.

IX. And be it further enacted by the Authority aforesaid, That at the same time when the Persons concerned in this Act shall take the aforesaid Oaths of Supremacy and Allegiance, they shall likewise make and subscribe this Declaration following, under the same Penalties and Forfeitures as by this Act is appointed;

'I, A.B., do declare, That I do believe that there is not any Transubstantiation[1] in the Sacrament of the Lord's Supper, or in the Elements of Bread and Wine, at or after the Consecration thereof by any Person whatsoever.'

XIV. Provided also, That any Person who by his or her Neglect or Refusal, according to this Act, shall lose or forfeit any Office, may be capable by a new Grant of the said Office, or of any other, and to have and hold the same again, such Person taking the said Oaths, and doing all other things required by this Act, so as such Office be not granted to, and actually enjoyed by, some other Person at the time of the regranting thereof.

---

[1] Catholic belief in the conversion of bread and wine, after consecration at Mass, into the actual body and blood of Christ.

11
The Declaration for Liberty of Conscience (1687)

Source: D. Oswald Dykes (ed.), *Source Book of Constitutional History from 1660*, Longmans, Green and Co., London, New York, Toronto, 1930, pp.247–50.

James II regarded Nonconformists as his natural allies: they suffered almost as much as Catholics from the Test Acts. Their lack of enthusiasm for his cause during the next year, when England was invaded by William of Orange, showed that he had seriously miscalculated.

His Majesty's gracious Declaration to all his loving subjects for liberty of conscience

JAMES R.

'It having pleased Almighty God not only to bring Us to the Imperial Crowns of these Kingdoms through the greatest difficulties, but to preserve Us by a more than ordinary Providence upon the Throne of our Royal Ancestors; there is nothing now that We so earnestly desire, as to establish our Government on such a foundation as may make Our subjects happy, and unite them to us by inclination as well as duty: Which We think can be done by no means so effectually as by granting to them the free exercise of their Religion for the time to come, and add that to the perfect enjoyment of their Property, which has never been in any case invaded by Us, since Our coming to the Crown; which being the two things men value most, shall ever be preserved in these Kingdoms, during Our reign over them, as the truest methods of their peace and Our glory. We cannot but heartily wish, as it will easily be believed, that all the people of Our Dominions were members of the Catholic Church; yet We humbly thank Almighty God, it is, and hath of long time been Our constant sense and opinion (which upon divers occasions We have declared) that Conscience ought not to be constrained, nor people forced in matters of mere Religion: It has ever been directly contrary to Our inclination, as We think it is to the interest of Government, which it destroys by spoiling trade, depopulating countries, and discouraging strangers; and finally, that it never obtained the End for which it was employed; And in this We are confirmed by the reflections We have made upon the conduct of the four last reigns. For after all the frequent and pressing endeavours that were used in each of them, to reduce these Kingdoms to an exact Conformity in Religion, it is visible the success has not answered the design, and that the difficulty is invincible. We therefore, out of Our Princely care and affection unto all Our loving Subjects, that they may live at ease and quiet, and for the increase of trade, and encouragement of strangers, have thought fit by virtue of Our Royal Prerogative to issue forth this Our Declaration of Indulgence; making no doubt of the concurrence of Our two Houses of Parliament, when We shall think it convenient for them to meet.

'In the first place We do declare, That We will protect and maintain Our Archbishops, Bishops, and Clergy, and all other Our subjects of the Church of England, in the free exercise of their Religion, as by law established, and in the quiet and full enjoyment of all their possessions, without any molestation or disturbance whatsoever.

'We do likewise declare, that it is Our Royal Will and Pleasure, That from henceforth the execution of all and all manner of penal laws in matters ecclesiastical, for not coming to Church, or not receiving the Sacrament, or for any other non-conformity to the Religion established, or for, or by reason of, the exercise of Religion in any manner whatsoever, be immediately suspended; and the further execution of the said penal laws and every of them is hereby suspended.

'And to the end that by the liberty hereby granted, the peace and security of Our Government in the practice thereof, may not be endangered, We have thought fit, and do hereby straightly charge and command all Our loving subjects, That, as We do freely give them leave to meet and serve God, after their own way and manner, be it in private houses or places purposely hired or built for that use; so that they take especial care that nothing be preached or taught amongst them which may any ways tend to alienate the hearts of Our people from Us or Our Government; and that their meetings and assemblies be peaceably, openly, and publicly held, and all persons freely admitted to them; and that they do signify and make known to some one or more of the next Justices of the Peace what place or places they set apart for those uses.

'And that all Our subjects may enjoy such their Religious assemblies with greater assurance and protection, We have thought it requisite, and do hereby command, that no disturbance of any kind be made or given unto them, under pain of Our displeasure, and to be further proceeded against with the utmost severity.

'And for as much as We are desirous to have the benefit of the service of Our loving subjects, which by the Law of Nature is inseparably annexed to, and inherent in, Our Royal Person: and that none of Our subjects may for the future be under any discouragement or disability, (who are otherways well inclined and fit to serve Us) by reason of some oaths or tests that have usually been administered on such occasions: We do hereby further declare, That it is Our Royal Will and Pleasure That the oaths commonly called, *The oaths of Supremacy and Allegiance*, and also the several Tests and Declarations mentioned in the Acts of Parliament made in the 25th and 30th years of the reign of Our late Royal Brother King Charles the Second, shall not at any time hereafter be required to be taken, declared, or subscribed by any person or persons whatsoever, who is, or shall be, employed in any office or place of trust, either civil or military, under Us or in Our Government. And We do further declare it to be Our Pleasure and Intention from time to time hereafter, to grant Our Royal Dispensations under Our Great Seal to all Our loving subjects so to be Employed, who shall not take the said oaths, or subscribe or declare the said tests or declarations in the above-mentioned Acts and every of them.

'And to the end that all Our loving subjects may receive and enjoy the full benefit and advantage of Our gracious Indulgence hereby intended, and may be acquitted and discharged from all pains, penalties, forfeitures, and disabilities by them or any of them incurred or forfeited, or which they shall or may at any time hereafter be liable to, for or by reason of their Non-conformity, or the exercise of their Religion, and from all suits, troubles, or disturbances for the same: We do hereby give Our free and ample Pardon unto all Non-conformists, Recusants,[1] and other Our loving subjects, for all crimes and things by them committed or done contrary to the penal laws formerly made, relating to Religion, and the profession and exercise thereof. Hereby Declaring that this Our Royal Pardon and Indemnity shall be as good and effectual to all intents and purposes as if every individual person had been therein particularly named, or had particular pardons under Our Great Seal, which We do likewise declare, shall from time to time be granted unto any person or persons desiring the same; Willing and requiring Our Judges, Justices, and other Officers, to take notice of and obey Our Royal Will and Pleasure herein before declared.

'And although the freedom and assurance We have hereby given in relation to Religion and Property might be sufficient to remove from the minds of Our loving subjects all fears and jealousies in relation to either; Yet We have thought fit further to declare, That We will maintain them in all their properties and possessions, as well of Church and Abbey lands, as in any other their lands and properties whatsoever.

'Given at our Court at Whitehall, the Fourth day of April, 1687. In the Third year of Our Reign.'

[1] Refusers: those who rejected the Anglican rite.

12
The Bill of Rights (1689)

Source: D. Oswald Dykes (ed.), *Source Book of Constitutional History from 1660*, Longmans, Green and Co., London, New York, Toronto, 1930, pp.105–8.

This bill was based on the Declaration of Rights made in February, 1689, '. . . King James the second having abdicated the government . . .'. The

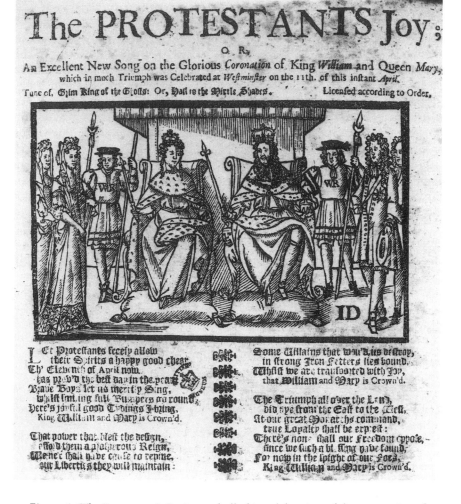

Figure 6 'The Protestant's Joy' . . . a ballad in celebration of the coronation of William and Mary, April 21st, 1689.

members of the body which enacted it had been elected in the constituencies but not summoned by royal writ, so it was a 'convention' rather than a 'parliament'. Strictly speaking, if James had abdicated, his infant Catholic son should have been his heir. Instead the crown was jointly vested in his eldest Protestant daughter by his first marriage and her husband: William and Mary, prince and princess of Orange. Should they die without children, Mary's younger Protestant sister Anne would succeed.

An Act declaring the Rights and Liberties of the
Subject, and Settling the Succession of the Crown.
(I Wm. & Mary, sess. 2, cap. 2)

Whereas the Lords Spiritual and Temporal, and Commons, assembled at Westminster, lawfully, fully, and freely representing all the Estates of the People of this Realm, did upon the Thirteenth day of February in the year of our Lord one thousand six hundred eighty-eight present unto their Majesties then called and known by the names and style of William and Mary, Prince and Princess of Orange, being present in their proper persons, a certain Declaration in writing, made by the said Lords and Commons in the words following, viz.—

Whereas the late King James the Second, by the assistance of divers evil Councillors, Judges, and Ministers employed by him, did endeavour to subvert and extirpate the Protestant Religion, and the laws and liberties of this Kingdom;

1. By assuming and exercising a power of Dispensing with and Suspending of laws, and the execution of laws, without consent of Parliament;
2. By committing and prosecuting divers worthy Prelates, for humbly petitioning to be excused from concurring to the said assumed power;
3. By issuing and causing to be executed a Commission under the Great Seal for erecting a Court called the Court of Commissioners for Ecclesiastical Causes;
4. By levying Money for and to the use of the Crown, by pretence of Prerogative, for other time, and in other manner, than the same was granted by Parliament;
5. By raising and keeping a Standing Army within the Kingdom in time of Peace, without consent of Parliament, and quartering Soldiers contrary to law;
6. By causing several good subjects, being Protestants, to be disarmed, at the same time when Papists were both armed and employed contrary to law;
7. By violating the freedom of election of Members to serve in Parliament;
8. By Prosecutions in the Court of King's Bench, for matters and causes cognizable only in Parliament; and by divers other arbitrary and illegal courses;
9. And whereas of late years, partial, corrupt, and unqualified persons have been returned and served on Juries in trials, and particularly divers Jurors in trials for High Treason, which were not Freeholders;
10. And excessive Bail hath been required of persons committed in criminal cases, to elude the benefit of the laws made for the liberty of the subjects;
11. And excessive Fines have been imposed; and illegal and cruel punishments have been inflicted;
12. And several grants and promises made of Fines and Forfeitures, before any conviction or judgment against the persons, upon whom the same were to be levied.

All which are utterly and directly contrary to the known laws and statutes and freedom of this Realm.

And whereas the said late King James the Second having abdicated the Government and the Throne being thereby vacant, His Highness the Prince of Orange (whom it hath pleased Almighty God to make the glorious Instrument of Delivering this Kingdom from Popery and arbitrary power) did (by the advice of the Lords Spiritual and Temporal and divers principal Persons of the Commons) cause Letters to be written to the Lords Spiritual and Temporal, being Protestants; and other Letters to the several Counties, Cities, Universities, Boroughs, and Cinque-ports,[1] for the choosing of such persons to represent them, as were of right to be sent to Parliament, to meet and sit at Westminster upon the two and twentieth day of January in this year one thousand six hundred eighty and eight, in order to such an Establishment as that their Religion, Laws, and Liberties might not again be in danger of being subverted: Upon which Letters Elections having been accordingly made,

And thereupon the said Lords Spiritual and Temporal, and Commons, pursuant to their respective Letters and Elections, being now assembled in a full and free Representative of the Nation, taking into their most serious consideration the best means for attaining the ends aforesaid; Do in the first place (as their Ancestors in like case have usually done) for the vindicating and asserting their ancient Rights and Liberties, Declare

1. That the pretended power of Suspending laws, or the execution of laws, by Regal authority, without consent of Parliament, is illegal.
2. That the pretended power of Dispensing with laws, or the execution of laws, by Regal authority, as it hath been assumed and exercised of late, is illegal.
3. That the Commission for erecting the late Court of Commissioners for Ecclesiastical Causes, and all other Commissions and Courts of like nature, are illegal and pernicious.
4. That levying of money for the use of the Crown, by pretence of Prerogative, without grant of Parliament, for longer time, or in other manner, than the same is or shall be granted, is illegal.
5. That it is the right of the subjects to Petition the King, and all Commitments and Prosecutions for such petitioning are illegal.
6. That the raising or keeping of a Standing Army within the Kingdom in time of peace, unless it be with the consent of Parliament, is against the law.
7. That the subjects which are Protestants, may have Arms for their defence suitable to their conditions, and as allowed by law.
8. That Election of Members of Parliament ought to be free.
9. That the Freedom of Speech, and Debates or Proceedings in Parliament, ought not to be impeached or questioned in any Court or place out of Parliament.

10. That excessive Bail ought not to be required, nor excessive Fines imposed, nor cruel and unusual punishments inflicted.
11. That Jurors ought to be duly impanneled and returned, and Jurors which pass upon men in trials for High Treason ought to be Freeholders.
12. That all Grants and Promises of Fines and Forfeitures of particular persons before conviction are illegal and void.
13. And that for redress of all grievances, and for the amending, strengthening, and preserving of the laws, Parliaments ought to be held frequently.

And They do claim, demand, and insist upon all and singular the premises, as their undoubted rights and liberties; And that no Declarations, Judgments, Doings, or Proceedings, to the Prejudice of the People in any of the said Premisses, ought in any wise to be drawn hereafter into consequence or example.

To which demand of their rights they are particularly encouraged by the Declaration of His Highness the Prince of Orange, as being the only means for obtaining a full redress and remedy therein.

Having therefore an entire confidence, that His said Highness the Prince of Orange will perfect the deliverance so far advanced by Him, and will still preserve them from the violation of their rights, which they have here asserted, and from all other attempts upon their Religion, Rights, and Liberties.

II. The said Lords Spiritual and Temporal, and Commons, assembled at Westminster, do Resolve, that William and Mary Prince and Princess of Orange be, and be declared, King and Queen of England, France, and Ireland, and the Dominions thereunto belonging, to hold the Crown and Royal Dignity of the said Kingdoms and Dominions to them and said Prince and Princess during their lives, and the life of the Survivor of them; And that the sole and full exercise of the Regal Power be only in, and executed by, the said Prince of Orange, in the names of the said Prince and Princess, during their joint lives; And after their deceases, the said Crown and Royal Dignity of the said Kingdoms and Dominions to be to the Heirs of the Body of the said Princess, and for default of such Issue to the Princess Anne of Denmark, and the Heirs of her Body; And for default of such Issue to the Heirs of the Body of the said Prince of Orange. And the Lords Spiritual and Temporal, and Commons, do pray the said Prince and Princess to accept the same accordingly.

[1] Channel ports which traditionally enjoy special privileges.

190

13
Scots Acts Anent [in relation to] Peace and War (1703)

Source: D. Oswald Dykes (ed.), *Source Book of Constitutional History from 1660*, Longmans, Green and Co., London, New York, Toronto, 1930, pp.137–40.

This act and the Act for the Security of the Kingdom, 1704 (see above III.4) reflect the concern of the Scots nation that their interests should not be entirely submerged in those of their larger neighbour.

OUR Sovereign Lady, with Advice and Consent of the Estates of Parliament, Statutes, Enacts, and Declares, That after her Majesty's Decease, and failing Heirs of her Body, no person being King or Queen of Scotland and England, shall have the sole power of making War with any Prince, Potentate or State whatsoever without consent of Parliament; and that no Declaration of War without consent foresaid, shall be binding on the Subjects of this Kingdom, Declaring always, that this shall no ways be understood to impede the Sovereign of this Kingdom to call forth, command, and employ the Subjects thereof to suppress an Insurrection within the Kingdom, or repel any Invasion from abroad, according to former Laws; and also Declaring, that everything which relates to Treaties of Peace, Alliance and Commerce, is left to the Wisdom of the Sovereign, with consent of the Estates of Parliament who shall declare the War: And her Majesty with Consent foresaid, Repels, Casses [makes void], and Annuls all former Acts of Parliament, in so far as they are contrary hereunto or inconsistent herewith.

14
The Act of Union with Scotland (1706)

Source: D. Oswald Dykes (ed.), *Source Book of Constitutional History from 1660*, Longmans, Green and Co., London, New York, Toronto, 1930, pp.144–56.

One hundred years after the union of the crowns in the house of Stuart, and despite the reservations of many Scots, the Act of Union recognized what was an economic and political reality by the early eighteenth century. The provisions of the act did much to safeguard the culture of the Lowland Scots. Highlanders, many of whom were still Catholic, continued to be regarded as second-class citizens.

An Act for an Union of the two Kingdoms of England and Scotland.

MOST GRACIOUS SOVEREIGN,

Whereas Articles of Union were agreed on, the Twenty-second day of July in the fifth year of your Majesty's Reign, by the Commissioners nominated on behalf of the Kingdom of England, under your Majesty's Great Seal of England, bearing date at Westminster the Tenth day of April then last past, in pursuance of an Act of Parliament made in England, in the Third year of your Majesty's Reign, and the Commissioners nominated on behalf of the Kingdom of Scotland, under your Majesty's Great Seal of Scotland, bearing date the Twenty-seventh day of February in the Fourth year of your Majesty's Reign, in pursuance of the Fourth Act of the Third Session of the Present Parliament of Scotland, to treat of and concerning an Union of the said Kingdoms: And whereas an Act hath passed in the Parliament of Scotland, at Edinburgh the Sixteenth day of January in the Fifth year of your Majesty's reign, wherein 'tis mentioned, that the Estates of Parliament considering the said Articles of Union of the two Kingdoms, had agreed to and approved of the said Articles of Union, with some Additions and Explanations, and that your Majesty, with advice and consent of the Estates of Parliament, for establishing the Protestant Religion and Presbyterian Church Government within the Kingdom of Scotland, had passed in the same Session of Parliament an Act, intituled, An Act for the Securing of the Protestant Religion and Presbyterian Church Government, which by the tenor thereof was appointed to be inserted in any Act ratifying the Treaty, and expressly declared to be a fundamental and essential condition of the said Treaty of Union in all Times coming: the tenor of which Articles, as ratified and approved of, with additions and explanations by the said Act of Parliament of Scotland, follows:

Article I. That the Two Kingdoms of England and Scotland shall upon the First day of May which shall be in the year One thousand seven hundred and seven, and for ever after, be united into one Kingdom by the name of Great Britain; and that the Ensigns Armorial of the said United Kingdom be such as Her Majesty shall appoint, and the Crosses of St. George and St. Andrew be conjoined in such manner as Her Majesty shall think fit, and used in all Flags, Banners, Standards and Ensigns, both at Sea and Land.

Article II. That the Succession of the Monarchy to the United Kingdom of Great Britain, and of the Dominions thereunto belonging, after Her most Sacred Majesty, and in default of Issue of her Majesty, be, remain, and continue to the most excellent Princess Sophia. Electoress and Duchess Dowager of Hanover and the Heirs of her Body being Protestants, upon whom the Crown of England is settled by an Act of Parliament made in England in the Twelfth year of the Reign of his late Majesty King William the Third, intituled, An Act for the further Limitation of the Crown, and better securing the Rights and Liberties of the Subject [Act of Settlement]: And that all Papists, and persons marrying Papists, shall be excluded from, and for ever incapable to inherit, possess, or enjoy the Imperial Crown of Great Britain, and the Dominions thereunto belonging, or any part thereof; and in every such case the Crown and Government shall from time to time descend to, and be enjoyed by such Person, being a Protestant, as should have inherited and enjoyed the same in case such Papist, or Person marrying a Papist, was naturally dead, according to a Provision for the Descent of the Crown of England made by another Act of Parliament in England in the First year of the Reign of their late Majesties King William and Queen Mary, intituled, An Act declaring the Rights and Liberties of the Subject, and Settling the Succession of the Crown [the Bill of Rights].

Article III. That the United Kingdom of Great Britain be represented by One and the same Parliament, to be styled, the Parliament of Great Britain.

Article IV. That all the Subjects of the United Kingdom of Great Britain shall, from and after the Union, have full Freedom and Intercourse of Trade and Navigation to and from any Port or Place within the said United Kingdom, and the Dominions and Plantations thereunto belonging: . . .

[Articles VI to XV provide for equality of taxation and make other financial provisions.]

Article XVI. That from and after the Union, the Coin shall be of the same standard and value throughout the United Kingdom, as now in England, and a Mint shall be continued in Scotland, under the same Rules as the Mint in England, . . .

Article XVII. That from and after the Union, the same Weights and Measures shall be used throughout the United Kingdom, as are established in England, . . .

Article XVIII. That the Laws concerning Regulation of Trade, Customs, and such Excises to which Scotland is, by virtue of this Treaty, to be liable, be the same in Scotland from and after the Union as in England; and that all other Laws in use within the Kingdom of Scotland, do after the Union, and notwithstanding thereof, remain in the same force as before, (except such as are contrary to, or inconsistent with this Treaty) but alterable by the Parliament of Great Britain; . . .

Article XIX. That the Court of Session, or College of Justice, do after the Union, and notwithstanding thereof, remain in all time coming within Scotland, as it is now constituted by the Laws of that Kingdom, and with the same Authority and Privileges as before the Union, subject nevertheless to such Regulations for the better Administration of Justice as shall be made by the Parliament of Great Britain; . . .

And that the Court of Justiciary do also after the Union, and notwithstanding thereof, remain in all time coming within Scotland, as it is now constituted by the Laws of that Kingdom, and with the same Authority and Privileges as before the Union, subject nevertheless to such Regulations as shall be made by the Parliament of Great Britain, and without prejudice of other Rights of

Justiciary.

. . . And that all other Courts now being within the Kingdom of Scotland do remain, but subject to alterations by the Parliament of Great Britain; . . .

Article XXI. That the Rights and Privileges of the Royal Burghs in Scotland, as they now are, do remain entire after the Union, and notwithstanding thereof.

Article XXII. That by virtue of this Treaty, of the Peers of Scotland at the time of the Union, Sixteen shall be the number to sit and vote in the House of Lords, and Forty-five the Number of the Representatives of Scotland in the House of Commons of the Parliament of Great Britain; and that when Her Majesty, her Heirs or Successors, shall declare her or their Pleasure for holding the First or any subsequent Parliament of Great Britain, until the Parliament of Great Britain shall make further provision therein, a Writ do issue under the Great Seal of the United Kingdom, directed to the Privy Council of Scotland, commanding them to cause Sixteen Peers, who are to sit in the House of Lords, to be summoned to Parliament, and Forty-five Members to be elected to sit in the House of Commons of the Parliament of Great Britain, according to the Agreement in this Treaty, in such manner as by an Act of this present Session of the Parliament of Scotland is or shall be settled; . . .

Article XXV. That all Laws and Statutes in either Kingdom, so far as they are contrary to, or inconsistent with, the Terms of these Articles, or any of them, shall from and after the Union, cease and become void, and shall be so declared to be, by the respective Parliaments of the said Kingdoms.

As by the said Articles of Union, ratified and approved by the said Act of Parliament of Scotland, relation being thereunto had, may appear; And the Tenor of the aforesaid Act for Securing the Protestant Religion and Presbyterian Church Government within the Kingdom of Scotland, is as follows:—

'Our Sovereign Lady, and the Estates of Parliament, considering that by the late Act of Parliament for a Treaty with England for an Union of both Kingdoms, it is provided, That the Commissioners for that Treaty should not treat of or concerning any alteration of the Worship, Discipline, and Government of the Church of this Kingdom as now by Law established: Which Treaty being now reported to the Parliament, and it being reasonable and necessary that the true Protestant Religion, as presently professed within this Kingdom, with the Worship, Discipline, and Government of this Church, should be effectually and unalterably secured: Therefore Her Majesty, with advice and consent of the said Estates of Parliament, doth hereby establish and confirm the said true Protestant Religion, and the Worship, Discipline, and Government of this Church, to continue without any alteration to the People of this Land in all succeeding generations; and more especially her Majesty, with advice and consent aforesaid, ratifies, approves, and for ever confirms the Fifth Act of the First Parliament of King William and Queen Mary, intituled, an Act ratifying the Confession of Faith and settling Presbyterian Church Government; with all other Acts of Parliament relating thereto, in prosecution of the Declaration of the Estates of this Kingdom, containing the Claim of Right, bearing date the Eleventh of April one thousand six hundred and eighty-nine: And Her Majesty, with advice and consent aforesaid, expressly provides and declares, that the foresaid true Protestant Religion, contained in the above-mentioned Confession of Faith, with the Form and Purity of Worship presently in use within this Church and its Presbyterian Church Government and Discipline (that is to say) that Government of the Church by Kirk Sessions, Presbyteries, Provincial Synods, and General Assemblies, all established by the foresaid Acts of Parliament, pursuant to the Claim of Right, shall remain and continue unalterable, and that the said Presbyterian Government shall be the only Government of the Church within the Kingdom of Scotland.

'And further, for the greater security of the foresaid Protestant Religion, and of the Worship, Discipline, and Government of this Church, as above established, Her Majesty, with advice and consent foresaid, statutes and ordains, That the Universities and Colleges of Saint Andrews, Glasgow, Aberdeen, and Edinburgh, as now established by Law, shall continue within this Kingdom for ever; and that in all time coming no Professors, Principals, Regents, Masters or Others, bearing Office in any University, College, or School within this Kingdom, be capable or be admitted, or allowed to continue in the exercise of their said Functions, but such as shall own and acknowledge the Civil Government in manner prescribed or to be prescribed by the Acts of Parliament; as also that before or at their admissions they do and shall acknowledge and profess, and shall subscribe to, the foresaid Confession of Faith, as the Confession of their Faith, and that they will practise and conform themselves to the Worship presently in use in this Church, and submit themselves to the Government and Discipline thereof, and never endeavour directly or indirectly the prejudice or subversion of the same, and that before the respective Presbyteries of their Bounds, by whatever Gift, Presentation or Provision they may be thereto provided. . . . for establishing of the Church of Scotland within the Bounds of this Kingdom; as also the said Parliament of England may extend the additions and other provisions contained in the Articles of Union as above insert in favour of the Subjects of Scotland, to and in favour of the Subjects of England, which shall not suspend or derogate from the force and effect of this present ratification, but shall be understood as herein included, without the necessity of any new ratification in the Parliament of Scotland.

'And lastly, Her Majesty enacts and declares, that all Laws and Statutes in this Kingdom, so far as they are contrary to, or inconsistent with, the terms of these Articles, as above-mentioned, shall from and after the Union cease and become void.' . . .

X. May it therefore please your Most Excellent Majesty, that it may be enacted; and be it enacted by the Queen's most Excellent Majesty, by and with the advice and consent of the Lords Spiritual and Temporal, and Commons, in this present Parliament assembled, and by the authority of the same, That all and every the said Articles of Union as ratified and approved by the said Act of Parliament of Scotland, as aforesaid, and herein before particularly mentioned and inserted; and also the said Act of Parliament of Scotland for establishing the Protestant Religion, and Presbyterian Church Government within that Kingdom, intituled, Act for securing . . . and every Clause, Matter and Thing in the said Articles and Act contained, shall be, and the said Articles and Act are hereby for ever ratified, approved and confirmed.

XI. And it is hereby further enacted by the authority aforesaid, That the said Act passed in this present Session of Parliament, intituled, an Act for securing the Church of England as by Law established, and all and every the matters and things therein contained, and also the said Act of Parliament of Scotland, intituled, Act for securing the Protestant Religion and Presbyterian Church Government, with the Establishment in the said Act contained, be and shall for ever be held and adjudged to be, and observed as, fundamental and essential Conditions of the said Union; and shall in all times coming be taken to be, and are hereby declared to be, essential and fundamental Parts of the said Articles and Union; and the said Articles of Union so as aforesaid ratified, approved and confirmed by Act of Parliament of Scotland, and by this present Act and the said Act passed in this present Session of Parliament, intituled, An Act for securing the Church of England as by Law established, and also the said Act passed in the Parliament of Scotland, intituled, An Act for securing the Protestant Religion and Presbyterian Church Government, are hereby enacted and ordained to be and continue in all times coming the complete and entire Union of the two Kingdoms of England and Scotland.

XII. And whereas since the passing the said Act in the Parliament of Scotland, for ratifying the said Articles of Union, one other Act, intituled, An Act settling the manner of electing the Sixteen Peers and Forty-five Members to represent Scotland in the Parliament of Great Britain, hath likewise passed in the said Parliament of Scotland at Edinburgh the Fifth day of February One thousand seven hundred and seven, the tenor whereof follows:—

(Preamble.)

'Therefore Her Majesty, with advice and consent of the Estates of Parliament, statutes, enacts, and ordains, that the said Sixteen Peers who shall have right to sit in the House of Peers in the Parliament of Great Britain, on the part of Scotland, by virtue of this Treaty, shall be named by the said Peers of Scotland whom they represent, their Heirs or Successors to their Dignities and Honours, out of their own number, and that by open Election and Plurality of Voices of the Peers present, and of the Proxies for such as shall be absent, the said Proxies being Peers, and producing a Mandate in writing duly signed before witnesses, and both the Constituent and Proxy being qualified according to Law; declaring also, That such Peers as are absent, being qualified as aforesaid, may send to all such meetings Lists of the Peers whom they judge fittest, validly signed by the said absent Peers, which shall be reckoned in the same manner as if the Parties had been present, and given in the said List; and in case of the death or legal incapacity of any of the said Sixteen Peers, that the aforesaid Peers of Scotland shall nominate another of their own number in place of the said Peer or Peers in manner before and after mentioned: And that, of the Forty-five Representatives of Scotland in the House of Commons in the Parliament of Great Britain, Thirty shall be chosen by the Shires and Stewartries, and Fifteen by the Royal Boroughs.'

15
Two *Nu-Pieds* poems of 1639

Source: Diarie ou Journal du Voyage du Chancelier Séguier en Normandie après la sédition des Nu-Pieds (1639–40), A. Floquet, Paris, 1842, pp.407–8, 415–17. Translated by Angela Scholar.

The *nu-pieds* were the bare-footed salt panners of Mont St Michel in Normandy. Other peasants, artisans and minor nobles (*hobereaux*) took the name when they all rose in rebellion in 1639 against the harsh economic conditions and heavy taxation which they suffered as a result of the expensive foreign wars waged by Louis XIII and Richelieu. The chancellor, Pierre Seguier (1588–1672), was sent to Rouen in 1640 to punish the rebels who had, by then, been defeated. Some were hanged and the *parlement* of Rouen was suspended and exiled. The chancellor recorded the following rebel poems in the Journal which he kept as a record of his journey to Normandy.

A.   *Manifesto of the noble and invincible Captain Jean Nu-pieds, general of the army of suffering*

Let the factions grown rich on taxation
Oppress the poor people with plots and sedition,
Let them summon their minions and henchmen,
And with schemes bring their land to perdition.
Let them strut in their satin and velvet,
And mock us who pay for their vanity and pride;
Though bare-foot, a *nu-pieds*, I will not stand by,
But will put down their treacherous ambition.

Let them run to the *partisans*[1] for help,
Let them hurry to Paris to seize the *gabelle*,
I with my peasants, burning with zeal,

Will seek out the treachery they try to conceal.
How can I watch while they brazenly steal,
Crushing the poor with a weight they can't bear?
When I look at the people so bowed down with care,
Though just a *nu-pieds*, I must help their despair.

Against Senate and people Caesar schemed and was slain,
Thus Brutus avenged the whole Roman state,
Catalina fell to the people's just hate
For crimes too abhorrent, too numerous to name:
How, then, could I watch a whole people languish,
By tyrants oppressed, by outsiders betrayed?
Or stand by while schemers reduce them to anguish?
I'm just a *nu-pieds*, yet I'll come to their aid.

Why should I tremble at threats and at blows?
My people as valiant as soldiers will prove,
Shoulder to shoulder in bold serried rows
Alongside brave peasants, they'll stand unmoved.
Agents of tyranny they'll face, and tax-grabbers,
Hyrcanian[2] oppressors of nations and lands,
Against tyrants, conspirators and robbers,
Normandy, Brittany and Poitiers will stand.

Fair Paris, first city in all of the land
Show us your virtue, support the *souffrans*[3]
Give comfort and aid to this brave fertile band
Of the most valiant sons of Rouen and Caen.
Valognes and Saint-Lô. Carentan and Bayeux.
Domfront, Vire, Coutances. Falaise and Lisieux.
Avranches and Évreux, Dol, Gougères and Rennes,
Help succour our *nu-pieds*, most valorous of men.

Courtiers, it's time to abandon your mistresses,
Your finery and foppery have brought you disgrace,
The people are sick of your craven caresses,
And can't bear to see you so decked out in lace,
Saint-Malo is calling, Tomblaine and Granville,
All sovereign sea-ports, close by Saint-Michel,
They'll give, when you need it, refuge and relief,
Along with Jean Nu-pieds, your colonel-in-chief.

'What is it that moves you', some *nu-pieds* might ask me,
'To struggle so hard with the grim *partisans*?'
When I see cruel tyranny allied with vile blasphemy,
Then I must take up arms to support the *souffrans*,

To help them is good works, to aid them is piety:
While my purpose holds firm, with the help of the nations[4]
To overturn slavery, institute liberty,
And see freedom triumphant in each class and station.

Colonel Mondrin[5] beseeches the ancient nobility
Of all cantons and regions to reject the *gabelle*,
To boldly resist, to fight and break free
From the burden of imposts and taxes as well.
Towns, likewise, and cities can advance this great cause,
If to succour Jean Nu-pieds they swiftly unite,
In spite of the edict, against greedy tax-laws,
Which will bring us all else to prompt ruin and blight.

[1] A speculator in government finance.
[2] A remote province of the ancient Persian Empire.
[3] Those who suffer.
[4] 'Nations' probably refers to Bretons, Poitevins, etc., rather than to foreign countries.
[5] Assumed name of one of the leaders of the revolt.

B.   *To Normandy*

Fair Normandy, rise and rebel.
For what is it they give to you
In payment for long service true?
They give the harsh *gabelle*.
Is this the hoped-for recompense
For loyalty to the Kings of France,
For fighting to preserve in peace
Their royal crown, their fleur-de-lys,
Defending them, time and again,
From England and from hostile Spain?

It's time to show posterity
By feats of arms and martial skill
Duke William is with us still.
You're mightier than when, setting forth,
You came here from the distant north.
Your arm is more than well prepared
To put all tyrants to the sword,
Until they cry in fear and dread
'Preserve us from the Normans, Lord'.

But could it be that it's too late?
The cardinal and armies take
Our riches, goods, all we possess,
And leave us in profound distress.

How, then, when nothing's left at all
Can we achieve the miracle
And rise above our desparate plight?
Yet surely the old proverb's right
That urges us to new endeavour,
Saying 'Better late than never'.

So help valorous *nu-pieds*
Your Norman towns will show the way
And bring forth soldiers quick to rise
And rally where his banner flies.
The time has come, it's plain to see,
To fight and die for liberty,
Resist oppression and unite
With Valognes, Rouen, Chartres;
Since, if for Chartres you will not fight,
Where, Normans, is your heart?

And you, our noble general,
The colonel of our suffering land,
Who slew the traitor Poupinel[1]
With a just avenging hand.
You must seize Mesnil-Garnier[2] too,
He's plotting now to ruin you.
Accept the good advice I give,
Don't let him any longer live.
Gather the people and conspire
To go and set his house on fire.

Too long, Mortain, we've suffered you.
So let's unleash without delay
Ten thousand weapons on Beaupré,[3]
Until, this time, one blow strikes true.
Don't think we're easy to deceive,
Our enemies we'll not believe,
Nor the false news they put about.
Mortain himself, beyond a doubt,
Imposed the infamous *gabelle*
And raised the paper tax as well.

And you, our nation's noble class,
The fairest jewel in the crown,
But now the stuff of comic farce,
Of satire from l'Hôtel de Bourgogne.[4]
How can you endure this blow,
Nobility brought down so low,

A puppet in a comedy?
Rise and reassert your state,
Prove the offence has been too great,
Avenge in blood the perfidy.

Let Jean Nu-pieds espouse your cause;
He'll soon avenge you, soon repeal
And free you from the harsh *gabelle*;
He'll crush the cruel tax-laws.
He'll rid you of the people who
Get rich quick by defrauding you,
Your property and fatherland.
For he it is whom God's good hand
Has sent at last to Normandy
To institute true liberty.

Come, cowardly commissioners,
Come and indict us who dares.
Boidrot, Les Sablons, brave *nu-pieds*,[5]
Despise you and your musketeers.
They mock your orders and your writs,
They thumb the nose at your edicts;
Our general, too, gives not a fig,
So, come, judge him without appeal.
Then come and see the grave he's dug
For you, alongside Poupinel.

[1] A legal official, the first to be assassinated by the rebels.
[2] A hated tax farmer who escaped.
[3] The vicomte of Mortain who was threatened but not killed.
[4] The older of the two theatres in Paris at this time.
[5] Assumed names of the rebel leaders.

16
Guez de Balzac: on royal authority (1631)

Source: Guez de Balzec: *Oeuvres*, Paris, 1665, vol. 2, pp.61–3, translated by W.F. Church, in *Richelieu and Reason of State*, Princeton University Press, Princeton, 1972, p.246.

Jean Louis Guez de Balzac (1594–1654) was a prominent writer who was employed by Cardinal Richelieu to support the absolutist policies of the royal government. In this extract he praised prudence, a traditional kingly virtue, as a means of justifying the harsh and repressive measures

Richelieu and Louis XIII were employing to establish security in the state. Although this extract comes from a work entitled *The Prince* (1631), Balzac was not emulating the treatise of the same name by Niccolò Macchiavelli. He insisted that absolute royal power could only be justified if the monarch was governing according to a Christian code of ethics.

Prudence[1] must modify justice in many things. Prudence should prevail when justice would move too slowly and never be complete, and prudence must prevent crimes whose punishment would be either impossible or dangerous. Justice is rendered only according to the actions of men, but prudence has its rights over their thoughts and secrets. It extends into the future; it concerns the general welfare; it provides for the good of posterity. And for these it must everywhere make use of means which the laws do not ordain but necessity justifies, and which would not be entirely good if they were not for a good end.

Public utility often benefits from injury to individuals . . . Life is redeemed by abstinence, suffering, and even the loss of a part that is willingly sacrificed to save the whole. Although the king has preserved the dignity and reputation of the crown on occasions when others would have thought it necessary to do anything to save the state, although even in the greatest extremities he has attempted if possible to avoid using disagreeable remedies, although in a word he is infinitely sensitive to the misery and complaints of his people, he has been unable to avoid weakening them while curing their ills and taking from their blood and treasure the means of achieving their own salvation. But we should willingly endure brief pain that brings long prosperity. We may not honourably seek relief from a burden that we share with our master, and when the prince puts forth great effort and does not spare himself, it is just that the subjects exert themselves on their part and that no one in the realm remain indolent or cowardly while he labors and risks his life.

[1] Prudence was one of the Cardinal Virtues (the others were Justice, Temperance and Fortitude) which political theorists in the middle ages thought should be attributes of a good ruler.

17

Extracts from de Morgues, writings in defence of the Queen Mother (1631)

Source: M. De Morgues, *Diverses pièces pour la défense de la Royne Mère du Roy trés-chrétien, Louis XIII*, n.p., 1637, vol. 1, pp.1–109, translated by W.F. Church, in *Richelieu and Reason of State*, Princeton University Press, Princeton, 1972, pp.213, 215.

Matthieu de Morgues (1582–1670) was initially a supporter of the policies of Cardinal Richelieu, at home and abroad. He eventually became disillusioned with the royal regime, and by the 1630s was a loyal supporter of Marie de' Medici, the Queen Mother, and her disaffected followers. This was the context of his bitter denunciation of Richelieu as the cause of France's troubles, which were contained in the tract from which the following extracts are taken, *The Very Humble, Very True and Very Important Remonstrance to the King* (1631).

A.

Sire, you are the sovereign judge of all your people. God has given you the sword of justice as well as of war. False witnesses, produced by those who control your affairs and report to you as counsel before a court, are those who now condemn men although you sometimes order their arrest. I say sometimes because I know that arrests and imprisonments are often made without your knowledge. If you are informed, evidence is falsified and favourable information suppressed . . . In order to magnify matters of small importance, they allege the safety of your person and your state; they enter the formidable charge of *lèse-majesté* [treason] in the highest degree and say that your authority will be lost if those whom they wish to destroy are not condemned. If the sovereign courts remonstrate against edicts that oppress the people, if frontier provinces point to their privileges which Your Majesty has confirmed, if they oppose the introduction of changes that will ruin them, all are reduced to questions of authority. Petitions are called rebellion; no mention is made of kindness, clemency, or justice, only severity, rigor, and force. No one points to the people's misery, the disorder caused by war, the ravages of disease, the extent of famine . . . They try to persuade you that it is good policy to lose the hearts of men in order to preserve the body of your state, as if it could survive without that which gives it life and strength for your service.

B.

It is most important that Your Majesty examine the aims of those who would undertake purposeless wars and refuse to terminate them . . . This is abominable before God and punishable under justice in all the states of the globe.

Sire, good and wise kings are persuaded to undertake war only because of necessity and wage it solely to establish peace in their states or gain it for their allies. When peace is proposed and the occasion arises for giving or receiving it without loss of reputation, it must be embraced as a daughter of God, sister of justice, mother of abundance, guardian of piety, and the most treasured gift that heaven may send earth or kings may give their subjects . . . Nothing disturbs him [Richelieu] like fear of peace, because a tormented mind fears tranquillity more than confusion. Arrest his ambition, his avarice, and his violence, Great King. Call to yourself those who by natural rights should be near you and merit it because of their virtue . . . Realize the condition of finances and the position of your arms; relieve your poor people, and God will give you perfect health, peace of mind, peace of home and abroad, a better council than you now have, faithful officials, an obedient realm, and will crown you with all manner of benedictions.

18
Speech by Charles I to the Lords and Commons (1626)

Source: S.R. Gardiner, *Constitutional Documents of the Puritan Revolution 1625–1660*, Oxford Univesity Press, Oxford, 1962, pp.5–6. (First published 1906.)

Charles I referred to the support he and Buckingham had enjoyed from parliament whilst he was Prince of Wales. They had returned from their humiliating expedition to Spain and joined with the Commons and Lords in persuading the reluctant James I to declare war against that country. Charles was concerned in 1626 to defend Buckingham from impeachment by parliament, hence his assertion that he possessed absolute power to call or dismiss it.

Then his Majesty spoke again:—
    I must withall put you in mind a little of times past; you may remember, that in the time of my blessed father, you did with your counsel and persuasion persuade both my father and me to break off the treaties. I confess I was your instrument for two reasons; one was, the fitness of the time; the other because I was seconded by so great and worthy a body, as the whole body of parliament; then there was nobody in so great favour with you as this man whom you seem now to touch, but indeed, my father's government and mine. Now that you have all things according to your wishes, and that I am so far engaged, that you think there is no retreat; now you begin to set the dice, and make your own game; but I pray you be not deceived, it is not a

parliamentary way, nor is it a way to deal with a King.

Mr Cook told you, it was better to be eaten up by a foreign enemy, than to be destroyed at home; indeed, I think it more honour for a King to be invaded, and almost destroyed by a foreign enemy, than to be despised by his own subjects.

Remember that parliaments are altogether in my power for their calling, sitting and dissolution; therefore as I find the fruits of them good or evil, they are to continue or not to be. And remember, that if in this time, instead of mending your errors, by delay you persist in your errors, you make them greater and irreconcilable. Whereas on the other side, if you go on cheerfully to mend them, and look to the distressed state of Christendom, and the affairs of the kingdom as it lieth now by this great engagement; you will do yourselves honour, you shall encourage me to go with parliaments; and I hope all Christendom shall feel the good of it.

19
Sir Robert Filmer, extract from *Patriarcha* (*c*.1640)

Source: Sir Robert Filmer, *Patriarcha and Other Writings*, edited by J.P. Sommerville, Cambridge Texts in the History of Political Thought, Cambridge University Press, Cambridge, 1991, p.7.

For details see above, II.35.

This lordship which Adam by creation had over the whole world, and by right descending from him the patriarchs did enjoy, was as large and ample as the absolutest dominion of any monarch which hath been since the creation. For power of life and death we find that Judah, the father, pronounced sentence of death against Thamar, his daughter-in-law, for playing the harlot. 'Bring her forth', saith he, 'that she may be burnt' [Genesis 38:24]. Touching war, we see that Abraham commanded an army of 318 soldiers of his own family [Genesis 14:14]; and Esau met his brother Jacob with 400 men at arms [Genesis 33:1]. For matter of peace, Abraham made a league with Abimelech, and ratified the articles by an oath [Genesis 21:23–4]. These acts of judging in capital causes, of making war, and concluding peace, are the chiefest marks of sovereignty that are found in any monarch.

20
Mary Astell, *A Serious Proposal to the Ladies* (1694–7)

Source: Mary Astell, *A Serious Proposal to the Ladies for the Advancement of their True and Greatest Interests*, parts I and II, R. Wilkin, London, 1697, pp.30, 47–9, 50–2.

Mary Astell (1666–1731) was the daughter of a coal-merchant in New-castle. After her father's death, with no regular means of support, she moved to London and settled in Chelsea. With the help of Archbishop Sancroft, who may have been impressed by her sincerity and piety, she became a professional writer. Most of her works were devotional, but her main importance for modern readers lies in *A Serious Proposal to the Ladies* from which extracts are printed below. This laid out in reasoned and elegant prose the case for women being given a voice in political life and education.

A.

. . . When a poor young lady is taught to value nothing but her clothes, she's very fine when well accoutred; when she hears say, that 'tis wisdom enough for her to know how to dress herself, that she may become amiable in his eyes, to whom it appertains to be knowing and learned; who can blame her if she lay out her industry and money on such accomplishments, and sometimes extends it farther than her misinformer desires she should?

B.

. . . since God has given women as well as men intelligent souls, why should they be forbidden to improve them? Since he had not denied us the faculty of thinking, why should we not (at least in gratitude to him) employ our thoughts on himself their noblest object; and not unworthily bestow them on trifles and gaieties and secular affairs? Being the soul was created for the contemplation of truth as well as for the fruition of good, is it not as cruel and unjust to exclude women from the knowledge of one as from the enjoyment of the other? . . . What is it but the want of an ingenious education, that renders the generality of feminine conversations so insipid and foolish and their solitude so insupportable? Learning is therefore necessary to render them more agreeable and useful in company, and to furnish them with becoming entertainments when alone . . .

C.

We pretend not that women should teach in the Church, or usurp authority where it is not allowed them; permit us only to understand our own duty, and not be forced to take it upon trust from others; to be at least so far learned, as to be able to form in our minds a true idea of Christianity, it being so very necessary to fence us against the danger of these last and perilous days, in which deceivers, a part of whose characters it is to lead captive silly women, need not creep into houses since they have authority to proclaim their errors on the house top. And let us also acquire a true practical knowledge, such as will convince us of the absolute necessity of holy living as well as of right believing, and that no heresy is more dangerous than that of an ungodly and wicked life. And since the French tongue is understood by most ladies, methinks they may much better improve it by the study of Philosophy (as I hear the French ladies do), Descartes, Malebranche and others, than by reading idle novels and romances. 'Tis strange we should be so forward to imitate their fashions and fopperies, and have no regard to what really deserves our imitation! And why shall it not be thought as genteel to understand French philosophy, as to be accoutred in a French mode? Let therefore the famous Madame d'Acier,[1] Scudery[2] etc. and our own incomparable Orinda[3] excite the emulation of English ladies.

The ladies, I'm sure, have no reason to dislike this proposal, but I know not how the men will resent it to have their enclosure broke down, and women invited to taste of the tree of knowledge they have so long unjustly monopolized. But they must excuse me, if I be as partial to my own sex as they are to theirs, and think women as capable of learning as men are, and that it becomes them as well.

[1] Anne Dacier, a French classicist and translator of several Greek and Latin texts.
[2] Madelaine de Scudery.
[3] Katherine Philips, an admired contemporary poet.

21

An Agreement of the People (1647)

Source: A. Hughes (ed.), *Seventeenth Century England: A Changing Culture*, Ward Lock/The Open University, 1980, vol. 1, *Primary Sources*, pp.179–81.

The 'Agreement' encapsulates many of the main demands which had been recently developed by Levellers. These were an amorphous selection of politically radical London artisans and small traders, troopers and junior officers in the New Model Army. John Lilburne and William Walwyn, leading London Levellers, may have had a hand in this document, which proposed several of the principles which were debated at Putney at a meeting of the General Council of the Army in late October 1647. They were rejected by the senior generals led by Oliver Cromwell: those who refused to accept the decision were brutally repressed. (See also I.18, above.)

An Agreement of the People for a firm and present peace upon grounds of common right.

Having by our late labours and hazards made it appear to the world at how high a rate we value our just freedom, and God having so far owned our cause as to deliver the enemies thereof into our hands, we do now hold ourselves bound in mutual duty to each other to take the best care we can for the future to avoid both the danger of returning into a slavish condition and the chargeable remedy of another war; . . .

Since, therefore, our former oppressions and scarce-yet-ended troubles have been occasioned, either by want of frequent national meetings in Council, or by rendering those meetings ineffectual, we are fully agreed and resolved to provide that hereafter our representatives be neither left to an uncertainty for the time nor made useless to the ends for which they are intended. In order whereunto we declare:

That the people of England, being at this day very unequally distributed by Counties, Cities, and Boroughs for the election of their deputies in Parliament, ought to be more indifferently proportioned according to the number of the inhabitants; . . .

II

That, to prevent the many inconveniences apparently arising from the long continuance of the same persons in authority, this present Parliament be dissolved upon the last day of September which shall be in the year of our Lord 1648.

III

That the people do, of course, choose themselves a Parliament once in two years, . . .

IV

That the power of this, and all future Representatives of this Nation, is inferior only to theirs who choose them, and doth extend, without the consent or concurrence of any other person or persons, to the enacting, altering, and repealing of laws, to the erecting and abolishing of offices and courts, to the appointing, removing, and calling to account magistrates and officers of all degrees, to the making war and peace, to the treating with foreign States, and, generally, to whatsoever is not expressly or impliedly

reserved by the represented to themselves:
Which are as followeth.

1 That matters of religion and the ways of God's worship are not at all entrusted by us to any human power, because therein we cannot remit or exceed a tittle of what our consciences dictate to be the mind of God without wilful sin: nevertheless the public way of instructing the nation (so it be not compulsive) is referred to their discretion.

2 That the matter of impresting and constraining any of us to serve in the wars is against our freedom; and therefore we do not allow it in our Representatives; . . .

3 That after the dissolution of this present Parliament, no person be at any time questioned for anything said or done in reference to the late public differences, otherwise than in execution of the judgments of the present Representatives or House of Commons.

4 That in all laws made or to be made every person may be bound alike, and that no tenure, estate, charter, degree, birth, or place do confer any exemption from the ordinary course of legal proceedings whereunto others are subjected.

5 That as the laws ought to be equal, so they must be good, and not evidently destructive to the safety and well-being of the people.

These things we declare to be our native rights, and therefore are agreed and resolved to maintain them with our utmost possibilities against all opposition whatsoever; being compelled thereunto not only by the examples of our ancestors, whose blood was often spent in vain for the recovery of their freedoms, suffering themselves through fraudulent accommodations to be still deluded of the fruit of their victories, but also by our own woeful experience, who, having long expected and dearly earned the establishment of these certain rules of government, are yet made to depend for the settlement of our peace and freedom upon him that intended our bondage and brought a cruel war upon us.

22

Thomas Hobbes, *Leviathan* (1651)

Source: Thomas Hobbes, *Leviathan or the Matter, Form and Power of a Commonwealth Ecclesiastical and Civil*, edited by M. Oakshott, Blackwell, Oxford, 1946, pp.113–15, 144–5.

Thomas Hobbes (1588–1679) worked as a tutor and secretary for various noble patrons, especially the earls of Devonshire. He travelled widely on the continent and had contacts with philosophers such as Mersenne, Gassendi and Descartes. Alarmed by the conflict between king

209

and parliament he fled to Paris in 1640; many of his major works, including the *Leviathan*, were composed there. He returned to England in 1651, the year of the publication of *Leviathan*, and lived quietly under Cromwell and, after the Restoration, under Charles II. He was suspect to royalists and parliamentarians alike who condemned his doctrine that power could legitimately be exercised by the strongest body in the state. His version of a contract which only bound subjects to obey 'Leviathan' their sovereign, without any guarantee that he would rule justly, seemed amoral.

Chapter XVIII: Of the rights of sovereigns by institution

A *commonwealth* is said to be *instituted*, when a *multitude* of men do agree, and *covenant, every one, with every one*, that to whatsoever *man*, or *assembly of men*, shall be given by the major part, the *right* to *present* the person of them all, that is to say, to be their *representative*; every one, as well he that *voted for it*, as he that *voted against it*, shall *authorize* all the actions and judgments, of the man, or assembly of men, in the same manner, as if they were his own, to the end, to live peaceably amongst themselves, and be protected against other men.

From this institution of a commonwealth are derived all the *rights*, and *faculties* of him, or them, on whom the sovereign power is conferred by the consent of the people assembled.

First, because they covenant, it is to be understood, they are not obliged by former covenant to any thing repugnant hereunto. And consequently they that have already instituted a commonwealth, being thereby bound by covenant, to own the actions, and judgments of one, cannot lawfully make a new covenant, amongst themselves, to be obedient to any other, in any thing whatsoever, without his permission. And therefore, they that are subjects to a monarch, cannot without his leave cast off monarchy, and return to the confusion of a disunited multitude; nor transfer their person from him that beareth it, to another man, or other assembly of men: for they are bound, every man to every man, to own, and be reputed author of all, that he that already is their sovereign, shall do, and judge fit to be done: so that any one man dissenting, all the rest should break their covenant made to that man, which is injustice; and they have also every man given the sovereignty to him that beareth their person; and therefore if they depose him, they take from him that which is his own, and so again it is injustice Besides, if he that attempteth to depose his sovereign, be killed, or punished by him for such attempt, he is author of his own punishment, as being by the institution, author of all his sovereign shall do: and because it is injustice for a man to do any thing, for which he may be punished by his own authority, he is also upon that title, unjust. And whereas some men have pretended for their disobedience to their sovereign, a new covenant, made, not with men, but with God; this also is unjust: for there is no covenant with God, but by

210

mediation of somebody that representeth God's person; which none doth but God's lieutenant, who hath the sovereignty under God. . . .

Secondly, because the right of bearing the person of them all, is given to him they make sovereign, by covenant only of one to another, and not of him to any of them; there can happen no breach of covenant on the part of the sovereign; and consequently none of his subjects, by any pretence of forfeiture, can be freed from his subjection. That he which is made sovereign maketh no covenant with his subjects beforehand, is manifest; because either he must make it with the whole multitude, as one party to the covenant; or he must make a several convenant with every man. With the whole, as one party, it is impossible; because as yet they are not one person: and if he make so many several covenants as there be men, those covenants after he hath the sovereignty are void; because what act soever can be pretended by any one of them for breach thereof, is the act both of himself, and of all the rest, because done in the person, and by the right of every one of them in particular. Besides, if any one, or more of them, pretend a breach of the covenant made by the sovereign at his institution; and others, or one other of his subjects, or himself alone, pretend there was no such breach, there is in this case, no judge to decide the controversy; it returns therefore to the sword again; and every man recovereth the right of protecting himself by his own strength, contrary to the design they had in the institution. It is therefore in vain to grant sovereignty by way of precedent covenant. The opinion that any monarch receiveth his power by covenant, that is to say, on condition, proceedeth from want of understanding . . .

The obligation of subjects to the sovereign, is understood to last as long, and no longer, than the power lasteth, by which he is able to protect them. For the right men have by nature to protect themselves, when none else can protect them, can by no covenant be relinquished. The sovereignty is the soul of the commonwealth; which once departed from the body, the members do no more receive their motion from it. The end of obedience is protection; which, wheresoever a man seeth it, either in his own, or in another's sword, nature applieth his obedience to it, and his endeavour to maintain it. And though sovereignty, in the intention of them that make it, be immortal; yet is it in its own nature, not only subject to violent death, by foreign war; but also through the ignorance, and passions of men, it hath in it, from the very institution, many seeds of a natural mortality, by intestine discord.

23
Extracts from Louis XIV's *Mémoires*

Source: Jean Longnon (ed.), *Mémoires de Louis XIV*, Éditions Jules Tallandier, Paris, 1927, pp.60–1, 254–5, 287. Translated by A. Lentin.

Louis XIV dictated his *Mémoires* between 1666 and 1668 as a justification for his policies since assuming his sole rule in 1661 and as an introduction to his principles of government for the use of his son and heir-apparent, the Grand Dauphin. As such, the *Mémoires* (*un mémoire* includes the sense of a report or memorandum as well as of personal reminiscences) were highly confidential and were only published long after Louis' death. While some recent scholars have questioned how far they record Louis' own words, they were unquestionably written on his authority and constitute an important document of state.

A. *Louis XIV on obedience to the king (c.1667)*

It must certainly be agreed that, however wicked a prince may be, rebellion by his subjects is always infinitely criminal. He who set kings to rule over men, wished them to be respected as His lieutenants, reserving to Himself alone the right to examine their conduct. It is His will that every born subject should obey without question: and this law, so express and so universal, is not simply laid down for the sake of princes, but is salutary for the very peoples on whom it is enjoined, and who can never violate it without exposing themselves to evils far more terrible than those from which they claim to be protecting themselves. No maxim is more firmly established by Christianity than this duty of humble submission by the subjects to those who are set over them.

B. *Louis XIV on his policy towards the Huguenots (c.1671)*

I thought, my son, that the best way gradually to reduce the number of Huguenots in my realm was to put no pressure at all on them through any new restriction against them, and to observe the rights which they had acquired under the reigns of my predecessors; but also to grant them nothing more, and indeed to confine their scope within the strictest limits compatible with justice and propriety.

. . . But as for favours which depended on me alone, I resolved, and I have since adhered to this quite punctiliously, to grant none to persons of that religion. In this I have acted out of generosity, not out of spite, in order thereby to induce them to consider for themselves from time to time and without constraint, whether it was reasonable of them deliberately to deprive themselves of the advantages which they could share with my other subjects.

212

However, in order to enhance their opportunities of hearing, more willingly than hitherto, that which could disabuse them, I also resolved to win over, even by rewards, those ready to prove themselves tractable; and to encourage the bishops as much as possible to work for their instruction . . .

However, my son, I am still far from having exhausted all my ideas for bringing back to the fold those who sincerely persist in these pernicious errors by reason of their birth, upbringing and, most often, their great and unenlightened zeal. So I shall have, I hope, other occasions to mention these to you in the later parts of these *Mémoires*, without revealing in advance plans to which time and circumstances may bring a thousand changes.

C.   *Louis XIV on war, peace and prestige (1710)*

This extract is from a draft manifesto, written during a period of negotiation after successive defeats in the War of the Spanish Succession. Louis broke off negotiations because of the humiliating nature of the terms offered.

I have carried on this war [War of the Spanish Succession] with the grandeur and pride befitting this realm; through the valour of my nobles and the zeal of my subjects I have succeeded in my designs for the good of the State; I have devoted all my care and attention to that end. I have also taken the steps which I considered necesary to fulfil my duties and to make known the tender love I have for my peoples, by securing for them through my efforts lasting peace for the remainder of my reign, in order henceforth to think only of their happiness.

Having extended the boundaries of this realm and protected my frontiers with the important towns which I have taken, I have listened to the proposals of peace which have been made to me, and I have perhaps exceeded, in these negotiations, the bounds of wisdom, in order to attain so great an achievement. I may say that I have acted out of character and done great violence to my nature in order to bring speedy peace to my subjects at the cost of my reputation or at least of my personal satisfaction and perhaps of my glory, which I have willingly risked for the sake of those who have caused me to acquire it.

24
Bossuet on the Divine Right of Kings

Source: J.B. Bossuet, *Textes Choisis et Commentés*, edited by H. Bremond, Librairie Plon, Paris, 1913, vol. II, pp.124, 201. Translated by A. Lentin.

Jacques-Bénigne Bossuet (1627–1704) was France's leading churchman under Louis XIV. An eloquent preacher, appointed tutor to the Grand Dauphin in 1670, he became Bishop of Meaux from 1681, and was in effect primate of the Gallican church. A tireless apologist of Catholic orthodoxy, Bossuet was in the forefront of the campaign to eradicate heresy, especially Protestantism, in France. (See above I.19 and II.33.)

A.   *From a letter to Louis XIV (1675)*

You were born, Sire, with a great love of justice, a goodness and mildness which cannot be valued too highly; and it is in these qualities that God has laid down most of your duties, as we learn from these words of Scripture: 'Mercy and truth preserve the king; and his throne is upholden by mercy' [Proverbs 20:28]. You must therefore understand, Sire, that the throne that you occupy belongs to God; that you represent him there and that you must reign there in accordance with his laws. The laws which he has given you require that your power should be fearsome only to the wicked among your subjects, and that your other subjects should be able to live in peace and quiet, whilst rendering obedience to you. Your peoples, Sire, look forward to seeing you practise more than ever these laws which Scripture lays down for you. Your Majesty's lofty profession of your desire to amend in your life what was displeasing to God [i.e. his adulteries] has filled them with consolation: it convinces them that Your Majesty, by dedicating himself to God, will be more than ever attentive to the very strict obligation which He imposes on you, to take account of their misery; and on this they base their hope of the relief in which they stand in great need. I am not unaware, Sire, how hard it is to accord them this relief amidst a great war [the war with Holland], when you are obliged to go to such extraordinary expenses in order both to resist your enemies [Holland, Spain, the Holy Roman Empire and the electorate of Brandenburg] and to retain your allies [Sweden and some German principalities]. But the war which obliges Your Majesty to incur such great expenses obliges you at the same time not to let the people, through whom alone you can support these expenses, to be overburdened.

B. *From 'Polity drawn from Holy Writ' (1709)*

A divine element attaches to the prince and inspires fear in the peoples. For that very reason, let the king not forget himself. 'I have said,' – it is God who speaks – 'I have said: Ye are gods; and all of you are children of the most High. But ye shall die like men, and fall like one of the princes' [Psalm 82:6–7]. 'I have said: Ye are gods'; that is to say, you possess in your authority and you wear on your brow a divine character. 'Ye are children of the most High'; it is He who has established your authority for the good of mankind. But, o gods of flesh and blood, o gods of mud and dust, 'ye shall die like men, and fall like one of the princes!' Greatness distinguishes men for a little time; a common fate makes them equal in the end.

25
Jean de la Bruyère: *Characters* (1688)

Source: The Characters of Jean de la Bruyère, translated by Henri van Laun, Routledge, London, 1929, pp.184, 212–13, 248–9, 264–6.

Jean de la Bruyère (1645–96) rose from humble origins. Under Bossuet's patronage he was introduced to the court of Louis XIV in 1684 as tutor to the Duke of Bourbon, grandson of the Grand Condé. Four years later he published his *Characters*, which enjoyed a notable success and soon established itself as a classic of French literature, running to nine editions in de la Bruyère's own lifetime. Ostensibly drawn from the ancient Greek author, Theophrastes, the *Characters* comprise moral and satirical observations on French society.

A. *Of the Court (i)*

(6.) People who live in the provinces consider the court admirable; but if they visit it, its beauties diminish, like those of a fine drawing of perspective viewed too closely.

(7.) It is difficult to get accustomed to the spending of our lives in antechambers, courtyards, or on staircases.

(8.) The court does not satisfy a man, but it prevents him from being satisfied with anything else.

(9.) A cultured gentleman should have some experience of the court; as soon as he enters it he will discover a new world, as it were, wholly unknown to him, where vice and politeness have equal sway, and where good and evil may be of use to him.

(10.) The court is like a marble structure, for the courtiers are very polished and very hard.

B. *Of the Court (ii)*

(74.) . . . This nation has, besides, its God and its king: the high and mighty among them go at a fixed time every day to a temple they call a church; at the upper end of that temple stands an altar consecrated to their God, where a certain priest celebrates some mysteries, called by them holy, sacred, and formidable. The high and mighty men stand in a large circle at the foot of the altar, with their back to the priest and the holy mysteries, and their faces towards their king, who is seen kneeling in a raised and open pew, and towards whom all minds and all hearts seem directed. However, a certain kind of subordination is to be observed whilst this is going on; for this people seem to adore their prince, and their prince appears to worship God. The natives of this country call it . . . It is situated about forty-eight degrees northern latitude, and more than eleven hundred leagues by sea from the Iroquois and Hurons [Versailles].

(75.) Whoever will consider that a king's presence constitutes the entire happiness of courtiers, that their sole occupation and satisfaction during the whole course of their lives is to see and be seen by him, will in some measure understand how to behold God may constitute the glory and felicity of the saints.

C. *Of the Sovereign and the State (i)*

(9.) Even in the most remote antiquity, and in all ages, war has existed, and has always filled the world with widows and orphans, drained families of heirs, and destroyed several brothers in one and the same battle. Young Soyecourt![1] I mourn your loss, your modesty, your intelligence, already so developed, so clear, lofty, and communicative; I bewail that untimely death which carried you off, as well as your intrepid brother, and removed you from a court where you had barely time to show yourself; such a misfortune is not uncommon, but nevertheless should be deplored! In every age men have agreed to destroy, burn, kill, and slaughter one another, for some piece of land more or less; and to accomplish this with the greater certainty and ingenuity, they have invented beautiful rules, which they call 'strategy'. When anyone brings these rules into practice, glory and the highest honours are his reward, whilst every age improves on the method of destroying one another reciprocally. An injustice committed by the first men was the primary occasion for wars, and made the people feel the necessity of giving themselves masters to settle their rights and pretensions. If each man could have been satisfied with his own property and had not infringed on that of his neighbours, the world would have enjoyed uninterrupted peace and liberty.

[1] Adolphe de Belleforière, Chevalier de Soyecourt, a captain of the gendarmes of the Dauphine, died two days after the battle of Fleurus (1 July 1690), of wounds received in this battle, in which his elder brother, the Marquis of Soyecourt, was also killed . . . de la Bruyère was a friend of the family.

D. *Of the Sovereign and the State (ii)*

(27.) To call a king the father of his people is not so much to eulogise him as to call him by his name and to define what he is.

(28.) There exists a sort of interchange or permutation of duties between a sovereign and his subjects, and between them and him; and I shall not decide which are most obligatory and most difficult. On the one hand, we have to determine what are the bounden duties of reverence, assistance, service, obedience, and dependence, and on the other what are the indispensable obligations of goodness, justice and protection. To say the prince can dispose of the lives of the people, is to tell us only that through their crimes men have become subjected to the laws and justice which the king administers; to add that he is absolute master of all his subjects' goods without any considerations, without rendering any accounts, or without discussion, is the language of flattery, the opinion of a favourite who will recant on his deathbed.[1] . . .

Which condition seems to you the most delicious and the most unfettered, that of the sheep or the shepherd? Was the flock made for the shepherd or the shepherd for the flock? This is an artless representation of a nation and its prince, but then the prince must be good.

A gorgeous and sumptuous monarch is like a shepherd adorned with gold and jewels, with a golden crook in his hands, with a collar of gold about his dog's neck, and a silken and golden string to lead him. What is his flock the better for all this gold, or what avails it against the wolves?

[1] Such was, however, the opinion of Louis XIV himself, who states in his *Mémoires*: 'Kings are absolute masters, and naturally dispose fully and entirely of all the property possessed by the clergy and laity'.

26

Saint-Simon from his *Memoirs* on the reign of Louis XIV

Source: Memoirs of the Duke of Saint-Simon on the Reign of Louis XIV and the Regency, translated from the French by Bayle St John, Samuel Bangster & Sons, London, 1902, vol. III, pp.216–19, 229–35, 249–51, 272–3.

For details of Saint-Simon, see III.8, above.

A. *The abilities of the King*

Louis XIV was made for a brilliant Court. In the midst of other men, his figure, his courage, his grace, his beauty, his grand mien, even the tone of his voice and majestic and natural charm of all his person, distinguished him till his death as the King Bee, and showed that if he had only been born a simple private gentleman, he would equally have excelled in fêtes, pleasures, and gallantry, and would have had the greatest success in love. The intrigues and adventures which early in life he had been engaged in . . . had exercised an unfortunate influence upon him: he received those impressions with which he could never after successfully struggle. From this time, intellect, education, nobility of sentiment, and high principle, in others, became objects of suspicion to him, and soon of hatred. The more he advanced in years the more this sentiment was confirmed in him. He wished to reign by himself. His jealousy on this point unceasingly became weakness. He reigned, indeed, in little things; the great he could never reach: even in the former, too, he was often governed. The superior ability of his early ministers and his early generals soon wearied him. He liked nobody to be in any way superior to him. Thus he chose his ministers, not for their knowledge, but for their ignorance; not for their capacity, but for their want of it. He liked to form them, as he said; liked to teach them even the most trifling things. It was the same with his generals. He took credit to himself for instructing them; wished it to be thought that from his cabinet he commanded and directed all his armies. . . .

This vanity, this unmeasured and unreasonable love of admiration, was his ruin. His ministers, his generals, his mistresses, his courtiers, soon perceived his weakness. They praised him with emulation and spoiled him. Praises, or to say truth, flattery, pleased him to such an extent, that the coarsest was well received, the vilest even better relished. . . .

And yet, it must be admitted, he might have done better. Though his intellect, as I have said, was beneath mediocrity, it was capable of being formed. He loved glory, was fond of order and regularity; was by disposition prudent, moderate, discreet, master of his movements and his tongue. Will it be believed? He was also by disposition good and just! God had sufficiently gifted him to enable him to be a good King; perhaps even *a tolerably great King!* . . .

It was his vanity, his desire for glory, that led him, soon after the death of the King of Spain, to make that event the pretext for war; in spite of the renunciations so recently made, so carefully stipulated, in the marriage contract. He marched into Flanders; his conquests there were rapid; the passage of the Rhine was admirable; the triple alliance of England, Sweden, and Holland only animated him. In the midst of winter he took Franche-Comté, by restoring which at the peace of Aix-la-Chapelle, he preserved his conquests in Flanders. All was flourishing then in the state. Riches everywhere. Colbert had placed the finances, the navy, commerce, manufactures, letters even, upon the highest point; and this age, like that of Augustus, produced in abundance illustrious men of all kinds, – even those illustrious only in pleasures. . . .

B. *The King's manners and tastes*

Never did man give with better grace than Louis XIV, or augmented so much, in this way, the price of his benefits. Never did man sell to better profit his words, even his smiles, – nay, his looks. Never did disobliging words escape him; and if he had to blame, to reprimand, or correct, which was very rare, it was nearly always with goodness, never . . . with anger or severity. Never was man so naturally polite, or of a politeness so measured, so graduated, so adapted to person, time, and place. Towards women his politeness was without parallel. Never did he pass the humblest petticoat without raising his hat; even to chambermaids, that he knew to be such, as often happened at Marly.[1] For ladies he took his hat off completely, but to a greater or less extent; for titled people, half off, holding it in his hand or against his ear some instants, more or less marked. For the nobility he contented himself by putting his hand to his hat. He took it off for the Princes of the blood, as for the ladies. If he accosted ladies he did not cover himself until he had quitted them. All this was out of doors, for in the house he was never covered. His reverences, more or less marked, but always light, were incomparable for their grace and manner; even his mode of half raising himself at supper for each lady who arrived at table. Though at last this fatigued him, yet he never ceased it; the ladies who were to sit down, however, took care not to enter after supper had commenced. . . .

He treated his valets well, above all those of the household. It was amongst them that he felt most at ease, and that he unbosomed himself the most familiarly, especially to the chiefs. Their friendship and their aversion have often had grand results. They were unceasingly in a position to render good and bad offices: thus they recalled those powerful enfranchised slaves of the Roman emperors, to whom the senate and the great people paid court and basely truckled. These valets during Louis XIV's reign were not less courted. The ministers, even the most powerful, openly studied their caprices; and the Princes of the blood, – nay, the bastards, – not to mention people of lower grade, did the same. The majority were accordingly insolent enough; and if you could not avoid their insolence, you were forced to put up with it. . . .

As for the King himself, nobody ever approached his magnificence. His buildings, who could number them? At the same time, who was there who did not deplore the pride, the caprice, the bad taste seen in them? He built nothing useful or ornamental in Paris, except the Pont Royal, and that simply by necessity; so that despite its incomparable extent, Paris is inferior to many cities of Europe. Saint-Germain, a lovely spot, with a marvellous view, rich forest, terraces, gardens, and water he abandoned for Versailles; the dullest and most ungrateful of all places, without prospect, without wood, without water, without soil; for the ground is all shifting sand or swamp, the air accordingly bad.

But he liked to subjugate nature by art and treasure. He built at Versailles, on, on, without any general design, the beautiful and the ugly, the vast and the mean, all jumbled together. His own apartments and those of the Queen, are inconvenient to the last degree, dull, close, stinking. The gardens astonish by their magnificence, but cause regret by their bad taste. You are introduced to the freshness of the shade only by a vast torrid zone, at the end of which there is nothing for you but to mount or descend; and with the hill, which is very short, terminate the gardens. The violence everwhere done to nature repels and wearies us despite ourselves. The abundance of water, forced up and gathered together from all parts, is rendered green, thick, muddy; it disseminates humidity, unhealthy and evident; and an odour still more so. I might never finish upon the monstrous defects of a palace so immense and so immensely dear, with its accompaniments, which are still more so. . . .

I am under the mark in saying that Versailles, even, did not cost so much as Marly.¹ . . .

¹ A favourite country residence not far from Versailles.

C. *The Revocation of the Edict of Nantes*

The profound ignorance in which the King had been educated and kept all his life, rendered him from the first an easy prey to the Jesuits. He became even more so with years, when he grew devout, for he was devout with the grossest ignorance. Religion became his weak point. In this state it was easy to persuade him that a decisive and tremendous blow struck against the Protestants would give his name more grandeur than any of his ancestors had acquired, besides strengthening his power and increasing his authority. Madame de Maintenon was one of those who did most to make him believe this.

The revocation of the edict of Nantes, without the slightest pretext or necessity, and the various proscriptions that followed it, were the fruits of a frightful plot, in which the new spouse was one of the chief conspirators, and which depopulated a quarter of the realm, ruined its commerce, weakened it in every direction, gave it up for a long time to the public and avowed pillage of the dragoons, authorised torments and punishments by which so many innocent people of both sexes were killed by thousands; ruined a numerous class; tore in pieces a world of families; armed relatives against relatives, so as to seize their property and leave them to die of hunger; banished our manufactures to foreign lands, made those lands flourish and overflow at the expense of France, and enabled them to build new cities; . . .

The King received from all sides news and details of these persecutions and of these conversions. It was by thousands that those who had abjured and taken the communion were counted; ten thousand in one place; six thousand in another – all at once and instantly. The King congratulated himself on his power and his piety. He believed himself to have renewed the days of the preaching of the Apostles, and attributed to himself all the honour. The bishops wrote panegyrics of him, the Jesuits made the pulpit resound with his praises. All France was filled with horror and confusion; and yet there never was so much triumph and joy – never such profusion of laudations! The monarch doubted not of the sincerity of this crowd of conversions; the converters took good care to persuade him of it and to beatify him beforehand. He swallowed their poison in long draughts. He had never yet believed himself so great in the eyes of man, or so advanced in the eyes of God, in the reparation of his sins and of the scandals of his life. He heard nothing but eulogies, while the good and true Catholics and the true bishops, groaned in spirit to see the orthodox act towards error and heretics as heretical tyrants and heathens had acted against the truth, the confessors, and the martyrs. They could not, above all, endure this immensity of perjury and sacrilege. They bitterly lamented the durable and irremediable odium that detestable measure cast upon the true religion, whilst our neighbours exulting to see us thus weaken and destroy ourselves, profited by our madness, and built designs upon the hatred we should draw upon ourselves from all the Protestant powers.

D. *The King with his armies*

I will not speak much of the King's manner of living when with the army. His hours were determined by what was to be done, though he held his councils regularly; I will simply say, that morning and evening he ate with people privileged to have that honour. When any one wished to claim it, the first gentleman of the chamber on duty was appealed to. He gave the answer, and if favourable you presented yourself the next day to the King, who said to you, 'Monsieur, seat yourself at table.' That being done, all was done. Ever afterwards you were at liberty to take a place at the King's table, but with discretion. The number of the persons from whom a choice was made was, however, very limited. Even very high military rank did not suffice. M. de Vauban, at the siege of Namur, was overwhelmed by the distinction. The King did the same honour at Namur to the Abbé de Grancey, who exposed himself everywhere to confess the wounded and encourage the troops. No other Abbé was ever so distinguished. All the clergy were excluded save the cardinals, and the bishops, peers, or the ecclesiastics who held the rank of foreign princes.

At these repasts everybody was covered [wore a hat]; it would have been a want of respect, of which you would have been immediately informed, if you had not kept your hat on your head. The King alone was uncovered. When the King wished to speak to you, or you had occasion to speak to him, you uncovered. You uncovered, also, when Monseigneur or Monsieur spoke to you, or you to them. For Princes of the blood you merely put your hand to your hat. The King alone had an arm-chair. All the rest of the company, Monseigneur included, had seats, with backs of black morocco leather, which could be folded up to be carried, and which were called 'parrots'. Except at the army, the King never ate with any man, under whatever circumstances; not even with the Princes of the blood, save sometimes at their wedding feasts.

27
Pierre Bayle, *The Great Contest of Faith and Reason*
(1686)

Source: Pierre Bayle, *The Great Contest of Faith and Reason*, translated and edited by Karl C. Sandberg, in *Milestones of Thought in the History of Ideas*, Frederick Ungar, 1963, pp.41–3, 51–2, 54–5.

Pierre Bayle (1647–1706), the son of a Huguenot minister, studied both Protestant and Catholic theology. After studying at the Jesuit Academy at Toulouse, and a brief period as a Catholic, he reconverted in 1670, and took up professorial posts at Protestant Academies at Geneva and Sedan. When the latter was closed by royal edict, he left France permanently in 1680 for Rotterdam, where he produced a stream of publications defending the Reformed Church against the background of the persecution of the Huguenots in France. (Also see above II.6.)

BAYLE, from 'A PHILOSOPHIC COMMENTARY UPON THESE WORDS OF JESUS CHRIST: "COMPEL THEM TO COME IN,"[1] WHEREBY IT IS PROVED BY MANY DEMONSTRATIVE REASONS THAT NOTHING IS MORE ABOMINABLE THAN TO MAKE CONVERSIONS BY FORCE' (1686)

I leave it to the theologians and the textual critics to explicate this passage by examining what precedes and what follows, by showing the force of the terms of the original, and of their various possible meanings, and of the meaning which they indeed do have in several places in the Scripture. As for myself, I aspire to write a new kind of commentary and to found it upon principles which are more general and more infallible than anything which the study of languages and criticisms and commonplaces could furnish me. I will not even try to discover why Jesus Christ used this expression *compel*, nor will I try to ascertain its legitimate meaning, nor will I try to discover whether there be some mystery lurking beneath its surface. I will limit myself to refuting the literal meaning which the persecutors give to it.

In order to refute it incontrovertibly I will base my argument upon this principle of natural light, that any literal meaning which entails the obligation to commit crimes is false. St Augustine himself sets down this rule for discerning between the figurative meaning and the literal meaning of the Scripture. Jesus Christ, he tells us, declares that if we do not eat the flesh of the Son of Man, we will not be saved. It seems that this interpretation enjoins us to commit a crime. These words must therefore be taken as a figure which enjoins us to participate in Communion and to bring to our remembrance for our edification that the Lord's flesh was crucified and wounded for us. This is not the place to examine whether or not these words prove that St Augustine was not of the opinion of the Roman Church, or whether or not he applies his own rule appropriately. Suffice it to say that he bases his reasoning upon this fundamental principle of Scriptual exegesis that *if a literal interpretation of the Scripture obliges men to commit crimes* or (to be perfectly clear) to perform acts which natural light, the precepts of the Decalogue [Ten Commandments], and the morality of the Gospel prohibit, we must assuredly conclude that its proponents have given the Scripture a false meaning, and instead of a divine revelation, they offer us nothing more than their own imaginations, passions, or prejudices. . . .

I know full well that there are axioms against which the most express and evident words of the Scripture would be powerless, as for example, the whole is greater than its parts; if from equal parts one takes away equal parts, the remainders are equal; it is impossible for two contradictory statements both to be true; or that the essence of a subject continues really to subsist after the destruction of the subject. Even if one were to show a hundred Scriptural passages contradicting these propositions, even if one were to perform thousands upon thousands of miracles, more than Moses and the Apostles, in order to establish a doctrine opposed to these universal maxims of common sense, people would still not be convinced. Rather, they would be persuaded either that the Scripture spoke only by metaphor or that these miracles came from the devil, for they cannot believe that the natural light of men which dictates these maxims is deceptive. . . .

It is then clear that the only legitimate way to inspire religion is to produce within the soul certain views and acts of will concerning God. Now since threats, persecutions, fines, exiles, beatings, tortures, and generally everything that is contained in the literal meaning of constraint cannot create these acts of will which constitute the essence of religion, it is clear that this use of constraint to establish a religion is false. Consequently, Jesus Christ did not command it.

I do not deny that the use of force produces within the soul certain views and acts of will, in addition to the external postures which are the usual signs of inward religion. These attitudes, however, are not toward God, but only toward the originators of the constraint. The persecuted judge that their persecutors are to be feared, and they indeed fear them. But those people who did not have the proper views concerning God beforehand and did not feel due respect, love, and fear for Him, do not acquire these ideas and feelings when someone forces them to go through the outward forms of religion. Likewise, those who held certain ideas of God beforehand and who believed that He was to be honored only in a certain way which was different than that of the persecutors, do not change their inward feeling toward God either. Their only new thoughts are to fear their persecutors and to retain their goods which are in danger. Thus, these manifestations of force accomplish nothing with respect to God, for the inward acts they produce have no relationship to Him. And as for the outward acts, it is evident that they are accepted by God only as they are accompanied by the inward dispositions of the soul which are the essence of religion. This should be sufficient to assure the solidity of this proof.

The nature of religion is a certain persuasion of the soul with regard to God which produces in the will the feelings of love, respect, and fear which this Supreme Being deserves, and in the members of the body the signs appropriate to this persuasion and disposition of the will. Therefore, if the outward signs are accompanied by an inappropriate or contradictory disposition of the soul, they are acts of hypocrisy, bad faith, or infidelity and revolt against conscience. . . .

To try to convert people by force to a religion they do not profess is consequently in evident contradiction with common sense and natural light, the general principles of reason, and, in a word, with the original and basic rule of discerning the true from the false, the good from the bad. . . .

It is commonly said that there is no more dangerous plague in a state than the multiplicity of religions, because it causes dissension between friends and neighbors, fathers and children, husbands and wives, and sovereigns and subjects. I answer that far from working against me, this argument is a very strong proof in favour of tolerance. If a multiplicity of religions is harmful to a state, it is only because one religion does not wish to tolerate another and sets out to crush it by persecution. *Hinc prima mali labes*, this is the source of the evil. If each religion practiced the tolerance which I advocate, a state divided by ten religions would enjoy the same peace and harmony as a city where all the different kinds of artisans live together in peace in spite of their differences. The only result of religious toleration would be an honest effort on the part of each sect to distinguish itself by its piety, its virtuous acts, and its learning. Each one would make it a matter of pride to show by its good works that it was the most favored of God. Each would even show forth more devotion to the state if the sovereign protected all of them and judged them all with equity. Now such an honest emulation among them would obviously be the source of an infinite amount of good, and consequently nothing would be more apt to restore the Golden Age than toleration. Certainly the harmony which it would establish among several voices and instruments of varying tones and keys would not be any less pleasing than the uniformity of a single voice. But what stands in the way of this fine concert of diverse voices and sounds? It is the desire of one of the religions to exercise a cruel tyranny over the minds of others and to force others to sacrifice their consciences. It is the unjust partiality of kings who deliver the executive power of the state over to the raging and tumultuous desires of a populace of monks and religionists. In a word, all the strife comes not from tolerance, but from intolerance.

[1] Luke 14:23. In this passage Christ commands his servants 'to go out into the highways and hedges and compel them to come in, that my house may be filled'. In the fourth century AD, St Augustine cites the passage to justify the repression of heretics; and it was constantly invoked by the Catholic clergy in France (e.g. Bossuet) as authority for the forcible conversion of Huguenots.

28
Fénelon: Letter to Louis XIV (*c.*1694)

Source: Lettre à Louis XIV, avec une Préface de Henri Guillemin, c.*1694* from *Collection du Sablier,* Neuchâtel, series Ides et Calendes, Switzerland, 1966, pp.60–70. Translated by A. Lentin.

François de Salignac de La Mothe-Fénelon (1651–1715), churchman and writer, was well known for his piety and saintliness. A popular instructor of converts from Protestantism, he preferred persuasion to force. In 1689, under Bossuet's patronage, he became tutor to Louis XIV's grandson, the Duke of Burgundy, and was made Archbishop of Cambrai in 1695. Fénelon, however, became associated with Quietism, a religious movement which aroused the suspicions of Bossuet and was condemned as heretical. In 1699 Louis confined him to the see at Cambrai. The same year, Fénelon published his best known work, *The Adventures of Télémaque,* an allegorical account of the upbringing of the ideal ruler, which was read by many as a veiled critique of Louis' rule. He wrote this letter to Louis XIV around 1694. It is doubtful that Louis ever received it, and it was not published until long after.

Your name has become hateful and the entire French nation intolerable to all our neighbours. None of our former allies has been retained, because all that was desired were slaves. For over twenty years, bloody wars have been sparked off. For example, Sire, in 1672 your Majesty was induced to embark on war with Holland for the sake of your glory . . . I mention this war in particular because it has been the source of all the others. Its only cause was a desire for glory and vengeance which can never justify a war; hence all the frontiers which you have extended as a result of that war were unjustly acquired from the start. It is true, Sire, that the subsequent peace treaties appear to cover up and make good that injustice, since they have assigned to you the conquered places; but an unjust war is no less unjust for being successful. Peace treaties signed by the vanquished are not freely signed. Men sign with a knife at their throat, they sign in spite of themselves, in order to avoid still greater losses; they sign as men surrender their purse when it is a case of your money or your life. Thus, Sire, one must go back to the origin of that war with Holland if one is to consider all your conquests in God's presence.

It is useless to say that they were necessary to the State: other people's property is never necessary to us. What we really need is to do strict justice. You should not even claim the right to keep certain places as guarantees of the security of your frontiers. It is for you to seek that security by means of good alliances, your own moderation, or places in the rear which you can fortify. In any event, our concern for security never entitles us to take our neighbour's land. Take advice from men of learning and integrity: they will tell you that what I say is as clear as daylight. . . .

That war is also the true source of all the evils suffered by France. Ever since that war, you have always sought to dictate peace from above and to lay down conditions instead of drawing them up with equity and moderation. Hence lasting peace has been impossible. Your enemies, having been shamefully humiliated, have had one sole aspiration: to recover and to unite against you. Is it any wonder? You did not even keep to the terms of that peace which you laid down with such arrogance. In time of peace you waged war and made enormous conquests. You set up a *Chambre des réunions* [courts set up by Louis XIV to give legal sanction to his annexations] so as to be judge and litigant at the same time, thus adding insult and mockery to usurpation and aggression. You scrutinised the treaty of Westphalia[1] for ambiguous terms in order to take over Strasbourg. None of your ministers had ever dared, after so many years, to cite those terms in any kind of negotiation in order to show that you had the slightest claim to that town. Such conduct has united and inspired the whole of Europe against you. Even those who have not dared to declare themselves openly, impatiently desire (to say the least) to see you weakened and humiliated, as the only way to bring liberty and peace to all the Christian nations. You, Sire, who could gain such lasting and peaceful glory by being a father of your subjects and an arbiter to your neighbours, have become the common enemy of your neighbours and have the reputation of a hard taskmaster within your kingdom. . . .

Your peoples, however, whom you ought to love as your children, and who hitherto have been so devoted to you, are starving to death. Agriculture is all but abandoned; the towns and the countryside are being depopulated; all trades languish and no longer feed the workers. All trade is at an end. You have thus destroyed half of the real strengths within your State in order to make and to defend vain conquests outside it. Instead of extracting money from this poor people, the people should be given alms and food. The whole of France is no more than one great hospital, desolate and unprovided for. The magistrates are brought low and exhausted. The nobility, whose property is all under order of distraint, only survives by virtue of suspending decrees. You are importuned by the crowd of grumbling petitioners. You have brought all these difficulties upon yourself, Sire; for since the whole kingdom has been ruined, everything lies in your hands, and no-one can live except by your bounties. So flourishes this great kingdom under a king every day held out to be the people's joy, and who would indeed be so had he not been poisoned by flattering counsels.

The whole truth must be told: the very people which so adored and trusted you, begins to lose its love, its trust and even its respect for you. Your victories and conquests no longer delight it: it is full of bitterness and despair. Little by little the flame of sedition is everywhere arising. Men think that you have no pity for them in their misfortunes, that you care only for your authority and your glory. If, they say, the king had a father's heart for his people, would he not glory in providing bread for them and in giving them breathing-space after so many ills, rather than in keeping a few frontier towns which lead to war? What is the answer to that, Sire? Popular uprisings, for so long unknown, are becoming commonplace. Not even Paris, so close to you, is exempt. The magistrates are obliged to tolerate the insolence of the insurgents and to bribe them into submission; thus those who ought to be punished, are rewarded. You are reduced to a shameful and deplorable extremity: either to leave sedition unpunished and to increase it by this impunity, or inhumanly to put down peoples whom you bring to despair by tearing from them, through your taxes for this war, the bread which they try to earn by the sweat of their brow.

But while they lack bread, you yourself lack money, and you refuse to see the extremity to which you are reduced. Because you have always enjoyed good fortune, you cannot imagine that you might ever cease to do so. You fear to open your eyes; you fear having to lose some of your glory. This glory, which hardens your heart, means more to you than justice, than your own tranquillity, than the lives of your peoples, who are dying every day from diseases caused by the famine; more, in word, than your eternal salvation, which is incompatible with this idol of glory.

Such, Sire, is your situation. You live as if with a fatal blindfold across your eyes; you flatter yourself with ephemeral successes which decide nothing, and you take no overview of things in general, which are gradually falling into irremediable decline. Whilst you encounter the field of battle and the enemy cannon in some rude combat, while you storm towns, you have no idea that you are fighting on ground which sinks beneath your feet, and that you will fall despite your victories.

Everyone sees, and none dares make you see. Perhaps you will see when it is too late. True courage consists in never flattering oneself and in firmly deciding to do what has to be done. You readily listen, Sire, only to those who flatter you with vain hopes. The men whom you reckon the most reliable are those whom you fear and avoid most. You ought to place yourself in the vanguard of truth, since you are king, to urge men to tell you the truth without softening it, and to encourage those who are too timid. On the contrary, you seek only to avoid looking beneath the surface; but God will one day contrive to lift the veil that covers your eyes and show you what you seek to avoid. He has long since held his arm raised above you, but he is slow to strike because he feels pity for a prince who all his life has been surrounded by flatterers, and also because your enemies are his too. But he will contrive to distinguish his just cause from yours, which is unjust, and to bring you low in order to convert you; for you will be a Christian only in humiliation. You do not love God; you do not even fear him except with a slavish fear; you fear hell, not God. Your religion only consists in superstitions, in petty superficial practices.

[1] 1648, ending the Thirty Years' War.

29
Two contemporary pamphlets

A. *Pamphlet by Andrew Fletcher (1697)*

Source: Andrew Fletcher of Saltoun, *A Discourse Concerning Militias and Standing Armies with relation to the past and present Governments of Europe and of England in particular*, London, 1697, pp.6–7.

Andrew Fletcher (1655–1716) was laird of Saltoun in East Lothian, Scotland. He was exiled in the early 1680s after he had vigorously opposed the policies of Charles II and the Duke of York. Described by the English envoy to France as 'an ingenious but a violent fanatic', he supported Monmouth and participated in his invasion in 1685. He withdrew before its collapse, either because the proclamation of Monmouth as king offended his republican sentiments, or because he had murdered a fellow rebel. He was reinstated by William of Orange but opposed the king, taking every opportunity to limit royal power and enhance the independence of Scotland.

In our time most princes in Europe are in possession of the sword, by standing mercenary forces kept up in time of peace, and absolutely depending on them, I say that all such governments are changed from monarchies to tyrannies. Nor can the power of granting or refusing money, though vested in the subject, be a sufficient security for liberty, where a standing mercenary army is kept in time of peace: for he that is armed, is always master of the purse of him that is unarmed. And not only that government is tyrannical, which is tyrannically exercised; but all governments are tyrannical, which have not in their constitution a sufficient security against the arbitrary power of the prince.

B. *Pamphlet by John Toland (1698)*

Source: John Toland, *The Militia Reformed or an easy scheme of furnishing England with a constant landforce, capable to prevent or subdue any foreign power; and to maintain perpetual quiet at home, without endangering the public liberty,* printed by John Darby, sold by Andrew Bell, London, 1698, pp.73–4.

John Toland (1670–1722) was born a Catholic near Londonderry in Ireland. His conversion to Protestantism gave him access to educated radical circles in northern Europe. His publication of *Christianity not Mysterious* in 1696 caused a great stir as it was one of the earliest works which contained deist (belief in a god but not in a creed dependent on revelation) ideas. He eked out a precarious living supported by various enlightened patrons and published a large number of his own subversive tracts as well as the works of Harrington and other radical thinkers.

When a mercenary army is once routed and dispersed, then all is irrecoverably lost, because either that you cannot presently take the field again, or you can only oppose the enemy with undisciplined multitudes. Now we may easily conceive why a militia of freemen are for venturing a battle whenever they are favoured with an opportunity of doing it, whereas mercenaries are observed to decline fighting as much as they can . . . for the first are sure of making good their losses by a rotation of their fellows, and the latter wait for advantages, because the loss of one battle is enough to ruin them. From all that is premised, I think I may conclude, that to make successive levies of our free militia out of the several parts of England, and corroborated with some auxiliary regiments, is the best method of waging the wars abroad.

30
John Locke, *Two Treatises of Government* (1690)

Source: John Locke, *Two Treatises of Government,* a critical edition, by P. Laslett, Cambridge University Press, Cambridge, 1967, pp.398–401.

John Locke (1632–1704) studied the classics at Christ Church, Oxford. He refused to become a cleric but managed to remain as a lecturer until his disgrace after the Exclusion Crisis. He also studied medicine and, by 1667, was mainly living in the household of Anthony Ashley Cooper

(1672, earl of Shaftesbury) as his personal physician. He became involved in the earl's political activities and his own opinions appear to have become more radical. At the time of Shaftesbury's disgrace and flight, he too found it prudent to leave England for Holland (1683). Locke returned to England after the Glorious Revolution and was given an undemanding post as commissioner of appeals (£200 per annum). He lived partly in London and partly with his friends Lord and Lady Masham in Essex. (Also see above, III.12.)

Of Paternal, Political, and Despotical Power, considered together.
Though I have had occasion to speak of these separately before, yet the great mistakes of late about Government, having, as I suppose, arisen from confounding these distinct Powers one with another, it may not, perhaps, be amiss, to consider them here together.

170. *First* then, *Paternal* or *Parental Power* is nothing but that, which Parents have over their Children, to govern them for the Children's good, till they come to the use of Reason, or a state of Knowledge, wherein they may be supposed capable to understand that Rule, whether it be the Law of Nature, or the municipal Law of their Country they are to govern themselves by: Capable, I say, to know it, as well as several others, who live, as Free-men, under the Law. ... the *Paternal* is a natural *Government*, but not at all extending it self to the Ends, and Jurisdictions of that which is Political. The *Power of the Father doth not reach* at all to the *Property* of the Child, which is only in his own disposing.

171. *Secondly, Political Power* is that Power which every Man, having in the state of Nature, has given up into the hands of the Society, and therein to the Governors, whom the Society hath set over it self, with this express or tacit Trust, That it shall be employed for their good, and the preservation of their Property; Now this *Power*, which every Man has *in the state of Nature*, and which he parts with to the Society, in all such cases, where the Society can secure him, is, to use such means for the preserving of his own Property, as he thinks good, and Nature allows him; and to punish the Breach of the Law of Nature in others so, as (according to the best of his Reason) may most conduce to the preservation of himself, and the rest of Mankind. So that the *end and measure of this Power*, when in every Man's hands in the state of Nature, being the preservation of all of his Society, that is, all Mankind in general, it can have no other *end or measure*, when in the hands of the Magistrate, but to preserve the Members of that Society in their Lives, Liberties, and Possessions; and so cannot be an Absolute, Arbitrary Power over their Lives and Fortunes, which are as much as possible to be preserved; but a *Power to make Laws*, and annex such *Penalties* to them, as may tend to the preservation of the whole, but cutting off those Parts, and those only, which are so corrupt, that they threaten the sound and healthy, without which no severity is lawful. And this *Power has its Original only from*

Compact and Agreement, and the mutual Consent of those who make up the Community.

172. *Thirdly, Despotical Power* is an Absolute, Arbitrary Power one Man has over another, to take away his Life, whenever he pleases. This is a Power, which neither Nature gives, for it has made no such distinction between one Man and another; nor Compact can convey, for Man not having such an Arbitrary Power over his own Life, cannot give another Man such a Power over it; but it is *the effect only of Forfeiture,* which the Aggressor makes of his own Life, when he puts himself into the state of War with another. For having quitted Reason, which God hath given to be the Rule betwixt Man and Man, and the common bond whereby humane kind is united into one fellowship and society; and having renounced the way of peace, which that teaches, and made use of the Force of War to compass his unjust ends upon an other, where he has no right, and so revolting from his own kind to that of Beasts by making Force which is theirs, to be his rule of right, he renders himself liable to be destroyed by the injured person and the rest of mankind, that will join with him in the execution of Justice, . . .

31
Christopher Wren: a letter of 1665

Source: Christopher Wren, *Parentalia, or Memoirs of the Family of Wren,* London, 1750, pp.261–2.

Christopher Wren (1632–1723), a founder and President of the Royal Society (knighted in 1673), was the foremost architect of the late seventeenth century. His visit to France in 1665 brought him into contact with French classicism at its height, and had a crucial influence on his own development.

The Louvre for a while was my daily object; where no less than a thousand hands are constantly employed in the works; some in laying mighty foundations, some in raising the stories, columns, entablements[1] &c. with vast stones, by great and useful engines; others in carving, inlaying of marbles, plastering, painting, gilding, &c. Which altogether make a school of architecture, the best probably, at this day in Europe . . . Monsieur Colbert, the Superintendant, comes to the works of the Louvre, every Wednesday, and, if business hinders not, Thursday. The workmen are paid every Sunday duly. Monsieur Abbé Charles introduced me to the acquaintance of Bernini, who shewed me the designs of the Louvre, and of the King's statue . . .

Bernini's design of the Louvre I would have given my skin for, but the old reserved Italian gave me but a few minutes view; it was five little designs on paper, for which he hath received as many thousand pistoles:[2] I had only time to copy it in my fancy and memory; I shall be able by discourse and a crayon to give you a tolerable account of it.

[1] Horizontal platforms supporting statues.
[2] Gold coin, worth about £1.

32
The Fountains at Boughton (1712)

Source: John Morton, *Natural History of Northamptonshire*, R. Knaplock and R. Wilkin, London, 1712, pp.491–2.

John Morton (*c.*1671–1726), naturalist and Fellow of the Royal Society, was curate and Rector of Great Oxendon, Northamptonshire, in the reign of Queen Anne. He was the author of *The Natural History of Northamptonshire* (1712), from which the description of the gardens at Boughton is taken.

The seat at Boughton is particularly observable for its spacious, elegant and delightful gardens, and for its sumptuous water-works. Below the western front of the house are three more remarkable parterres [level spaces with flowerbeds, etc.]: the parterre of statues, the parterre of basins, and the water parterre, wherein is an octagon basin whose circumference is 216 yards, which in the middle of it has a Jet d'Eau [fountain] whose height is above 50 feet, surrounded with other smaller jets d'Eaus . . . The canal at the bottom of all, is about 1500 yards in length in four lines falling into each other at right angles. At the lower end of it is a very noble cascade. The walls on each side of the cascade at the head of the basin that it falls into, are adorned with vases and statues. The cascade has five falls. The perpendicular about seven feet. A line or range of jets d'eau, in number thirteen, are placed at the head of the cascade, and possess the interval where the water enters upon its first fall. These throw *up* their water, as that of the canal descends. A very agreeable and charming entertainment both to the eye and ear, and a lovely refreshment to the standers-by, in a hot and sultry air.

33
D'Avenant's adaptation of *Macbeth* (an extract from Act II Scene 1) (1674)

Source: C. Spenser (ed.), *D'Avenant's Macbeth from the Yale Manuscript*, Yale University Press, New Haven, 1961, p.96.

William D'Avenant (1606–88) was a poet, playwright and impresario. Poet laureate in 1638, he accompanied the Stuart court to exile in Paris during the Interregnum. On the Restoration, he was foremost in his efforts to revive English drama, banned under Cromwell. Reputed to be Shakespeare's godson, he adapted Shakespearean plays to suit the taste of contemporary audiences. Passages amended by D'Avenant are italicized.

Macb. Go bid your Mistress, when *she is undrest,*
To strike *the Closet-bell, and I'll go* to bed.
Is this a dagger which I see before me?
The *hilt draws* towards my hand; come, let me *grasp* thee:
I have thee not, and yet I see thee still;
Art thou not, fatal Vision, sensible
To feeling as to sight? or, art thou but
A dagger of the mind, a false creation
Proceeding from the brain, *opprest with heat.*
My eyes are made the fools of th'other senses;
Or else worth all the rest: I see thee still,
And on thy blade *are stains of reeking* bloud.
It is the bloudy business *that* thus
Informs *my eye-sight*; now, *to half the world*
Nature seems dead, and wicked dreams *infect*
The *health of* sleep; now witchcraft celebrates
Pale *Heccate*'s Offerings; *now* murder *is*
Alarm'd by his *nights* Centinel: the wolf,
Whose howl*ing seems the watch-word to the dead:*
But whilst I *talk*, he lives: *hark, I am summon'd;*
O *Duncan*, hear it not, for 'tis a *bell*
That rings my Coronation, and thy Knell.

34
Dryden on Louis XIV (1692)

Source: John Dryden, 'A Discourse concerning the Origins and Progress of Satire', reprinted in G.R. Noyes (ed.), *The Poetical Works of Dryden*, The Riverside Press, Cambridge, Mass., 1950, p.286.

John Dryden (1631–1700), the leading poet and literary critic under Charles II and James II, succeeded D'Avenant as poet laureate from 1668 to 1688. As a dramatist, he was an important contributor to the revival of the post-Restoration English theatre. In the extract he refers to Boileau, a prominent contemporary French literary critic.

If I would only cross the seas, I might find in France a living Horace and a Juvenal, in the person of the admirable Boileau; whose numbers are excellent, whose expressions are noble, whose thoughts are just, whose language is pure, whose satire is pointed, and whose sense is close; what he borrows from the ancients, he repays with usury of his own, in coin as good, and almost as universally valuable: for, setting prejudice and partiality apart, tho' he is our enemy, the stamp of a Louis, the patron of all arts, is not much inferior to the medal of an Augustus Caesar. Let this be said without entering into the interests of factions and parties, and relating only to the bounty of that king to men of learning and merit; a praise so just, that even we, who are his enemies, cannot refuse it to him.

35
Addison on the French

Joseph Addison (1672–1719), poet and essayist, was, with Richard Steele, the leading contributor to the periodical literature of the reign of Queen Anne in *The Tatler* and *The Spectator*. His continental Grand Tour of 1699–1704 brought him into contact with French men of letters, including the leading French literary critic, Boileau. Addison was a Whig, held office under Whig administrations and expressed strong Whig views in his periodicals.

A. *Addison on the French (1708)*

Source: Joseph Addison, 'The Present State of the War', reprinted in *Addison, Works*, edited by R. Hurd, Henry Bohn, London, 1854, vol. IV, pp.341–2.

The French are certainly the most implacable, and the most dangerous enemies of the British nation. Their form of government, their religion, their jealousy of the British power, as well as their prosecution of commerce, and pursuit of universal Monarchy, will fix them for ever in their animosities and aversions towards us, and make them catch at all opportunities of subverting our constitution, destroying our religion, ruining our trade, and sinking the figure which we make among the nations of Europe: not to mention the particular ties of honour that lie on their present King to impose on us a Prince, who must prove fatal to our country if he ever reigns over us.

B. *Addison on the influence of the French (1710)*

Source: Joseph Addison, *The Spectator*, 8 September 1710, reprinted in *Addison, Works*, edited by R. Hurd, Henry Bohn, London, 1854, vol. III, pp.11–15.

I have often wished, that as in our constitution there are several persons whose business it is to watch over our laws, our liberties, and commerce, certain men might be set apart as superintendents of our language, to hinder any words of a foreign coin from passing among us; and in particular to prohibit any French phrases from becoming current in this kingdom, when those of our own stamp are altogether as valuable. The present war has so adulterated our tongue with strange words, that it would be impossible for one of our great-grandfathers to know what his posterity has been doing, were he to read their exploits in a modern newspaper. Our warriors are very industrious in propagating the French language, at the same time that they are so gloriously successful in beating down their power. Our soldiers are men of strong heads for action, and perform such feats as they are not able to express. They want words in their own tongue to tell us what it is they achieve, and therefore send us over accounts of their performance in a jargon of phrases, which they learn among their conquered enemies. They ought however to be provided with secretaries, and assisted by our foreign ministers, to tell their story for them in plain English, and to let us know in our mother-tongue what it is our brave countrymen are about . . .

I remember in that remarkable year when our country was delivered from the greatest fears and apprehensions, and raised to the greatest height of gladness it had ever felt since it was a nation, I mean the year of Blenheim [1704], I had the copy of a letter sent to me out of the country, which was written from a young gentleman in the army to his father, a man of good estate and plain sense: as the letter was very modishly chequered with this modern military eloquence, I shall present my reader with a copy of it.

'Sir,
   Upon the junction of the French and Bavarian armies they took post behind

a great morass which they thought impracticable. Our general the next day sent a party of horse to reconnoitre them from a little *hauteur*, at about a quarter of an hour's distance from the army, who returned again to camp unobserved through several defiles, in one of which they met with a party of French that had been marauding, and made them all prisoners at discretion. The day after a drum arrived at our camp, with the message which he would communicate to none but the general; he was followed by a trumpet, who they say behaved himself very saucily, with a message from the Duke of Bavaria. The next morning our army, being divided into two corps, made a movement towards the enemy; you will hear in the public prints how we treated them, with the other circumstances of that glorious day. I had the good fortune to be in the regiment that pushed the *Gens d'Arms*. Several French battalions, who some say were a *Corps de Reserve*, made a show of resistance; but it only proved a gasconade, for upon our preparing to fill up a little fosse, in order to attack them, they beat the *Chamade*, and sent us *Charte Blanche*. Their commandant, with a great many other general officers, and troops without number, are made prisoners of war, and will, I believe, give you a visit in England, the *cartel* not being yet settled. Not questioning but these particulars will be very welcome to you, I congratulate you upon them, and am your most dutiful son,' &c.

The father of the young gentleman upon the perusal of the letter found it contained great news, but could not guess what it was. He immediately communicated it to the curate of the parish, who upon the reading of it, being vexed to see anything he could not understand, fell into a kind of passion, and told him, that his son had sent him a letter that was neither fish, flesh, nor good red herring.

36
Wycherley on a foolish francophile (1672)

Source: From *The Gentleman Dancing-Master*, in G. Weales (ed.), *The Complete Plays of William Wycherley*, New York University Press, New York, 1967, pp.133–4.

William Wycherley (1640–1716), one of the leading writers of Restoration comedy, was educated in France during the Interregnum. His plays include *Love in a Wood* (1671), his classic *The Country Wife* (1675) and *The Plain Dealer* (1676), based on Molière's *Le Misanthrope*.

The heroine, Hippolita, in love with Gerard, is to be forced by her father to marry her cousin, Mr Paris, who calls himself Monsieur de Paris, 'a vain coxcomb and rich city-heir, newly returned from France, and mightily affected with the French language and fashions'. In Act I Scene 1 Hippolita questions Paris about Gerard.

MONSIEUR. *Non, non*, they say he has good sense and judgment, but it is according to the account *Englis'* – for –
HIPPOLITA. For what?
MONSIEUR. For *Jarnie*[1] – if I think it –
HIPPOLITA. Why?
MONSIEUR. Why – why his tailor lives within Ludgate [i.e. Gerard does not have a French tailor], his *valet-de-chambre* is no Frenchman, and he has been seen at noon-day to go into an English eating-house.
HIPPOLITA. Say you so, Cousin?
MONSIEUR. Then for being well bred, you shall judge. First, he can't dance a step, nor sing a French song, nor swear a French *oat'*, nor use the polite French word in his conversation; and, in fine, can't play at Ombre [a card game], but speaks base good *Englis'* with the *commune* homebread pronunication, and, in fine, to say no more, he ne'er carries a snuff-box about with him.[2]
HIPPOLITA. Indeed.
MONSIEUR. And yet this man has been abroad as much as any man, and does not make the least show of it, but a little in his mien, not at all in his *discour, Jarnie*; he never talks so much as of St Peter's Church, and Rome, the Escurial, or Madrid, nay not so much as of Henry IV, of Pont-Neuf, Paris, and the new Louvre, nor of the *Grand Roi*.[3]

[1] *Jarnie* or *jarnidieu*, an oath, formed from '*je renie Dieu*' = 'sdeath, 'sblood.
[2] The snuff-box was a recent French importation.
[3] The Pont-Neuf bridge over the Seine was built by Henri IV, whose statue stands nearby. The new Louvre refers to the great colonnaded east front, built 1666–70. The *Grand Roi* is Louis XIV.

37

Stage directions by Thomas Shadwell for his production of Shakespeare's *The Tempest* (c.1673)

Source: E.J. Dent, *Foundations of English Opera: A Study of Musical Drama in England during the Seventeenth Century*, Cambridge University Press, Cambridge, 1928, pp.139–40.

Thomas Shadwell (1642–92) succeeded Dryden in 1688 as poet laureate. He was a dramatist and impresario under the Restoration. As poet laureate he instituted New Year and birthday odes.

Act I, Scene I

The front of the stage is opened, and the band of 24 violins, with the harpsicals and theorbos which accompany the voices, are placed between the pit and the stage. While the overture is playing, the curtain rises, and discovers a new frontispiece, joined to the great pilasters, on each side of the stage. This frontispiece is a noble arch, supported by large wreathed columns of the Corinthian order; the wreathing of the columns are beautified with roses wound round them, and several cupids flying about them. On the cornice, just above the capitals, sits on either side a figure, with a trumpet in one hand, and a palm in the other, representing Fame. A little further on the same cornice, on each side of a compass-pediment, lie a lion and a unicorn, the supporters of the royal arms of England. In the middle of the arch are several angels, holding the King's arms, as if they were placing them in the midst of that compass-pediment.

Behind this is the scene, which represents a thick cloudy sky, a very rocky coast, and a tempestuous sea in perpetual agitation. This Tempest (supposed to be raised by magic) has many dreadful objects in it, as several spirits in horrid shapes flying down amidst the sailors, then rising and crossing in the air. And when the ship is sinking, the whole house is darkened, and a shadow of fire falls upon 'em. This is accompanied by lightning, and several claps of thunder to the end of the storm.

38
Vauban's memorandum on frontier fortifications in Flanders (1678)

Source: G. Symcox (ed.), *War, Diplomacy and Imperialism, 1618–1763*, Macmillan, London, Basingstoke, 1974, pp.167–8. Translation from French.

Sebastien Le Prestre de Vauban (1633–1706) was a military engineer who fought in all the wars of Louis XIV's reign. He approached the art of warfare and, in particular, of constructing fortresses, defences and siege works, in a scientific manner. During Louis XIV's early campaigns his designs proved to be very successful. He also wrote prolifically on warfare and many other subjects.

The Frontier toward the Low Countries lies open and disordered as a consequence of the recent peace. There is no doubt that it will be necessary to establish a new frontier and fortify it so well that it closes the approaches into our country to an enemy while giving us access to his; that the fortified points that compose it will secure the river-crossings for us and provide

communication between the local government districts; that the for.
places should be large enough to contain not only the munitions required for
their own defense but also the supplies needed if we invade enemy territory. If
we assume all these to be necessary conditions, it appears that the frontier
would be very well protected if its defences were reduced to two lines of
fortifications, on the model of an army's order of battle, as follows:

The first line would be made up of thirteen fortified towns and two
fortresses: Dunkirk, Bergues, Furnes, the fort of la Kenocq, Ypres, Menin,
Lille, Tournai, the fort of Mortagne, Condé, Valenciennes, le Quesnoy,
Mauberge, or some other place on the river Sambre, Philippeville, and
Dinant.

The second line, of thirteen places, would comprise: Gravelines, Saint-
Omer, Aire, Béthune, Arras, Douai, Bouchain, Cambrai, Landrécies,
Avesnes, Mariembourg, Rocroi, and Charleville, making thirteen places all
told, and all of them large and strong.

In addition, the first line could be strengthened with canals or waterways
from the great canal of Ypres to the Lys, and between the Lys and the Scheldt,
along whose banks entrenchments could be dug in time of war, which
together with all the other fortifications listed above would secure all the
region behind them, while at the same time the canals would provide valuable
assistance for the movement of goods, and commerce.

Once the frontier is stabilized in this way and the fortified places finished
and well supplied, they will be extremely strong and the very best of their
kind. Moreover we have reason to hope that we shall be more often on the
offensive than our enemies, so that there will be no need for further fortifications. I am of the opinion that we should build no further fortifications
outside these two lines; on the contrary, I think that in the course of time it
would be best to destroy all the fortifications that do not form part of these
lines, or are situated deep inside the kingdom, for they serve only to
encourage rebellion by those bold enough to seize them. It is also probable
that by having ten less fortifications to guard, the king will save 30,000 men;
if we consider the events of the recent war, it is clear that if His Majesty had
had such a force at his disposal, he would have been able to conquer the rest of
the Low Countries.

In the event of a future war, the first enemy places to capture, in order to
break their frontier lines and invade their country, would be: toward the
coast, Dixmude, which would open our way to Nieuport, and make the fall of
that place inevitable; in the region of the Lys, Courtrai, which would lead to
Oudenarde and then Ath; in Hainault, the towns of Charlemont, Mons, and
then Charleroi; toward Lorraine, Luxembourg, which threatens twenty
leagues of our territory and would give us another twenty if we took it, while
making it easy for us to capture Trier, as well as Homburg and Bitsch.

With regard to Germany, if a war should break out in that direction, it is of
the utmost importance for us to take Strasbourg, which is much easier to

besiege and take than is generally believed, and whose capture would be of such value in carrying the war to the other side of the Rhine, that I can think of nothing more essential.

When I have visited the valley of the Meuse I shall give my opinion on the state of the frontier of Champagne and the Three Bishoprics.

39
Proceedings in the English Parliament, 9–12 November (1685)

Source: Debates of the House of Commons from 1667–1694, collected by the Hon. Anchitell Grey, London, 1763, vol. 8, pp.353–8.

Debates were not systematically recorded before the time of Hansard (1774). This account reflects the importance of the occasion when James II asked parliament for money to support a standing army. Details of the speakers in this extract follow: Sir Winston Churchill (1620–88) was a trained lawyer. Although he had fought with the royalists in the civil war he was out of sympathy with James's religious policy; Sir Richard Graham, 1st Viscount Preston (1648–95) was a staunch Anglican and an active supporter of King James; Richard Jones, 1st Earl of Ranelagh (1648–1712) was responsible for fiscal policy in Ireland under Charles II and became notorious for his corruption. He was saved from disgrace by the King's intervention; Sir Thomas Clarges (1618–95) was the brother-in-law of General Monck and credited with winning him over to support the Restoration. He was concerned that Catholics were a threat to the British state and was active in the Convention; Sir Hugh Cholmondley (1612–89) was a strong churchman loyal to both Charles II and James II. This brought about the loss of his local offices after the Glorious Revolution; Edward Seymour (1633–1708) was an outspoken critic of James II who maintained a steady opposition throughout this parliament.

Monday November 9, 1685.

The Parliament met, when his Majesty, in the House of Lords, made the following Speech . . .

My Lords and Gentlemen: After the storm that seemed to be coming upon us when we parted last, I am glad to meet you all again in so great peace and quietness. God Almighty be praised, by whose blessing that Rebellion was suppressed! But when we reflect what an inconsiderable number of men began it, and how they carried it on without opposition, I hope every body will be convinced that, the Militia, which has hitherto been so much depended upon, is not sufficient for such occasions; and that there is nothing but a good Force of well-disciplined Troops in constant pay, that can defend us from such, as, either at home or abroad, are disposed to disturb us: And, in truth, my concern for the peace and quiet of my Subjects, as well as for the safety of the Government, made me think it necessary to increase their number to the proportion I have done: That I owed as well to the honour as the security of the Nation; whose reputation was so infinitely exposed to all our neighbours, by having lain open to this late wretched attempt, that it is not to be repaired without keeping such a body of men on foot, that none may have the thought of finding us again so miserably provided.

It is for the support of this great charge, which is now more than double to what it was, that I ask your assistance in giving me a Supply answerable to the expenses it brings along with it: And I cannot doubt, but what I have begun, so much for the honour and defence of the Government, will be continued by you with all the cheerfullness and readiness that is requisite, for a work of so great importance.

Let no man take exception, that there are some Officers in the Army, not qualified, according to the late Tests for their Employments: These Gentlemen, I must tell you, are most of them well-known to me: And having formerly served with me on several occasions, and always approved the loyalty of their principles by their practice, I think them now fit to be employed under me: And will deal plainly with you, that, after having had the benefit of their service in such a time of need and danger, I will neither expose them to disgrace, nor myself to the want of them, if there should be an other Rebellion to make them necessary to me.

I am afraid some men may be so wicked as to hope and expect that a difference may happen between you and me on this occasion: But when you consider what advantages have arisen to us in a few months, by the good understanding we have hitherto had; what wonderful effects it hath already produced in the change of the whole Scene of Affairs abroad, so much more to the honour of the Nation, and the figure it ought to make in the World; and that nothing can hinder a farther progress in this way to all our satisfactions, but fears and jealousies amongst ourselves; I will not apprehend that such a misfortune can befall us, as a division, or but a coldness between me and you; nor that anything can shake you in your steadiness and loyalty to me: who, by God's blessing, will ever make you returns of all kindness and protection, with a resolution to venture even my own life in defence of the true interest of this Kingdom.

Thursday, November 12.

The House [of Commons] resolved itself into a Committee of the whole House, to take into consideration his Majesty's Speech . . .

Sir Winston Churchill. Some other than the Militia is necessary to be found: I move a Supply for the Army.

Lord Preston. We have lately had an unfortunate proof, how little we are to depend upon the Militia, and therefore we must all approve of his Majesty's increasing the Forces to what they are. France is formidable, now Holland's Forces are greatly increased, and we must be strong in proportion . . . Hence we may conclude, these Levies made by the King are just, reasonable, and necessary . . .

Earl of Ranelagh. The Question is, Whether a Supply, or not? I do not intend to arraign the Militia, but seeing a Soldier is a Trade, and must (as all other Trades are) be learned, I will show you where the Militias has failed . . . in June last, when the late Duke of Monmouth landed, and had but eighty-three men, and 300l. in Money, nay in spite of such other force as the King could spare hence, brought it as far as he did. If the King of France had landed then, what would have become of us? . . .

Sir Thomas Clarges . . . To come first to the Militia, who (let me tell you) had considerable service in the late Rebellion . . . A confidence betwixt the King and his people is absolutely needful, let it come whence it will; our happiness consists in it, His Majesty, on his first entrance on the Crown, told us, 'he had been misrepresented, and that he would preserve the Government in Church and State now established by Law, and would maintain us in all our just Rights and Privileges' . And pray let us not forget that there was a Bill of Exclusion debated in this House; I was here, and showed myself against it; the Arguments for it were, 'That we should, in case of a Popish Succession, have a Popish Army.' You see the Act of that already broken

Sir Hugh Cholmondley, I stand up for, and would not have the Militia reflected on, it was very useful in the late Rebellion of Monmouth; it kept him from Bristol and Exeter, and is as good an Army we can raise again at home . . .

Mr Seymour . . . for my part, I had rather pay double to those, (meaning keeping up the Militia) from whom I fear nothing, than holt so much to of whom I must ever be afraid, and, say what you will it is a standing

Supporting an Army is maintaining so many idle persons to lord the rest of the Subjects. The King declared, 'That no soldiers should private houses,' but they did: 'That they should pay for all things they but they paid nothing for almost all they took. And for Other employed not taking the Tests, it is dispensing with all the Laws at if these men be good and kind, we know not whether it proceeds generosity, or principles: For we must remember, it is Treason for be reconciled to the Church of Rome, for the Pope, by Law, is to this Kingdom . . .

40
Sir John Bramston's account of the debates of the King's speech (November 1685)

Source: Richard Griffin, Lord Braybrooke (ed.), *The Autobiography of Sir John Bramston*, Camden Society, no. XXXII, London, 1845, pp.211–15.

Sir John Bramston (1611–1700) was a lawyer and a friend of Edward Hyde, Earl of Clarendon. Created a Knight of the Bath by Charles II on his restoration, probably because of his family's loyalty to the monarchy, he entered parliament as a member for Essex. After James II's accession he became MP for the borough of Maldon, in Essex; he remained a staunch Protestant and a royalist. His autobiography is largely based on his recollections up until 1683, after which he began to keep a detailed diary.

In the debate there arose a question what the supply was demanded for: if for maintaining of a standing army, that is a thing not heard of, or known in our law; and though the raising of men for the defence of his Majesty and safety of the peace of the kingdom whilst there were rebels up in arms, and a pretender to the Crown, yet, that rebellion being quelled, and their general headless, the danger was over, and so no cause to continue the men any longer in arms. . . . But it was said, though the rebellion, at least the rebels in arms, were suppressed, yet the venom and seeds of that rebellion was not removed out of the hearts and minds of a very great part of the nation, who were apt still, if opportunity served, to rise, and that the militia as it is formed cannot be useful on such occasions. But it was insisted so strongly on behalf of the militia, that even in that rebellion they were useful, and might be made more, if the defects were taken into consideration. At length a question was stated by the chairman, that a supply should be granted to his Majesty. It was moved, and much insisted upon, for the addition of some words to the question, as, for his extraordinary occasions; others, for the support of the army; for it hath never been known that a supply was asked or granted and no cause shown for what. At last it was moved that a previous question should be put for these last words – for the support of the army – which being put, it passed in the negative, 225 being in the negative, 150 in the affirmative. Two things carried the odds to the negative; one by Sir Thomas Meeres, which would have it observed, that those who were to add the words were against any supply; the other was words which Mr Seymour said, that the militia might be made so useful that there would be no need of an army, and so no need of a supply; which alarmed the sword-men and the courtiers too, and made them conclude there was a design managed against any supply; which was not the thing intended, I presume, but they were not willing to establish an army officered by Papists. For though there were not many such yet amongst them, every man might see, by the same reason that these were dispensed with, all or as many as the King pleased might. So then the question was singly for a supply, and that passed without a negative; but in truth many were silent; one gentleman, I think, was singular, Sir Richard Temple. He contended earnestly and long, yea, and spoke often, and replied upon Sir Thomas Meeres, that it did not follow that those that were for having the additional words part of the question were against all supply; yet on the division he was for the negative, and was numbered amongst them; so that he spake one way and voted another; and yet I think he was the last that spoke before the committee divided.

On Friday the King's speech was again resumed . . . but a debate arose upon the penning of the order, so it was not clear whether to proceed farther on supply, or the other paragraph about the Popish officers not qualified. . . . On Saturday the 14th, the House . . . resolved into a committee, and the Solicitor taking the chair, there was a long and great silence. At length Sir Edmund Jennings broke the ice (as I was told, for I was not there), and when I came in Sir Thomas Clarges was speaking, and did it with more temper than he uses. Every man that spoke did it with great tenderness and deference to the King, and at length the debates ended, and a committee appointed to draw up an Address to his Majesty, wherein the House should declare the breach of the law, and danger the officers not qualified were in, with a desire that his Majesty would be pleased to take care to free the subjects from their fears; and that a Bill, if his Majesty please shall be prepared to indemnify those officers which have not taken the Test from the inabilities and penalties of the law. It was said by many, and denied by none, that nothing but a law could secure them . . . Some would have it penned that those officers might be removed. That was too harsh a word some thought, and so left [it] to the committee to take the same words which were in a former Address on the same subject to the last King, Charles II.

On Monday the 16 . . . the House resolved into a committee of the whole House to consider further of a supply. Several sums were mentioned, 200,000l. 400,000l. 700,000l. and twelve hundred thousand. The Lord Camden moved the first, alleging that, there being in bank 400,000l. of the money given for suppressing the rebellion, and that the charge of the additional forces raised on that occasion was 300,000l for a year, there would be sufficient by this addition to keep up the army for a year and a quarter, if only 100,000l were remaining; but on the debate that sum seemed to be waved, and a question, after much debate, was put upon the second sum. The committee divided, and was carried in the negative, though it did plainly appear there was sufficient to keep the army 2 years and half. The question for 700,000l. was put, and upon the division the Yeas were 213, the Noes 193.

41
Vauban's memorandum concerning privateering (1695)

Source: G. Symcox (ed.), *War, Diplomacy and Imperialism, 1618–1763,* Macmillan, London, Basingstoke, 1974, pp.237–42.

Privateers were private persons who sailed armed vessels by commission from their government. They were authorized (normally but not invariably during the time of war) to use them against hostile nations, especially by capturing merchant shipping.

One does not need to be very learned to know that the English and Dutch are the main pillars of the Alliance; they support it by making war against us in concert with the other powers, and they keep it going by means of the money that they pay every year to the Duke of Savoy, the German princes, and the other allies . . . France should therefore consider England and Holland as its real enemies; not content to make open and unremitting war on us by land and sea, they also stir up as many foes as they can by means of their money.

Now this money does not come from their own countries; we know that they only have what trade brings them. Nor does it derive from the products of their own soil, which provides them with very little, and not enough to suffice for the necessaries of life, as do the grain, wine, brandy, salt, oil, hemp, canvas, timber, and all the thousand other commodities that abound in our land. Nevertheless, these products and certain others of their own are so abundant there that they are able to send them to the farthest parts of the globe, obtaining in return great quantities of bullion and other valuable articles which they export all over Europe at a great profit. Their trade is carried on almost completely by sea and hardly at all by land, for this is the way in which they have built up and maintained it in all the inhabited lands of Europe, Asia, Africa, and America, where these two nations carry on their commerce with all possible ingenuity and intelligence, making use of that prodigious number of ships that ply continually between their own countries and the remotest parts of the earth where they have trading posts for all kinds of goods. By this means the English and Dutch have made themselves the masters and dispensers of the most solid money in Europe, the most considerable part of whose wealth indubitably lies in their hands. This is the secret of the abundance of their goods and it is this that furnishes them with the means to carry on the war against us. In a word, this is the source of all the evils that we are suffering, and we must fight it with all our strength and industry, but intelligently, and choosing methods that will bring success . . .

The only suitable means . . . is privateering warfare, which is a covert and indirect form of war whose effects they will fear all the more because it strikes them in the very sinews of war; this in turn will be of great advantage to us since not only will they be unable to prevent the destruction of their commerce, but also because of the vast expenditure they will be forced to make, ruining themselves without being able to find a proper remedy. At the same time, they cannot attack us in this way, for we have little or no overseas territory, which, in any case, we can afford to neglect for a time in order to favour the privateers, since whatever we make by overseas trade cannot compare with what can be won through privateering, which should be encouraged in every way as long as the war lasts.

. . . all the commerce of the Spaniards, the English, the Dutch, and the other northern states, trafficking with Italy, the Levant, and the Barbary coast, has to pass within reach of Marseilles, Toulon, and our other Mediterranean ports; and whether it passes close to our coast or far out at sea makes no difference to a privateer, for these distances count for little at sea.

Dunkirk is just as admirably situated to attack the trade of England and Scotland, the Spanish Netherlands, Holland, Denmark, Sweden, Norway, Muscovy, and Greenland, and the herring, cod, and whale fisheries in those waters, as well as merchant shipping coming from the Mediterranean, Spain, Africa, and the East or West Indies, should it escape the privateers of Brest and Saint-Malo, whether it travels up the Channel or round the north of Scotland. Le Havre, Saint-Malo, and Brest can send out privateers against England, Scotland, and Ireland, through the Channel or round the west of Ireland and the north of Scotland, while those from Dunkirk ravage the east of England and Scotland, and the north and west of the Spanish Netherlands and Holland . . .

Finally, this kingdom possesses the materials with which to build all the ships that would be required, and there are many officers who would like nothing better than to serve on them; there are also plenty of people who would contribute to the cost if they saw a chance of profit and honour . . .

We must therefore fall back on privateering as the method of conducting war which is most feasible, simple, cheap, and safe, and which will cost least to the state since any losses will not be felt by the King, who risks virtually nothing. It should be added that it will enrich the country, train many good officers for the King, and in a short time force his enemies to sue for peace on far more reasonable conditions than he could otherwise hope for . . .

42
Saint-Simon's frustrations at his failure to be promoted in the army (after 1697)

Source: *Mémoires complets et authentiques du duc de Saint-Simon*, Paris, 1829, vol. 3, pp.262–6. Translated by Clive Emsley.

For details of Saint-Simon's career, see above III.8. *Ordre de Tableau* was a system of promotion based on seniority, and Saint-Simon felt that its use impeded the advance of able men who came from good families.

The disbandments which followed the Peace of Ryswick were large and strange . . . My regiment was disbanded . . . the remnants were transferred to the Regiment of Duras, and my company was incorporated into that of the Count of Uzès . . . This left me in the same situation as others, though this did not console me. Officers without companies were attached to other regiments; I was attached to that of Saint-Moris. He was a gentleman of Franche-Comté who I had never before met, and whose brother was a well-regarded lieutenant general. Soon afterwards the pedantry which was always part of life in the army, required two months presence with the regiments to which men were attached. This seemed harsh to me. I did not intend to shirk, but as I had endured a variety of inconveniences and as I had been advised to take the soothing waters of Pombières, I requested to travel there rather than passing the next three years in exile with a regiment in which I knew no-one and where I had nothing to do. The king did not seem to find this wrong. I often went to Marly; he spoke to me sometimes . . . in a word he treated me well, and better than others of my age and condition.

However some officers' places were filled with men who were my inferiors; veteran officers obtained regiments because of long service . . . The promotion which had been talked of never came my way. The times had gone when you could take advantage of dignity and birth . . .

[When war came again] promotions were announced and everyone was surprised by the great number . . . I avidly scanned the cavalry promotions to see if my name was there. I was absolutely astonished to find five men who were my inferiors on the list . . . It was difficult to feel more stung than I did. I found equality confusing the *Ordre de Tableau* sufficiently humiliating, but the preference given to the Count of Ayen, in spite of his nepotism, and to the four other gentlemen was particularly insupportable. I remained silent, however, so as not to do anything at the wrong moment in my anger. Marshal de Lorge [my father-in-law] was outraged for me and for himself; his brother was hardly less so, for the lack of consideration shown to them . . . They both suggested that I resign. Frustration increased my desire; I thought of my age, the beginning of the war, renouncing every hope of advancement in the profession of arms, the boredom of leisure, the pain of summers hearing talk of war, of expeditions, of the advancement of men who distinguished themselves, who won reputation, and all this powerfully restrained me. Thus I passed two months agonizing, resigning every morning, and yet unable soon afterwards to make up my mind to do it.

At last, pushed to the limit with myself and pressed by the two marshals, I resolved to seek further advice from others. I chose Marshal de Choiseul, under whom I had served and who was a good judge in these matters, de Beauvilliers, the Chancellor, and de la Rochefoucauld. I had already complained to them; they were indignant at the injustice, but the three latter were courtiers.

. . . the three courtiers were of the same opinion as the three marshals; they all told me forcefully that it was shameful and unacceptable that a man of my birth and dignity, who had served with honour, assiduity and approbation through four campaigns at the head of a smart and gallant regiment, should be discharged with his company, without reason, stuck with a similar number on the same rank, see five of his subordinates promoted over him, and should, at the beginning of a war, be without regiment, company, or troops, and only be at the call of Saint-Moris. That a duke and a peer of my birth, established as I was, and with a wife and children, should not serve as a *haut-le-pied* [run-around] in the armies, and see men so different from myself, inferior to me, all with employment in regiments . . . and that if this injustice was done when my father-in-law and his brother were living and serving as marshals of France, dukes, and captains in the royal bodyguard, what could I hope for when they were gone?

. . . At last I did it, and when I acted, I followed the advice of the same people; I did not let drop a word of discontent, I let my omission from the promotions speak for me; the king's anger was inevitable.

43
A priest's description of the *milice* (1711)

Source: René Lehoreau, *Cérémonial de l'Église d'Angers 1692–1721*, edited by F. Lebrun, Klincksiek, Paris, 1967, p.205. Translated from French by Clive Emsley.

René Lehoreau (1671–1752) was born at le Pommeraie, Anjou. He was ordained as a priest in 1695 and became a chaplain at Angers cathedral and, later, a canon of St Leonard de Chemille. He left a huge manuscript in three volumes in which he recorded many details of religious and social life in Angers.

On 9 March the parishes brought their militiamen to the Town Hall [in Angers]. These militiamen were unmarried youths from each parish in the diocese . . . Those who drew the lot were obliged to go to war on behalf of all the lads in their parish, and they each received a bounty from the other lads, an *écu* of three pounds or 100 *sous*,[1] depending on the numbers. The larger parishes furnished two, three, even four men. You have never seen greater sorrow in the parishes given the treatment which is meted out to them on the march. They are bound and chained like veritable animals, and treated even more shamefully. They are chained two by two, four by four and, when they arrive in each town or village, they are housed in barns and stables, sleep on straw, still chained, and guarded by armed townsmen. They die in considerable numbers, or desert when the opportunity presents itself; and these troops have never made it into the army. The families of these young men are devastated, but also responsible for their sons who they must hand over to the captains dead or alive. It is this which empties the parishes of young men and which makes cultivation difficult since, at the time of the ballot, the young men take flight and wander here and there. But their fathers and mothers remain responsible, and this results in their having to purchase militiamen in the absence of the sons . . . You never see so many peasants marry as in time of war, so as to escape the army.

[1] A sou was worth about one shilling.

44
Soldiers as salt smugglers (1711)

Source: B. Briais, *Contrebandiers du sel: La vie des faux sauniers au temps de la gabelle*. Aubier, Paris, 1984, p.183. Translated from French by Clive Emsley.

The sale of contraband salt was generally welcomed by the common people, who wished to avoid the full rigours of the *gabelle* tax. When carried out on a large scale by well-armed soldiers, however, it could lead to disorderliness and even to brigandage.

Not only does the disorder caused by troops involved in salt smuggling continue, but it is getting worse. Their audacity is without limit and I have received a letter from Riom reporting that those in the province of the Auvergne cross and recross the walls of that town in broad daylight, and in large groups, shouting out the places where they are going to sell salt.

On the 12 of this month ten or twelve dragoons arrived in Château-Chinon, where there is a salt store, put their smuggled salt under one of the town gates and publicly announced the sale of their merchandise at 8 sous the pound.

A month ago, when I was finishing an inspection and leaving Sancoins (in the Cher) where there is also a store, fifteen or sixteen dragoons and cavalrymen from those quartered in Berry and Cosne-sur Loire arrived and also announced the sale of their smuggled salt, then, having had something to eat, they moved on. The receiver of the said store informs me that, since my departure, four hundred more have travelled through in broad daylight, full of insolence, threatening clerks and employees without distinction . . . These men have taken the mounts of several individuals, even priests, while on the road and take everywhere what they want, without payment. . . .

INDEX

absolutism 2, 6, 7, 11, 154–5
  limits of 13
Académie Française 64, 74
Act Anent Peace and War (1703) 155,
  191
Act of Union (1706) 155, 191–7
Addison, Joseph, on the French 7, 158,
  234–6
Agen, sedition at (1635) 10, 19–20
Agreement of the People (1647) 156,
  207–9
almshouses 122–5
Anglican Church
  Bishop Burnet's Espiscopal
    Responsibilities 95–6
  Canons (1640) 65, 88–90
  ecclesiastical courts at Stratford-upon-
    Avon 66, 99–101
  and the impeachment of Dr
    Sacheverell 6, 154, 171–2
  and James II 185
  visitation articles of the Diocese of
    Hereford 66, 101–2
Anne of Austria, Queen of France 59–60
Anne, Queen 88, 154, 166, 171
  and the Act of Union (1706) 196
  and the Bill of Rights (1689) 187, 190
  and the Scots Act of Security 167–8
  and the Scots Acts Anent Peace and
    War (1703) 191
Areopagitica (Milton) 65, 82–4
army
  and Louis XIV 221–2
  and the *milice* 159, 248–9
  New Model Army 208
  questioning need for standing army

157, 229
  by Parliament 158–9, 240–2, 243–4
  Saint-Simon on failure to be promoted
    159, 247–8
  and soldiers as salt smugglers 249–50
  see also warfare
Astell, Mary, *A Serious Proposal to the
    Ladies* (1694–7) 156, 206–7
Aylmer, Gerald 11

Balzac, Jean Louis Guez de, on royal
    authority (1631) 155–6, 201–2
Bate's Case, judgement of 10, 17–19
Baxter, Richard 5
  Account of his Ministry 65, 90–2
Bayle, Pierre 5, 63, 65
  Concerning Obscenities (1699) 65,
    84–6
  *The Great Contest of Faith and
    Reason* (1686) 157, 222–5
Beddard, Robert 2
beggars 121, 122, 126–7
Beuvelet, Mathieu, on marriage and the
    family (1669) 68, 135
Bill of Rights (1689) 6, 155, 186–90
Blenheim Palace 158
Bordeaux
  and the Duke of Épernon 12, 30, 31–2,
    42
  Ormée revolt 5, 42–3, 67, 114
Bossuet, Jacques Bénigne 6, 14, 48, 225
  on the Divine Right of Kings 156,
    214–15
  on marriage and the family (1687) 68,
    134–5
Boughton, fountains at (1712) 158, 232